PIERRE WITTMER

CAILLEBOTTE
and
HIS GARDEN
at
YERRES

Preface by BERNARD LORENCEAU

With excerpts from
Treatise on the Design and Decoration of Gardens
by Louis-Eustache Audot, Paris, 1859

HARRY N. ABRAMS, INC., *Publishers*, NEW YORK

To My Father

Editor, English-language edition: Mark Greenberg

A Note on the Titles, Dimensions,
and Attributions Used in This Book

Unless otherwise noted, all works reproduced are by Gustave Caillebotte.

TITLES
The titles or names of the works in the French edition are those used by Mademoiselle
Marie Berhaut in *Caillebotte, His Life and Work, a Descriptive Catalogue of the Paintings and
Pastels*, published by the Wildenstein Foundation Bibliothèque des Arts, Paris, 1978, or
have been taken from catalogues or other publications, especially those dealing with a
particular subject (see Bibliography). In the case of works handed down in families, the
names we give here are those used by those families. In the English edition, wherever
possible the titles are those from the 1976 Caillebotte exhibition as established by Kirk
Varnedoe.

SIZES
The dimensions are in centimeters, height followed by width. Where the works are
drawings, the dimensions of the sheet of paper are listed first, followed by the dimensions of
the drawing itself.

SIGNATURES AND STAMPS
Mademoiselle Marie Berhaut's indications have been followed. When reference is made to
works not included in her study, we have used her method, omitting details as to origins and
without giving particulars about the signatures or stamps.

LIBRARY OF CONGRESS CATALOGING-IN-PUBLICATION DATA
Wittmer, Pierre.
[Caillebotte au jardin.   English]
Caillebotte and His garden at Yerres / Pierre Wittmer; preface by Bernard
Lorenceau.
p.   cm.
Translation of: Caillebotte au jardin.
Includes bibliographical references (p.   ) and index.
ISBN 0-8109-3167-2 (cloth)
1. Caillebotte, Gustave, 1848–1894—Homes and haunts—France—
Yerres. 2. Gardens—France—Yerres.   I. Caillebotte, Gustave,
1848–1894. II. Title.
ND553.C243W5813   1991
759.4—dc20   91-300
               CIP

Copyright © 1990 Editions d'Art Monelle Hayot, Château de Saint-Rémy-en-l'Eau,
France
English translation copyright © 1991 Harry N. Abrams, Inc.

Published in 1991 by Harry N. Abrams, Incorporated, New York
A Times Mirror Company

Printed and bound in Hong Kong

Contents

Acknowledgments

The author wishes to thank the following people for their invaluable assistance in the writing of this book: the Conseiller d'Etat and Mrs. Jacques Chardeau; Dr. and Mrs. Patrick Chardeau; Aurélien, Dorthée, and especially Amaury Chardeau; Mr. and Mrs. Olivier Chardeau, Mr. and Mrs. Gilles Chardeau, Mrs. Thérèse Aubin, Mr. Dominique Chardeau, Mr. and Mrs. Jean Chardeau. We are especially grateful to Mr. Jean Chardeau for his advice. The publication of his book on Caillebotte's drawings, and his generous consent to put some of his research findings at our disposal have been of inestimable help. We are also indebted to Mr. Jean-Louis Daurelle and to Miss Marie-Jeanne Daurelle. We wish to thank Mr. Philippe Brame, Mr. Bernard Lorenceau and Mrs. Sylvie Brame for their never-failing assistance. Mr. Kirk Varnedoe, Director of the Department of Painting and Sculpture at the Museum of Modern Art in New York and a renowned Caillebotte specialist, lent us documents belonging to him, a generous gesture for which we are grateful.

Mrs. Claire Cogniet, Messrs. Robert and Manuel Schmit and Jean Gautier, curator of the Musée de Brunoy; Achim Moeller, Josefowitz, Gaston Dulière, the Ader-Picard-Tajan and Laurin-Guilloux-Buffetaud Research and Development Services; Rieunier; Bailly-Pommery of the Arcole Group; Sotheby's New York and Sotheby's Paris, have all graciously put their photo libraries at our disposition, for which we warmly thank them.

Our thanks also go to Mesdames René Hayot, Sylvie Dannaud, Caroline Durand-Ruel, Marianne Delafond, Geneviève Fossé, Myck Micheyl, Ledivelec-Gloeckner, Marie-Blanche d'Arnéville, Claire Bon, Annick Bourlet; J. Le Men, Archivist of the town of Gennevilliers; to Miss Marie Berhaut, Miss Anne Wittmer, Messrs. Robert Gérard, Jean-Pierre Altounian, Gérard Augis, Didier Leroy; Marc Lucas, Mayor of Yerres; Patrice Calvel, Jean-Pierre Nicol, Jacques Petit-Hory, O. K. Preis; Georges Queffurus, honorary archivist of the town of Yerres; Guy Quintrie Lamothe, William Wheeler, Boris Gogny-Goubert; Thibaud, Baudouin, Cyrille, and Aude Gogny-Goubert; Jean-Paul Le Garrec; and for her documentary assistance also to Mrs. Brigitte Le Garrec-Paris.

We express our gratitude as well for the immeasurable help of the Historical and Archeological Society of Corbeil, l'Essonne and Hurepoix; the Society of Friends of the Musée de Brunoy; the Society of Art, History and Archaeology of the Yerres Valley; the Vieilles Maisons Françaises; the National Society of Horticulture and the Historical Society of Montgeron.

Last but not least the editor gives special thanks to Mr. François Daulte, editor of Miss Marie Berhaut's *Descriptive Catalogue of Caillebotte's Works* published by the Wildenstein Foundation. Mr. Daulte has been a well-informed defender of Caillebotte in the magazine *Oeil* of which he is head.

PIERRE WITTMER

Foreword

Caillebotte, a highly intelligent man endowed with a wide-ranging mind, was a keen observer of his time and place, whose palette reflects the richness of his observation. His personal modesty, attested to in his work, has not brought him renown. He was a man with new ideas and no preconceptions. As an observer, he treated themes with which no one else had bothered. Studies and sketches for *The Floor Scrapers* date from 1875, those of house painters and sign painters from 1877. Edouard Manet executed *Street Pavers in the Rue Mosnier* in 1878; Maximilien Luce and others were to treat similar subjects later on. Caillebotte knew naval engineering, was interested in yachting, and was a sailor.

This man, an original in more than one field, found many means of expressing his originality. Generous and communicative, he gave away ideas to his friends and influenced them to take unexplored paths. His 1877 sporting scenes at Yerres, his plunging views of the Boulevard Haussmann in 1880, reveal a totally new, nearly photographic way of seeing things. His vision made a strong impression, which men who came after him would take up again.

Very early in my career, when I was looking for hitherto relatively unknown painters of quality, I became aware of Gustave Caillebotte. The first of his works I acquired, in Brussels in 1952, was *Still Life, Platter of Crayfish*, which he painted about 1881.

Caillebotte's family held an important place in his life and work, and so contacts with them played an important role in my research. Through an amateur printer I came to know descendants of his family. At that time the reputation of this fine artist was clouded by emotional issues and his aesthetic dimension escaped everyone. My strong conviction was that he deserved better, and I have strived to raise Gustave Caillebotte to his legitimate place.

Self-Portrait, *c. 1892*
Oil on canvas, 40 × 32 cm.

At the gallery at that time I had *The Orange Trees*, 1878, and *Madame Boissière Knitting*, 1877, which Caillebotte painted at Yerres; this last work was purchased by Madame Beck. I also had *Nude Woman on a Sofa*, 1873, now at the Art Institute of Minneapolis, and other masterpieces by this painter to whom I was immediately drawn.

The eye of a dealer examining a painting differs from that of the historian, who must rely on written data of historical or even scientific nature; the dealer's vision is more instinctive and more empirical. The painter's personal idiosyncrasies, his individual use of color and uniquely different approach to composition, his repetition of certain themes enable the dealer to recognize original work and distinguish real from fake. Nothing magic is involved here; works of art should be looked at without any a priori criteria. The dealer who limits himself to the study of only a few artists finds it easier to improve and deepen his knowledge. He will know that so-and-so is not likely to have created such and such a work as it isn't in his manner and doesn't jibe with his personal expression. Though the analytical process is intriguing, human beings are fallible, and so we must confine ourselves to our specialties. Even the possessor of a fine eye should remain modest—all the more the owner of a bad one.

Over the past forty years Caillebotte's worth has become clear; his works now bring the prices of Sisleys and Pissarros. Naturalistic and impressionistic in manner, his paintings are more solid than those of these two great Impressionists, chiefly because of his manner of arranging his themes on the canvas according to difficult axes with parallels going in definite directions, in such a way as to create astonishing effects. Caillebotte pointed the way and did not advertise the fact that he had done so.

Pierre Wittmer's study of the artist's youth and maturity, from the ages of twelve to thirty-one, complements previous ones and brings a new and original light to bear on the oeuvre. The garden at Petit Gennevilliers, on the edge of the Argenteuil basin, has disappeared. The historic garden at Yerres, evoking as it does the framework of the painter's life—summers he spent during an important period of his brief existence—has the value of a monument. I hope that the 1994 retrospective of Caillebotte's work, on the occasion of the hundredth anniversary of his death, will allow us at last to take the true measure of this important artist. Several heretofore unknown works will be shown then. My intention for the perpetuation of Gustave's fame is to see that they have the utmost exposure.

BERNARD LORENCEAU

Preface

In writing *Caillebotte and His Garden at Yerres* the author has attempted to suggest both a painting lesson in a park and a walk through the gardens of the Ile de France, which, before 1880, served as Gustave Caillebotte's inspiration. He was a lover of gardens, a painter, and an art patron and, from the period in question, a collector as well. The reader is invited to acquaint himself with the pleasures of a landscape park designed in the first half of the nineteenth century and then with paintings that Caillebotte created during the dozen or so years before 1879.

Beyond the simple aesthetic pleasure of our first encounter with the works Caillebotte painted in the countryside during this period (which was, incidentally, the period of his formation), these works present us with a challenge. As with all the Impressionists, and especially with those works the painters executed in familial surroundings, they carry a message that has become part of the culture of France and that must be decoded.

Art historians have studied Gustave Caillebotte's work and its relation to realism, naturalism, and Impressionism. They have analyzed its themes. The painter's insights, vision, methods, and the relation of his work to photography have been scrutinized and brilliantly described. His importance, originality, and modernity— not to mention his genius—are acknowledged. In order to know and appreciate him fully however, we need to call on disciplines not customarily used in the history of painting that will help us understand the customs and catch the meaning of a society that existed a hundred years ago. A knowledge of that society's philosophy and ideas, of the role that historical research played in it, as well as the growth of science at that time and its application to the medicine and hygiene of the period, are important to an understanding of its daily life. Themes in the artist's paintings relate to these things.

My aim is to connect Gustave Caillebotte's work prior to 1879 with the art of gardens. His father's acquisition, in 1860, of a property where the twelve-year-old Gustave spent his holidays turned the boy into a garden enthusiast. Less than ten years later he began to paint. The shapes of these gardens with their architectural features made an ineradicable mark on his aesthetic formation, awoke him to art, and stimulated his creative gifts. He turned to painting and, later, to collecting the work of friends whom he supported and defended. It can be argued that gardens provided the essential foundation for his work and even influenced his compositions based on other themes. Certain of his urban landscapes, for example *Place Saint Augustin, Misty Weather,* displayed at the fourth exhibition of 1879, and *The Boulevard Seen from Above,* 1880, seem to owe something to studies Caillebotte did at Yerres. My intention, however, is not to fix the artist forever on the estate at Yerres, no matter how important that period was to his life. That period, with all the sites that inspired Caillebotte, the picturesque valley with its wooded hillsides and well-kept gardens, constitutes only a facet of his work, although chronologically the first. His paintings of Paris, Normandy, Petit Gennevilliers, and the boat basin at Argenteuil also form a part of the message he left us.

The importance of the gardens at Yerres and the fact that they existed before the pictorial work was done lead me to surmise that they were created between 1814 and 1848 under the reigns of King Louis XVIII, Charles X, and Louis Philippe, a conclusion I base on an immensely popular work published in 1858, one year before the artist's father acquired the property at Yerres. A *Treatise on the Design and Ornamentation of Gardens* by Pierre Boitard, Louis Verardi, and Louis-Eustache Audot, who was also its publisher, not only brings the time and place to life but has a charm and wit of its own, which we can be sure delighted Gustave Caillebotte. It is filled with symbolism and significance. Unrevised, its references to design and painting reflect the preoccupations of the garden lover of the time and give us an idea of the value that the owners of country houses placed in those days on living well. Certain especially evocative descriptions seem to have a place in the intellectual thread running through the themes of Gustave Caillebotte, as well as, undoubtedly, those of other artists of the time. A mere reading of some of the book's stronger passages will bring to mind Claude Monet or Pierre Auguste Renoir. The attentive reader will enjoy discovering such parallels for himself.

Our study has to do with gardens created and maintained before 1880 and whose apogee can be fixed before that date, and it includes not only garden history but material on restoration and upkeep. It covers decorative planting, choices of ornamental trees and shrubs, conifers, fruit trees, and roses and the then-fashionable and popular varieties of flowers, as well as strategies for displaying them.

I have scheduled our tour to begin in the landscape park, after a glimpse of the river from the bridge. The hypothetical stroller will need two hours to cover the route, the sequence of which will be made clear in the chapter entitled, "The Reflection of a Dream." There we will place this landscape park within the chain of development of Western European garden design, between those gardens planned in France under the First Empire and those initiated under the Second Empire.

Indirectly and on another level, the same intellectual origins can be seen in

The Painter under His
Parasol, *c. 1878*
Oil on canvas, 80 × 65 cm.
Edouard Dessommes, a
friend of Caillebotte,
painting at Yerres in the
landscape park. In
Dessommes' studio on the
Rue du Rocher in Paris
Caillebotte painted Rooftop
View, Paris *in 1878.*
Dessommes also appears in
Game of Bezique, *in about*
1881.

A work of art is a bit of nature seen through a man's temperament.
EMILE ZOLA[1]

Gustave Caillebotte's work. The symbolism we find in gardens will enable us to understand his oeuvre. Given the importance of the gardens at Yerres in this artist's work, they become fundamental.

Truth need not be arrived at through the written word but may be absorbed directly from one human mind to another. A garden as a way of thinking and touching the human heart may lead to an understanding of man's essential nature and ultimate truth. *The Yerres, Effect of Rain* is impregnated with such Oriental mysticism. Here the artist seems to be in a contemplative state like that of monks viewing the sixteenth-century monastery garden at Ryojin, or like Roger Caillois meditating on the stones of Kyoto: "I speak of bare stones . . . within which a mystery slower, more vast and weightier than the destiny of an insubstantial species is at once hidden and revealed."

Before beginning our tour, some understanding of the art of gardens is needed so that we may go beyond a first and superficial impression of the paintings and pastels. In the chapter entitled "Yerres in the Second Half of the Nineteenth Century," I give a brief history of the region. This is followed by "The Impressionist Movement in Brie," and "A History of the Property."

The chapter entitled, "A Walk in the Family Park," and succeeding sections containing related information should be taken by the reader at his own speed, as by this point in the book he will understand its major principles and the trend of its underlying ideas. In "Saint Fiacre in the Yerres River Region," we touch on local gardening traditions. "In the Footsteps of Gustave Caillebotte" is intended to be useful in pinpointing works that have as their theme the landscape park and includes a map of the park's layout.

"The Park at Yerres, a Garden in Town," is chiefly intended to help the reader imagine what importance this landscape park must have had in its day in a region of more than one hundred thousand inhabitants spread over eight towns in the Yerres Valley. It will also compare the park to the Parc Monceau in Paris, which Caillebotte also painted.

The chapter entitled "A Lost Garden at Petit Gennevilliers," deals with the second of Gustave Caillebotte's two gardens. Here we find the garden amateur and orchid collector of about 1893 or 1894 secretly tending toward pictorial creation.

"On Observation and Color," deals with how color is first perceived, then assembled, by the artist. In the years around 1876 gardeners and painters were carrying on similar research into the composition of flowers and flower beds in the case of the former, and for the latter, into the arrangement of color on canvas.

"Day by Day," has as its subject a biographical sketch of Gustave Caillebotte, including a chronology of the events of his life from 1894 to 1897, centered around the period at Yerres and works painted there. Though not a true biography, this chapter should allow us, given what we now know of the artist's life, to understand him better.

Throughout the book I have used quotations to evoke the period and establish tone, as at that time reading was one of the leisurely delights of country living.

"The Yerres Region in Impressionist Exhibitions" establishes the importance of these locations in relation to the paintings themselves.

On October 10, 1855, Eugène Delacroix, on a holiday in Normandy, observed the effect of the west wind on the sea and ships with their exotic crews, and he reproached the marine painters of his day for slipshod work. "I seek accuracy of the imagination . . .," Delacroix wrote. "Color and form should cooperate. My accuracy . . . would consist in emphasizing the principal objects, while getting their relation to the figures. In sum, what I ask for in a seascape is what I insist on in any other subject . . ."

Gustave Caillebotte applied Delacroix's theory when, at the end of his short life, at Petit Gennevilliers, he painted sailboats in the boat basin at Argenteuil. Some of these craft are shown at anchor. Some, under way, are closer hauled than others. Some sail on the wind and some before it.

Here we have the very essence of imaginative accuracy. Even as early as Yerres Caillebotte took the greatest care with his figures and at the same time never neglected their settings. In working up both carefully, he followed the advice of Delacroix, who, on this point, may be said to have thought like a garden designer.

This is what gives the landscape park at Yerres its significance in our study of this fine, deeply human, and honest artist.

The Park of the
Caillebotte Estate at
Yerres, *1875 (detail)*

OPPOSITE:
"Environs of Paris,"
c. 1889
Prepared by A. H. Dufour;
steel engraving by F.
Lefèvre; topography by
Gérin; lettering by
Langevin.
Southeast of Paris: the
Yerres Valley between the
forest of Sénart to the south
and the wooded hills of the
Château de la Grange-du-
Milieu and the Château de
Grosbois; the Bois Notre-
Dame to the north of the
Reveillon, and the forest of
Armainvilliers to the north.

Sénart is to its neighboring villages, the lovely Yerres and Brunoy, as a green-wreathed Silenus pressing their grapes.

ROGER DE BEAUVOIR[2]

Yerres, then a village, is situated in the French district of Brie, 22 kilometers southeast of Paris in the Ile de France, and takes its name from the river whose lower course flows through it a distance of more than 2 kilometers from its junction above the town with the Reveillon, a small brook on the outskirts of Brunoy near the water mill of the renowned 1132 Benedictine abbey Notre Dame d'Yerres. Less than 4 kilometers away, at Villeneuve-Saint-Georges, after having flowed through Crosne and Montgeron, the Yerres empties into the Seine.

The village, which seems to have sprung up on the spot where the Roman road from Paris to Sens crossed the river—the ancient ford was located near the Caillebotte family property—grew up on the river's hilly right bank, around the

Mont Griffon, *watercolor, 25 × 34.5 cm. Painted at Yerres near the summit of the mountain. Mont Griffon can also be seen in Caillebotte's* Riverbank, *painted before 1879.*

parish church dedicated in the eleventh century to Saint-Loup and, in more modern times, to Saint-Honest; and around the fourteenth-century baronial château of the Courtenays. This château was later owned, in the sixteenth century, by the king's secretary and notary Dreux II Budé, brother of the celebrated Greek scholar and humanist Guillaume Budé. One can see the importance to the region of this feudal holding at Yerres; in the year 1504 ninety-nine fiefs were under its jurisdiction.

The wooded Mont Griffon, at 117½ meters, the highest point in the region, overlooks the town. Pleasant walks and charming scenic views are found here, and it

Mulard édit., - Yerres

This property was on the right bank of the river facing the Caillebotte property. One can glimpse the tower of Yerres' seignorial château, which stood on the square, at the upper end of Rue de Concy.

The seignorial château of Yerres and the bell tower of the Church of Saint-Honest. At the rear is the square. A laundress pushing a wheelbarrow on her way to the washhouse has paused for the photographer.

The park of the property. The country house or "manor," also sometimes referred to as "Les Charmilles." Along the river we see a gazebo, the walkway, a horse at the watering place (the old ford), the public washhouse, the bathhouse, and the bridge. We are looking from the property at 6 Rue de Concy toward the right bank of the river downstream of the bridge. The roof of the structure at the far left appears in Caillebotte's painting Fishing, 1878. The bathhouse and the bridge appear in Périssoire on the Yerres, 1878.

In the distance is the square. This picture was taken from the end of the bridge on the upstream side, with the photographer's back to the ornamental farm of the property belonging to Number 6 Rue de Concy.

56 bis — YERRES (S.-et-O.) — Le Lavoir et les Bains

YERRES (S.-et-O.). — Rue de Concy. — Le Lavoir et les Bains

is not far from a second château, that of La Grange du Milieu, built around 1617 by Comptroller General of Finance Charles Duret, Seigneur of Chevry and La Grange.

On the left bank the municipality's lands extend to the Sénart forest, an ancient royal hunting preserve. In the direction of Montgeron lies the ancient fief of Concy, once a farming area, while the Godeaux hillsides were planted with vineyards.

In 1836 Yerres had 967 inhabitants. In 1881 it comprised 1,429. At that time the villagers' occupations consisted of those common in the Brie country, which for centuries has been considered one of Paris's wheat-growing regions. Charcoal and

Landscape with Railway Tracks, *c. 1872,*
Oil on canvas, 81 × 116 cm.
The bridge spanning the right-of-way of the Compagnie
de Paris à Lyon et à la Méditerranée (P. L. M.). We are
looking in the direction of Montgeron and Villeneuve-
Saint-Georges. The Yerres Valley is to the right, the
Godeaux Hill to the left.

The Yerres River looking upstream from the bridge. On the left (and the river's left bank) are trees belonging to the family property of Gustave Caillebotte at 6 Rue de Concy. On the right (and the river's right bank) are trees growing on the property of the "Manor," the watering place, the old ford, and the public washhouse. Trees on both banks of the river create a characteristic arch over the water, resulting in the unique luminosity found in works having as their theme this section of the river.

Le Pont de l'Europe, *Variant, c. 1877*
Oil on canvas, 105 × 130 cm.
Stamped bottom right
According to Kirk Varnedoe, the person in the top hat is Gustave Caillebotte himself.

The bridge at Yerres, built in 1870. The photograph was taken after 1918. To the right is the roof of flat tiles of the public washhouse.

Yerres, the Rue de Concy. In the foreground on the left is the property of Gustave Caillebotte's family. We see the walls of the "casin." On the right is the Brault property; in the middle ground, the bridge over the river; and in the background, the square. On the left in front of the bridge we glimpse the small parcel of land bordering the road and the river, which corresponds to the access to the old ford that Monsieur de Vallençay moved to acquire on December 13, 1775, with a view to beautifying the site.

other forest products were produced. There was farming, and crafts relating to agriculture were practiced. Clay and silt soils encouraged the cultivation of grain crops. Sloping land was used for vineyards and orchards, especially apples. The valley's alluvial deposits favored poplar plantations and pastureland (a local name, "The Great Grassland," attests to this) and, in the plain of Concy, market gardening.

The many surviving houses having cellars intended for large-scale wine storage testify to the importance of viniculture here in the old days. The Normandie neighborhood and the Pas d'Ane were places dear to the hearts of vintners, and a chapel in the church was reserved for their patron, Saint Vincent.

The many springs flowing through fissures caused by Brie's millstone quarries encouraged the creation of parks and gardens, many of these during the eighteenth century. The seventeenth-century architect Jean Thiriot created an estate whose extremely Italianate park included, in the river bottom, a pavilion erected around a spring known as the Fontaine Budé.

After the Revolution, with its attendant disruption of the country's landed properties, vast old estates belonging to the aristocracy and the church were broken up and parceled out, and some very beautiful properties, with large parks and gardens, were created. The Yerres valley, in this lower part of the river's course, became a summer resort and hunting area popular with the Parisian middle class.

A famous eighteenth-century village fair traditionally took place during Pentecost

The Man on the Balcony, *c. 1880*
Oil on canvas, 116 × 97 cm.
Stamped bottom right
*Here we see Maurice Brault leaning on the balcony
railing of Gustave Caillebotte's apartment on the
Boulevard Haussmann, at the intersection of the Rue
Gluck, in Paris. We are looking west toward the Place
Saint-Augustin.*

COMMUNE de *Yerres*

TABLEAU DU CONSEIL MUNICIPAL (1870.)

(Nota.—Ce Tableau doit être dressé en 3 expéditions pour les communes des arrondissements autres que celui de Versailles, l'une pour la Mairie, la deuxième pour la Sous-Préfecture et la troisième pour la Préfecture.)

N°s D'ORDRE.	NOMS ET PRÉNOMS DES MEMBRES DU CONSEIL MUNICIPAL. (a)	QUALIFICATIONS PROFESSIONS OU FONCTIONS.	AGE.	NOMBRE du suffrages obtenus.	DÉSIGNER par les lettres R ou N si le Conseiller est réélu ou nouveau.	OBSERVATIONS. (b)
1	Blazy, Jule-Pierre	Négociant	40 ans	270	N.	N. D.
2	Gaudefroy, Jules-Prosper	Propriétaire	67	264	R.	
3	Féron, Jacques-Sévère	ex-Cultivat	54	264		
4	Raimojo, Jules	Négociant	52	257		N. D.
5	Perror, Auguste-Aimé	Propriétaire	59	223	N.	
6	Chaudée, Romain-Désiré	Maraud	37	190		
7	Bertrand, Jean-Baptiste	Adjoint-Vign	74	179	R.	
8	Blanchez, Louis-Charles	ex-colon	45	171		
9	Paysan, Victor-Léonard	ex-Vigneron	56	170	N.	
10	Bonvier, Jean-Marcelin	Propr-Rentier	52	167	R.	
11	Thomas, François	ex-Adjoint	57	166	R.	
12	Labance, Victor	Grainetier	54	158	N.	
13	Caillebotte, Martial	Propriét	71	139		N. D.
14	B⁾ Gourgaud de Mr Adjoint M	ex-Maire	47	132	R.	
15	Pranire, Claude-Joseph	ex-Rentier	65	105	N.	
16	Jean, Hippolyte	Entrepr de jard	46	99		

786. YERRES (S.-et-O.) — La Mairie

Yerres, the Town Hall

Roster of members of the Municipal Council of the Commune of Yerres in 1870. Martial Caillebotte, the artist's father, was then seventy-one years old.[3]

in the Camaldules Woods (from the name of a religious community of Italian origin, which established the second of their four convents in France in 1642).

It is easy to understand how by the second half of the nineteenth century Yerres might have been described as "one of the most enchanting little towns in the Paris area. Nowhere else can you see more charming country houses."

Paul Joanne in his *General Guide to France: the Environs of Paris, 1889 Edition, with Some Practical Notes Brought up to Date in 1892,* gives these particulars about Yerres: "To the south of the square[4] a path which crosses the river[5] bordering the estate formerly owned by Martial and Celeste Caillebotte connects Yerres two and a half kilometers farther on with the Montgeron train station."

The new bridge over the Yerres river, near the Caillebotte family property, was built in 1870. Its metal cross-brace construction recalls the superstructure of the great iron Pont de l'Europe, which the engineer Julien built over the rail tracks of the Gare Saint-Lazare in Paris. Gustave Caillebotte painted this bridge at various times from 1876 on.

Facing Number 6 Rue de Concy on the banks of the river is a property once owned by Gratien Milliet who in 1840 set up a limited partnership to merge the faience manufactory of Creil with that of Montereau. The new organization became "Faiences Creil-Montereau" and the name of the parent company "Leboeuf Milliet." In 1841 this became "Leboeuf, Milliet and Company," a title that continued until Gratien Milliet's death in 1875.

The residence that Gratien Milliet built on his property is known today as the "Brault house," Brault being the name of the family who owned it later on. A member of the Brault family, Maurice Brault, was a very close friend of Gustave Caillebotte, and Caillebotte painted him in 1876 in *The Card Game,* in 1880 in *The Man on the Balcony,* and in 1861 in *Game of Bezique,* in which Brault is shown playing cards with the artist's brother Martial. Their friendship lasted many years, as we can see in a letter Claude Monet wrote Gustave Caillebotte in 1890 about a subscription to buy Edouard Manet's painting *Olympia:*

Giverny, February 18, 1890

Dear friend,

As soon as you receive this letter, send me your contribution for Olympia. I must give this sum to Madame Manet. I have already paid 10,000 francs but must remit the remainder in order to have the painting delivered. I am counting on you. I would have advanced this sum for you but had to give 1,000 francs myself, over and above the unforeseen expense incurred in this transaction.

    Mr. Brault informed me that you will be returning any day.

    Therefore I shall expect to hear from you almost immediately.

I count on you.

With kindest regards,
Claude Monet

Château de la Grange du Milieu
Watercolor, 22 × 30 cm. In 1870 the Château belonged to the Comtesse du Taillis. The park had been redesigned "in the English manner" by the landscape architect Varé in 1847.

    The region suffered under the Franco-Prussian war of 1870–71, as can be seen in two documents of the time. One, a telegram, describes events in the woods of the Grange du Milieu Château near Limeil-Brevannes, a town bordering on Yerres:

Landscape with
Haystacks, *c. 1874*
Oil on canvas, 18 × 35 cm.[6]
Stamped, bottom left

January 8, 1871, 6:05 in the evening
Colonel le Mains in Creteil to General Ribout in Vincennes

This afternoon a heavy column of infantry was drawn up in battle formation on the road that runs parallel to that on the ridges behind the Château de Brevannes, undoubtedly to be reviewed by a high officer on his way through, since some time later, behind Meslay,[7] we again saw troops drawn up and distinctly heard three cheers. We continue to keep an eye out.

The second document, preserved in Yerres' municipal archives, is a report to the members of the town council by one Prudent Gaudefroy, who served as interim mayor from September 8, 1870 until April 14, 1871, in the absence of the elected official and his assistant.

Gaudefroy tells of having been required to transport provisions to Paris on September 8, 1870. He describes the interdiction on September 14, 1870, of all traffic save pedestrian and tells us that the local millers found it hard to get grain. Three bakers had their ovens requisitioned and Gaudefroy reports hostage taking and various taxations, the looting of farms, including one belonging to M. Paulmier at Concy, and many other woes.[8] We are also told that on March 13, 1871, the Comte du Taillis of the Château de la Grange du Milieu and his son-in-law the Baron Gourgaud and a M. Raingo set up a fund to aid the commune's workers, following a refusal of help by a M. Aubril, who then owned La Lethumière. M. Raingo's father-in-law was P. Debucourt's nephew J. P. Jazet, an aquatint engraver who, until his death on August 1, 1871, owned a charming country house at 16 Rue de la Grange in Yerres. Jules Raingo and his brother Alphonse manufactured clocks and bronzes in Paris, and Jules's niece Alice Raingo married first the art collector Ernest Hoschedé, then the painter Claude Monet. In 1876 Monet lived in the aforementioned La Lethumière, on the right bank of the river not far from Yerres' boundary with the town of Crosne.

OPPOSITE:
Loaded Haycart, *before*
1879
Oil on canvas, 36 × 47 cm.
Stamped lower right

This is the setting in which Gustave Caillebotte found himself in 1860 at the age of twelve. As a child and later as an adolescent living at home he prowled the Yerres valley's grasslands, the forest of Senart, the woods of the Château de la Grange du Milieu and those of the equally accessible Château de Grosbois. Every summer, perhaps even as early as Easter, he returned to Yerres and, at church or at village fêtes, came into contact with local farmers, gardeners, residents, and visitors. Long before he became a painter, his senses were stirred and his powers of observation sharpened by this initiation into country life.

Places that have inspired artists are usually considered to be of only secondary importance. A common belief is that only the works of art themselves count. Sites are thought to take on significance merely as they become parts of pictures. The Yerres river—thanks to its location and scenic attractions and for other reasons we shall consider later within the framework of descriptions of the park's design—was as important to Gustave Caillebotte as the Epte was to Claude Monet or Mont Saint-Victoire was to Paul Cézanne.

The artist adapts the reality of his world to his needs. Gustave Caillebotte gave the sites in which he lived a new and original and wholly personal dimension. His rendering of rural life evokes its perennial and cyclic nature, always leaving us with a sense of the rhythm of passing days and seasons. In every note he made on his paintings' sites and orientation we are reminded of this, and throughout our imaginary tour, "In the Footsteps of Gustave Caillebotte," we shall see this again in our every encounter with his work.

Throughout Caillebotte's career, motion is important. In his youthful *Yerres, Soldiers in the Woods* we see the smoke from soldiers' rifles and, in the park, the trajectory of their bullets.

If I stress the relation of the countryside to the art that is made from it, it is because specific regions are sometimes forgotten in discussions of artists' sources of inspiration.

Yerres, Woods at la Grange, Path of the Great "Ha-Ha", *before 1879*
Oil on canvas glued on cardboard, 31 × 43 cm. Stamped lower right[9]
To paint this scene, the artist placed himself in the center of the château's
façade overlooking its park, near the road leading west from Valenton to Yerres.
This path, rising to an elevation of about 86 meters, was sometimes
called the "Great Avenue of the Château." From it one has an open view onto
the Briard plateau, near Crosne.

The Impressionist Movement in Brie

Wednesday, May 5, off to Champrosay...

A picture should be sketched as though the weather were overcast, as if there were no sun, no distinct shadows, no light, no shade, and each object a colored mass reflecting differently on every side. Imagine in an outdoor scene on a gray day that objects are suddenly illuminated by a ray of sunshine. Then you have light and shadow as we commonly understand them, but as pure accidents.

EUGENE DELACROIX, 1852, *Journal*

The word "Impressionism" comes from a canvas Claude Monet painted of the outer harbor at Le Havre in 1870 and christened, *Impression, Sunrise*. This painting owned by Parisian merchant and art amateur Ernest Hoschedé, was first exhibited from April 15 to May 15, 1874, at 35 Boulevard des Capucines in Paris, on premises previously occupied by Felix Tournachon, known as Nadar. Many writers, including Alphonse Daudet,[10] lived at Champrosay at that time, on the Seine near the Forest of Sénart, and it was during this same year that Félicien Rops[11] wrote, "... There is perhaps much to hope for in a strange new painting movement which goes under the name of the School of Impressionism, characterized by the same kind of luminousness as in work being done a good deal now in Belgium, but rougher and better. It is full of grotesque stuff but there are three good men, Caillebotte, Degas and Monet, who show great strength and are very gifted..."

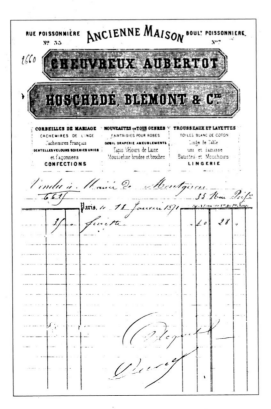

Bill from the firm of Chevreux, Aubertot, Hoschedé, Blémont and Company to the municipal offices of Montgeron dated Paris, January 18, 1871. The heading on this bill gives us some idea of Ernest Hoschedé's connections.

In September 1876, Pierre Auguste Renoir spent three weeks with Alphonse Daudet at Draveil-Champrosay and painted, among other works, a portrait of Julia Allard Daudet, who was Madame Alphonse Daudet, and *Banks of the Seine at Champrosay*. This last was exhibited in April 1877 at the third Impressionist show and was bought by Gustave Caillebotte who bequeathed it to the nation; today it hangs in the Musée d'Orsay in Paris.

That same year—which was also the year of the second Impressionist exhibition at the Durand-Ruel Gallery at 11 Rue Le Peletier, Paris, in April—Ernest Hoschedé

Harvest, Landscape with Five Haystacks, *before 1879*
Oil on cardboard, 25 × 32 cm.
Stamped lower right
The view is from Epinay-sous-Sénart. Near the road leading to that town is the curve of the Yerres River, which flows toward Boussy-Saint-Antoine. In the distance one can make out, on the right, the steeple of the church of Saint-Pierre-Saint-Eutrope (6th–7th century) at Boussy-Saint-Antoine, not far from the ancient seigneurial house, which in 1837 belonged to Auguste Prud'homme, a Parisian magistrate. To the left of the church is the seigneurial farm, which was once the property of the monks of Saint-Antoine of Viennois and which was restored in the seventeenth century.

and his wife, Alice, née Raingo, invited different painters during the summer to the Château de Rottembourg in the Yerres Valley at Montgeron.[12] In July Edouard Manet and his wife, Suzanne Leenhoff, spent a fortnight there. Manet does not seem to have found inspiration in the region but painted several portraits of family members, including one of Hoschedé himself. He also painted his friend Charles Durand or, as he was known, Carolus Duran. Duran's success as a popular painter of socialites and demimondaines fascinated Manet. To please Duran, Manet decorated one of the rooms of Le Moutier, Duran's house at Montgeron, with a design of parrots, and in turn Carolus Duran painted a splendid portrait of Manet.

In 1980, in his *Invitation to Giverny*, Gerald Van der Kemp wrote, "Wherever he lived, Claude Monet had a garden, at Ville d'Avray, Louveciennes, Argenteuil (where

Pierre-Auguste Renoir
Banks of the Seine at Champrosay, 1876
Oil on canvas, 55 × 66 cm. Signed lower right, "Renoir"
This painting was part of Gustave Caillebotte's collection

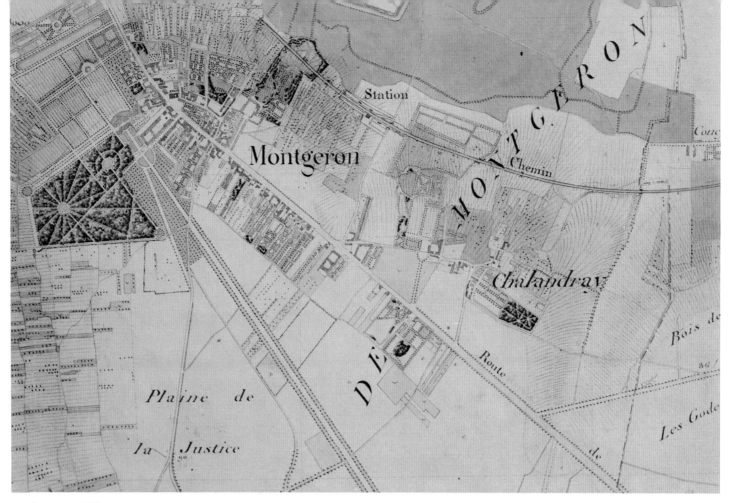

To this map of Montgeron, drawn about 1821, was added, around 1840, the projected railway line of the Compagnie de Paris à Lyon et à la Mediterranée. On the upper left is "Le Moutier," property of Carolus-Duran (1837–1917).

his taste for gardening was increased by contact with his friend Caillebotte) and at Vetheuil."

Claude Monet at this time was staying at Montgeron. His maternal grandfather, François-Léonard Aubrée, had been a native of Brunoy (Essonne). After retiring from the Finance Ministry and separating from his wife Marie-Françoise Toffard, Monet's

The Raingo-Hoschedé Château de Rottembourg, south façade. This façade is now integrated into monastery buildings, the château having become the property of a religious community. We see the north side of this château in Claude Monet's Turkeys.

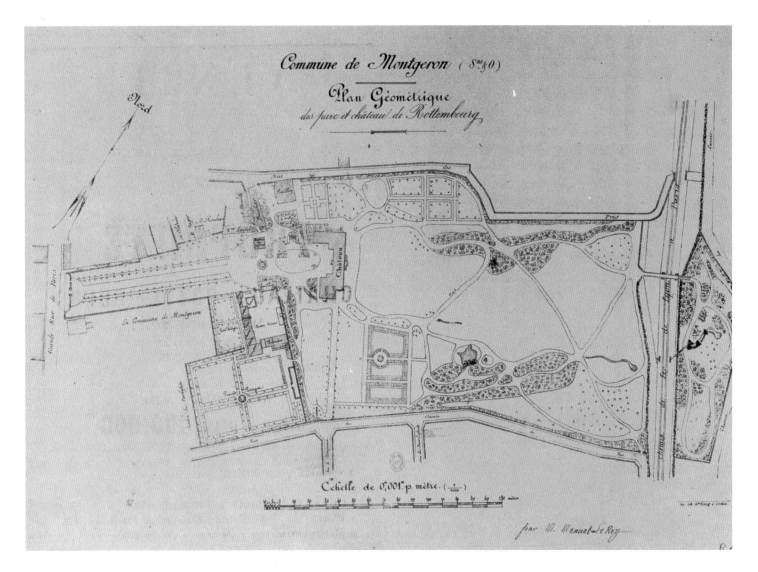

Map of the Château de Rottembourg and its park in about 1860. The lower part of the park, to the right, was cut by the railway line. A footbridge spans the tracks. On this map we see, from left to right, beginning in the lower section, the small kitchen garden, the large kitchen garden, the park grounds, and the flower garden overlooking the grotto on the edge of the ornamental pool.

grandfather settled at Villeneuve-Saint-Georges (Val-de-Marne) where, on the public road, he had a cerebral hemorrhage, was taken to the Madelonnettes infirmary, and died on January 2, 1844. Monet worked in the small house that Ernest Hoschedé lent him at La Lethumière, at Yerres.

Hoschedé commissioned Monet to paint a mural for the Château de Rottembourg's salon, and Monet executed four panels inspired by the park on the property. In *The Turkeys* we see the façade of the Château de Rottembourg as it appeared in 1876, overlooking the park with its lawn sloping toward Yerres. *In a Corner of the Garden at Montgeron*, or *Dahlias*, a small flower-covered hill in the foreground overlooks the lawn on the left and, near the flower garden on the right, the ornamental pool, as shown in the diagram. In the background, behind Crosne and Yerres on the other side of the river's right bank, we see the high land of the Brie plateau near Mont Griffon. A grotto on the edge of the ornamental pool is not shown.

The Pond at Montgeron features the lake with trees reflected in its flat, late-day surface. A figure appears in silhouette to the right at the water's edge, near the grotto. Under a spruce on the left is a boulder, which also appears in the foregoing work.

Edouard Manet
Madame Manet in the Greenhouse, *1879*
Oil on canvas, 81 × 100 cm.
*This portrait of Madame Manet shows her as she must
have looked several years earlier, when she came to
Montgeron.*

The last panel, *The Hunt* or *Park Avenue at Montgeron* shows Ernest Hoschedé hunting in the middle distance. Here the setting appears to be an avenue or service path through the forest of Sénart near Montgeron. On October 16, 1871, Aristide Subervielle, owner of the Château Sousy-sous-Etiolles (now Soisy-sur-Seine), acquired nine years of hunting rights, which he shared with the Count Cahen d'Anvers, who first rented, then bought the estate known as Les Bergeries in the hamlet of Mainville, at that time a dependency of the town of Draveil.

While at Montgeron, Claude Monet painted, in addition to preparatory work and studies made on the site itself for the decorative panels for the Château de Rottembourg, a portrait of Germaine Hoschedé with her doll, and three paintings called *Willow Grove at the Water's Edge, Yerres River near Montgeron; View of the River Yerres*; and *Willows on the Bank of the Yerres*. This last work was owned by Alexandre Berthier, Fourth Prince of Wagram, owner of the Château de Grosbois in Boissy-Saint-Léger.

At Yerres Monet also painted *The House at Yerres* showing a façade overlooking a park on the property of a M. Debatisse, a mechanical engineer. Other visitors at the Château de Rottembourg were the painter Léon-Germain Pelouse, who was to marry Ernest Hoschedé's sister, and Alfred Sisley. Other Impressionists were inspired by the Brie landscape. Sisley, working on the banks of the Seine near Saint-Mammès, painted the boundaries of Brie. From 1863 to 1864 Camille Pissarro visited Saint-Maur-des Fossés, La Varenne Saint-Hilaire and, around 1864 to 1865, painted *On the Banks of the Marne at Chennevières*. Paul Cézanne, while staying at Melun in the vicinity of Vaux-Le-Vicomte, painted *The Maincy Bridge*. Stanislas Henri Rouart contributed his *View of Melun* to the second painting exhibition in 1876, and his *Quai des Fourneaux at Melun* to the third exhibition in 1877.

Detail of a fountain in the farmyard of the Château de Rottembourg. This decorative structure is attributed to Alexandre-Théodore Brongniart. The drawing is by G. Quintrie-Lamothe.

Claude Monet
Turkeys, *1876*
Oil on canvas, 170 × 170 cm.
Signed and dated lower right, "Claude Monet, 77"
The north side of the Château de Rottembourg is
seen here from the lawn. The ornamental pool and
the grotto are concealed among the foliage on the
left. The evergreen trees in the center of the lawn,
in the middle of the composition, still exist.

IMPORTANT SITES AT YERRES, INCLUDING PLACES WHICH INSPIRED THE IMPRESSIONISTS

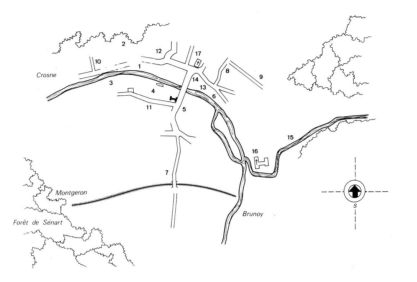

1. The Yerres River
2. Mont Griffon (altitude 117 meters)
3. The Great Meadow
4. The Caillebotte property, today Number 6 Rue de Concy
5. The Brault estate
6. Property of M. Debatisse, today Number 47 Avenue de l'Abbaye (Building B of the A. Calmette Center annex)
7. P. L. M. Railway bridge
8. Property of M. Jazet (Jules Raingo)
9. Old Raingo Way, today the Rue Raingo
10. Rue de la Lethumière, or Letumière
11. Meadow Cul-de-Sac
12. Le Buet property: owned in 1876 by a M. Beaure, a banker; today Number 1½ Rue René Coty[13]
13. The Budé Fountain (17th century)
14. Baronial Château d'Yerres, which in 1876 belonged to the family of Alexandre Hamelin, mayor of the Third Arrondissement in Paris
15. A brook: Le Reveillon
16. The Benedictine Abbey of Notre Dame d'Yerres
17. Parish church of "Saint-Honest"

Claude Monet
The Shoot, *1876*
Oil on canvas, 170 × 137 cm.
Signed and dated lower left, "Claude Monet 1876"

A History of the Property

The property at 6 Rue de Concy at Yerres lies between the Yerres river on the north, the meadow cul-de-sac to the south, the Rue de Concy to the east and, on the west, "The Meadow" or "Great Meadow." The Rue de Concy takes its name from an ancient fief in the land tenure of the seigneury of Yerres.

As far as we can tell, the property that was to become the Caillebotte estate belonged in the eighteenth century to Samuel Jacques Bernard, oldest son of Samuel Bernard, a French financier who founded the Guinea Company and lent important sums to Louis XIV and Louis XV. Samuel Jacques Bernard acquired the estate of Grosbois at Boissy-Saint-Leger on March 14, 1718, from Christian Louis de Montmorency-Luxembourg, Prince de Tingry, but Bernard was ruined by high living and speculation and by March 1731, was declared bankrupt and his holdings liquidated. On March 7 and 8 by a contract signed before a lawyer, one M. Tessier and his associate, notaries in Paris, a politician, Germain Louis de Chauvelin, France's Minister of Justice and Secretary of State for Foreign Affairs, acquired the Rue de Concy property along with the land and manor house of Grosbois with its seigneurial right pertaining to the land and castellan of Yerres. In March 1734, the marquisate of Grosbois, incorporating the fief of Narella at Yerres, was set up by letter and official seal and on April 19 registered with the Parliament in Paris and, on May 27th, with the government's Accounting Office.

On June 15, 1734, Chauvelin and his wife, referred to as "the former lord and lady of the manor at the aforesaid Yerres," sold Number 6 Rue de Concy to the King's Secretary Jacques Pajot, the deed witnessed by M. Tessier and his associate, notaries at Châtelet.

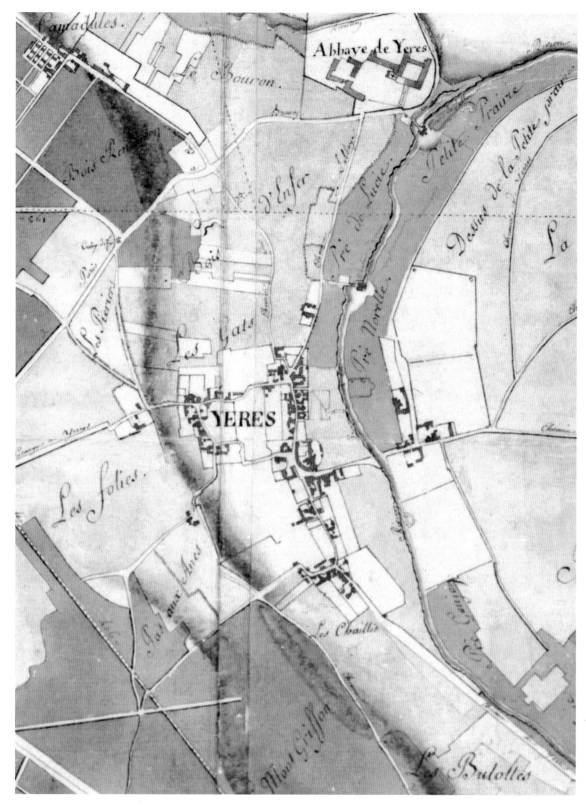

Yerres in an 18th-century administrative map

On April 29, 1750, and May 11, 1750, Pajot sold the place to Joseph Barthélémy and his wife Anne Françoise Virvoudet Barthélémy by deed executed before M. Ruelle and his associate, notaries at Châtelet. Around this time the property seems to have been rented to different people, notably to a M. Bergeons and to a M. Germain Combes.

Nearby, the Squire of Montgeron's two-arpent and forty-two-rod forest known as Les Rouches, which abutted the Narella farm and lands belonging to the Seminary of Saint-Sulpice in Paris, was awarded to Samuel Bernard's grandson Gabriel Henri Bernard, Marquis de Boulainvilliers, who from 1766 to 1792 was Provost of Paris.

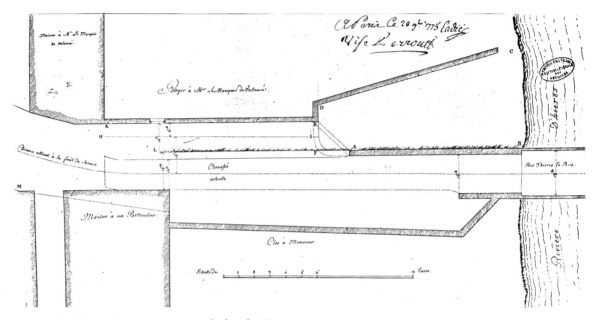

Map dated December 20, 1775, attached to the Marquis de Vallençay's petition

By 1775 the Marquis of Vallençay, Chamberlain to the Duke of Orleans, had a lifehold lease on what was to become the Caillebotte property and on December 13 of that year requested the right to acquire a small parcel of land on the edge of the road and the river next to the wooden bridge over the Yerres, with access to the old ford. After having obtained the authorization, and a report dated December 26, 1775, having been made by one M. Perronet, surveyor,[14] M. de Vallençay had this parcel of land enclosed.

On March 1, 1776, "the residents of the village of Hyerre bring to the attention [of the Count of Provence] the fact that M. de Vallençay has enclosed within his land a watering place which they need or which is at least very convenient for them. One of

*Upper end of the Rue de Concy, Yerres, in about 1800,
showing the seigneurial château's entrance on the square*

M. de Vallençay's own farmers is the most affected . . ." But nothing was done about this.

A notarized instrument drawn up at Brunoy on December 5, 1870, between Armand Louis Joseph Lelarge and one "Anne Françoise Virvoudet, widow of Sir Joseph Barthélémy, a bourgeoise presently residing at Brunoy in the Château de Grosbois, for herself as well as for her grandson, a minor," furnishes us with a description of the property as follows: "A large middle-class house with outbuildings presently occupied by the Marquis of Vallençay adjacent to the bridge of said place formerly known as the Fief of Nazelle,[15] consisting of several main buildings, each one equipped with kitchen, vestibule, dining room, drawing room, bedroom, dressing room, attic, and cellar; stable, coach house, parterres, shrubberies, small cottages, kitchen garden, orchard, and arable land, the whole consisting of sixteen arpents enclosed by walls and adjoining on its southern length, and separated from said southern length by the Great Meadow road, by the Tournelle lands belonging to the Concy farm; bounded on its northern length by the bridge and the Yerres River; and on its eastern side by the Nazelle crossroads and the street from the said bridge to Concy, the Godeaux and the Forest of Sénart; and on the west by lands and fields of the Messieurs of the Seminary of Saint Sulpice, which are part of the said Concy farm . . ."

In the nineteenth century the property belonged successively, from 1799 to 1806, to one Pierre Henri Chauveau and, from 1806 to 1824, to Alexandre Gaillot, Marquis of Mandat. Gaillot's father Jean, Marquis of Mandat and Commander in Chief of the Paris Garde Nationale, was in charge of the defense of the Tuileries at the time of the one-day insurrection of August 10, 1792, and was executed on the orders of the Revolutionary Commune.

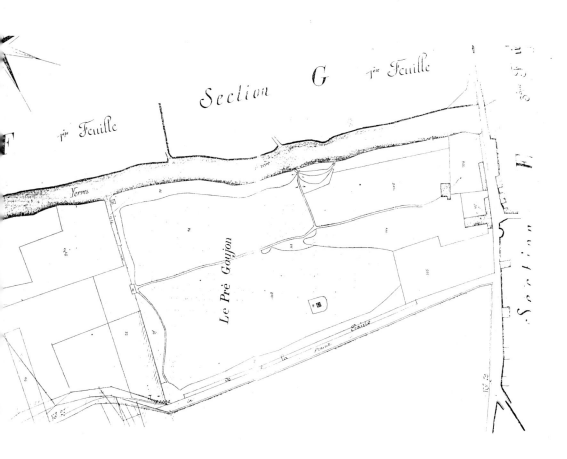

Survey map prepared in 1810: detail showing the property on the Rue de Concy, Yerres

About this time the poet Jean-François Ducis wrote the following poem, entitled, "The River Yerres":

From thy banks, charming Hière,
Not only waves glide by
But also the days of a hermit
Who seeks repose.
May this field be enriched by thy waters,
Be for me the boundaries of the world,
Be for me the universe.
May my soul dream only
Of this willow, that poplar
Overhanging thy wandering flood!
Thy hospitable bank abounds with cool grace.
Ah! Add if thou canst
The healing balm of forgetfulness.

Lith: de Frey.

Vue d'un Château de Henry IV, prise de la propriété de Mr Borrel à Yerres, (Environs de Paris)

A look at the land registry of 1810 reveals that the Caillebotte property with its buildings and park has not changed much. Only some outbuildings on the edge of the Meadow Cul-de-Sac, such as stables and aviaries and, in the park, some small cottages, a chapel, and orangery do not appear on the plan. The icehouse and the beginning of a future ornamental lake referred to as "the pond" are marked. Near the main house is the building that would eventually be altered into an alpine chalet, or Swiss house. At the far end of the park near the future gardens for flowers, vegetables, and roses a small canal evidently intended for irrigation and drainage had been dug perpendicular to the river.

From 1824 to 1843 the property belonged to a former majordomo to France's Minister of the Interior, Montalivet, one Pierre Frédéric Borrel who in 1816 acquired Balaine's famous Parisian restaurant Au Rocher de Cancale for the sum of 170,000 francs. Situated in the angle of Number 59 Rue de Montorgueil and Number 2 Rue Mandar in Paris, the Rocher de Cancale was, from 1808 on, a meeting place for the Taste Jury founded by Grimod de la Reynière and the Wednesday Club; the latter limited its reunions to seventeen diners who, fork in hand, bemoaned the hardships of the times and the sorrows of gourmands. The Literary and Bacchic Society of Vaudeville Dinners and the singers from the Caveau Moderne also met there. Since the restaurant was located near a shop that from 1780 to 1850 sold oysters from Etretat, it was naturally one of the best places to eat this delicacy in Paris. Grimod de la Reynière wrote, "At any hour of the year so many oysters are eaten that their discarded shells rise to the height of the tallest houses in that street and seem on the point of turning into real rock formations . . . The continuous relations that the oyster market gives this restaurant with Normandy and Brittany guarantee their superiority here. The same is true for the inestimable quality of game it brings in from those provinces. Furthermore the Rocher's wine cellar assures its marked preeminence over the Parc d'Etretat" (a neighboring rival). Desaugiers wrote in the *Journal des Gourmands et des Belles*:

This Rocher was ever the rock of chagrin
To the drinker of water
For its flanks are only lashed
By tides of wine.

Once a week Brillat-Savarin took such Parisian personalities as Talma and Cadet de Gassicourt to the famous Rocher to delight in a simple turbot on a spit. Borrel, who cared a great deal about quality, managed the place beautifully for twenty-five years, maintaining its spirit and tradition while at the same time expanding its operation. During Borrel's day the Rocher de Cancale received some unusual publicity from Honoré de Balzac who referred to it more than twenty times in *La Comédie Humaine*. Among the restaurant's clients were Victor Hugo in 1826, Alfred de Musset, and Alexandre Dumas Père. Around 1845 the restaurant disappeared.

Borrel acquired several other properties beside the one that interests us, among them Le Pré d'Espagnac, described as follows by Picard: "Not far away is a delightful

*Empire-style bedroom on the second floor as it looked at
the turn of the century*

*Details of frieze
in the loggia*

1. Northwest side

country house whose charmingly planted gardens are enhanced by a view over the river. A pavilion by the architect Liegeon takes the form of a temple with a dome supported by Ionic columns, and there are other sights to enchant the heart and mind. Once the property of the Baron d'Espagnac,[16] the estate now belongs to M. Philippe."

Certain installations appear to have been made in the estate's park at this time, specifically the exhedra that figures in Frey's lithograph and of which we shall speak later.

From 1843 to 1860 the property belonged to the widow of Martin Guillaume Biennais,[17] jeweler to France's first Consul and then to the Emperor, and to the kings of Holland and Westphalia. At the time of the Proclamation of Empire Biennais executed the imperial insignia for the coronation ceremony, including the gold laurel wreath Napoleon wore in David's celebrated painting; the great gold necklace of the Order of the Legion of Honor; and, in vermeil, the scepter, globe of the world, and hand of justice. In order to fill orders from his enormous clientele, Biennais' workshops on the Rue Saint Honoré employed as many as six hundred workers at a time and resembled an industrial empire.

Antiquity as revised and interpreted mostly by the architects Percier and Fontaine served Biennais as inspiration. Specialists in the Empire style rate his designs and execution highly. A favorite device of his was the frieze to which he liked to give a matte background and against which he deployed the entire Empire ornamental repertory, including such scenes as the Aldobrandini wedding, among his more popular themes.

Around this time Empire bedroom furniture executed for Murat, King of Naples, occupied the second floor of the property, which from 1860 to 1879 was to belong to

2. Southeast side

View of the lawn of the landscape park from the Empire-style bedroom on the "casin's" second-floor loggia

June 12, 1860, Yerres

To His Honor the Mayor:

I am the owner and purchaser, from the heirs of Madame Biennais, of a house situated at Yerres abutting the public road Number 72. This is to request the necessary authorization to replaster the façade of this house giving onto said road.

I have the honor, dear sir, to be your very humble servant.

For Monsieur Caillebotte, by the hand of Pommier

Correspondence relating to the restoration of the façade of the "casin": A request for authorization by one Pommier, contractor, for Martial Caillebotte, Senior, dated June 12, 1860

Martial Caillebotte and then his wife, Celeste Daufresne Caillebotte. The Caillebottes bought the place from the heirs of Madame Biennais.[18]

A description of Martial Caillebotte's purchase as recorded in the land registry reads, "The said Goujon field, the said village, the said large meadow, the said Narelle," and goes on to describe "the nature of the property" according to the parcels of land that made it up, as follows, "detached buildings, chapel, house, open land, meadow, ornamental wood, farm buildings, kitchen garden, flower beds, planted land, artificial lake, pasture, ha-ha." The last term requires some explanation. According to J. Lalos in 1824,

In order to preserve the views from a house and enjoy the landscape, one can construct ha-has, or large ditches dug at the boundaries of a park or garden. These ditches measure at least 12 feet in width by 7 or 8 feet deep and are lined with a masonry wall to prevent the earth from caving in. They may be lined only on the side facing outward, and a long slope constructed on the inner side. In this way the land can be cultivated to the foot of the wall without loss of usable land and at less expense. Such walls, of a pitch of 1 or 2 inches per foot according to the nature of the ground, are constructed of rough or dressed stone with a mortar of limestone and sand. If a course of cut stone can be added every 5 or so meters the construction becomes more solid. Such walls, raised only 2 feet above the natural level of the terrain, are topped by flat stone slabs or, where cut stone is lacking, by a row of bricks set edgewise. The indicated pitch is indispensable to contain the thrust of the earth.

Yerres, Watering Place, Public Washhouse and
Baths, the Stone Bridge that the Metal Bridge
Replaced in 1870, *before 1879*
Drawing on paper, (page) 20 × 31 cm.
(drawing) 18 × 30 cm.
This sketch was made by the young Caillebotte from the
riverbank of his family's property at 6 Rue de Concy in
Yerres and focuses on the river's right bank downstream
of the bridge. This is the same site as the postcard on
page 19 and the painting Périssoires on the Yerres.

Millstone rock with limestone and sand mortar are materials traditionally used in Brie. A ha-ha originally constructed at the boundary of the landscape park and the flower, fruit, and vegetable gardens may explain the existence of the canal of which we shall speak later.

"A map of the property of M. Caillebotte residing at Yerres (Seine-Oise)" may date from a period of reconstruction following his purchase, since we know that in June 1860, Martial Caillebotte had the stucco façade of the Italianate house, or "casin," as it was called, restored. On this map[20] we see the landscape garden, the perimeter road, the paths, the wood, the icehouse, the grotto, the Belvedere or gazebo, the cottage, the avenue leading to the openwork gate, the chapel, the flower, fruit, and vegetable gardens, the rosarium (in this last we can make out a structure composed of metal arches, probably an arbor for climbing roses), the canal and the stone bridge over it leading to a wetland, and the property's meadow in common with the so called "Great Meadow."

In the meadow, near four of the seven rows of trees growing parallel to the river

Yerres, August 16, 1873

To the Mayor of Yerres
Dear Sir:

I have the honor of enclosing the agreement that Monsieur Brault and I have entered into to remit 800 francs to your municipality for repair of the wall, which goes from the bridge along the southern slope toward the river.

Monsieur Labarre, appointed by the municipal council, agrees that there is no reason to shorten the wall. The conditions in our agreement are those that Monsieur Pommier had submitted. He should give you a copy of his contract with us.

It will give us great pleasure to have this business straightened out promptly so that the work can be accomplished during warm weather.

Please accept, dear sir, the assurance of my greatest respect.

Martial Caillebotte

Letter from Martial Caillebotte (Senior) to the Mayor of Yerres, dated Yerres, August 6, 1873, concerning the repair of a wall

OPPOSITE:

The Park of the Caillebotte Estate at Yerres, *1875 (detail).*[19]

View from the lawn of the "casin's" colonnade as it looks today

(the poplars that we see in Caillebotte's 1878 paintings *The Yerres River Valley* and *The Meadow at Yerres*, we find the outlines of a structure that may have been the country house in his *Luncheon of the Boaters Beside the Yerres* executed around 1872 and that Kirk Varnedoe in 1976 dubbed *The Swamp* ("La Grenouillière"). In the meadow a row of trees at right angles to the river provided a curtain of poplar foliage veiling the western limit of the property where it abutted the "Great Meadow."

On the river's edge—on the northwest side of the landscape park not far from the lower end of the canal—a square outline may mark the site of a rustic pavilion such as a summerhouse or a scenic lookout over the river and over the contiguous park belonging to the estate known as Le Buet, or it may have been a water mill intended to

A drawing room on the "casin's" ground floor at the turn of the century. Here was where Gustave Caillebotte painted Billiards, *c. 1875.*

irrigate the flower and kitchen gardens. Remains of a water mill can be seen to the right of the wall enclosing the kitchen garden near the canal.

Also discernible on this plan are the bridge constructed of rough timbers and dressed wood spanning the narrow end of the pond, and the outline of a structure at the river's edge[23] downstream from where the pond's narrow end begins, either a fisherman's house, a rustic dwelling, or a dock. One can also see the property's washhouse on the riverbank, the greenhouse, well, Swiss-style house, Italianate house (or "casin"), lawn, exhedra, fountain, ornamental farm, and aviary. Many different paths lead to these different places.[24]

In 1879 the Caillebotte property was acquired by Pierre Ferdinand Dubois in whose family it remained until the second half of the twentieth century. At that time it consisted of a total of 11 hectares (2.47 acres per hectare), including the landscape

The orangery in March, 1916, on a day of hoar frost[21]

The chapel in the park, January, 1918[22]

park of 7 hectares; the flower, fruit, and vegetable gardens enclosed by walls (2 hectares); and the meadow (2 hectares). It employed five gardeners, although after 1938 there were only three. Some light metal frames are still found in the rose garden. The buildings of the so-called ornamental farm still have their decorative facings of brick and timberwork. The wood paneling of the dining room in the Italianate house frames large canvases painted in the manner of Jean-Baptiste Camille Corot.

After 1965 one of the owners of the property added a second porch separating the exhedra from the rest of the park. To the terrace of the small pavilion situated on the right of the main terrace near the exhedra a half story has been added. The architecture of this pavilion, and more particularly of the second-floor dormer window, is inspired by the "Petit Château" at Chantilly, constructed about 1550 by the architect Jean Bullant II for the High Constable Anne, First Duke of Montmorency. The interior of the Italianate house has been changed significantly to give second-story rooms, previously oriented to the north, a view of the south, an alteration achieved by shifting a service corridor. The room giving onto the loggia to the west, where some parts of the First Empire decoration still remain, was not touched as it is situated at the building's far end.

The municipality of Yerres acquired the property by a decree dated February 12, 1975, in Paris, of the Secretary of State for Cultural Affairs, which reads,

Article First, the entirety formed in the commune of Yerres by the Caillebotte property shall be classed among the sites of the Department of Essonne, demarcated as follows: the Rue de Conçy (C.D. number 31), the meadow cul-de-sac, the boundary between parcels 32 and 31 Section AO of the land registry of Yerres and an artificial line extending this boundary to the Yerres River, and the Yerres River to the Rue de Conçy (point of departure).

The above specifications do not include the lower end of the property beyond the old ha-ha and the blue gate, which was the site of the flower garden where, in 1877, Gustave Caillebotte painted *The Gardener* in the vicinity of the greenhouses. Also excluded from the town's protection is the spot that inspired *Yerres, in the Kitchen Garden, Gardeners Watering the Plants*.

Aerial photograph of the property at Yerres: The course of the Yerres river can be seen at the top

A Walk in the Family Park at Yerres

A single turn around a garden is a voyage from which one always returns contented and usefully stimulated.

ANTOINE JOSEPH DEZALLIER D'ARGENVILLE, 1739

SAINT FIACRE IN THE YERRES REGION

Before we begin our tour let us have a look at the role gardening plays in Brie and examine the manner in which the traditions of the Briard gardener arose and spread through the Yerres valley, for these traditions are reflected in Caillebotte's work. Caillebotte painted the Chapter House at Meaux, which is the high holy place of the cult of Saint Fiacre, and he depicted the Benedictine Abbey at Yerres where the movement originated in the valley.

Engraving of Saint Fiacre by Israel Silvestre (1621–91), after Jacques Callot (c. 1592–1635)

Saint Fiacre patron of Brye,
Alone of this name, I beg thee,
Intercede for me
With God the Creator.
Glorious Saint of Scotland born,
Certain am I that God gave thee
Power over men and women;
Thanks to thee dangers
Are expelled from their bodies and souls.
By thy intercession they are cured of languishing ills,
Fevers, chancres, infection,
Fractures, deadly stones,
Growths filled with decay and disease and foulness
And filth which enters the body
Together with an onrush of blood,
Humors which attack the belly, menstrual flux, worms
And many other evils which physicians cannot cure.
Saint Fiacre helps him who prays devoutly to him;
May my soul have access to eternal glory,
May my body enjoy great health.

Meaux, Effect of Sunlight on the Old Chapterhouse, *before 1879*
Oil on cardboard, 37 × 49 cm.
Stamped lower left
This rectangular building, dating from the end of the twelfth century when Meaux was part of western Champagne, was built near the Cathedral of Saint Etienne, to the right of the Episcopal Palace. Two large rooms surmount a vaulted cellar. The lower of the two, also vaulted and divided into naves, serves as a sacristy. The upper room is covered with planking supported by a central row of columns. The artist may have painted this high place of the cult of Saint Fiacre on the occasion of a visit to his jurist friend Albert Courtier, Notary at Meaux.

YERRES (s.-et-o.) - Ancienne Abbaye d'Yerres (Porte du Prieuré)

L. Combes, Edit.
L.H. Paris

What we see on the left side of this old postcard was represented in reverse by Gustave Caillebotte. The house known as "Le Val Ombré" is on the left, and "Les Vallées" is to its right, in the center. Perhaps Caillebotte worked from a photographic negative in his studio, or he may have used a mirror, an unusual technique for a landscape painter working on the site. Dress designers employ mirrors during corrections on the model to show up imperfections. Use of a rear-view mirror may have helped Caillebotte frame his composition better. He resorted to this method in Self-Portrait in Front of the Easel, c. 1879, *where Renoir's* Le Moulin de la Galette *hanging on a wall in his apartment, appears reversed. In a* Café, 1880, *and* Paris, Profile of Painter at Work in a Voltaire Armchair *are also reverse images.*

Saint Fiacre, whose dates are about 610 to 670, was a Scottish recluse who immigrated to Gaul. His hermitage near Meaux became first a monastery, then grew into the town of Breuil (Saint-Fiacre in Brie). He is the town's patron saint, and the patron saint of gardeners including market gardeners and, by a play on words in the French, of coachmen (*fiacre* = coach). The cult of Saint Fiacre, whose feast day is August 30, appears to have been practiced at Yerres since the eighth century at the Benedictine Abbey of Notre Dame d'Yerres, where the saint's relics were enshrined.

By the end of the fifteenth century Jeanne de Rauville, a native of Meaux, became Abbess. One of the first measures inaugurated during her tenure, which lasted from 1460 to 1487, was the renovation of the Abbey's buildings, which had been damaged by the Hundred Years War of 1337 to 1453. To finance this work, Jeanne de Rauville sold her own personal property, including a house at Saint Fiacre, near Meaux. During the sixteenth century while Dreux Budé II was Seigneur of Yerres, the Abbey's influence expanded and in March 1518, François I proclaimed two fair days, which had originally been set aside by Louis XI: the Day of Sainte Croix in May and, on August 30, the Day of Saint Fiacre. The latter-day François had moved from September 1. Until that time it had been devoted to Saint Gilles and Saint Leu. During this period all the parishes in the province recited the prayer from a 1509 book of hours, which is at the beginning of this chapter.

In 1599 Henry IV granted the Guild of Master Gardeners status comparable to that accorded other professions, and thereafter in Paris master gardeners enjoyed all the perquisites of their new rank, including an office on the Rue des Rosiers (a street name that appears as early as 1230), a chapel at Saint-Nicolas-des-Champs, a coat of arms ("sable with three garden lilies silver in leaf and stem vert resting in two chiefs of the shield and tapering, one chief azure charged with a gold sun") and a holy patron, who was Saint Fiacre.

Yerres, Close of the Abbesses, before 1879
Oil on cardboard, 33 × 49 cm.
Stamped lower right
The site of this painting is the first road from Yerres to Brunoy, from the intersection of the present-day Rue du Clos des Nonnains d'Hyères and the Rue du Réveillon. This road was the only link between Yerres and Brunoy until the construction, in 1737, of a right of way, which passed around the Abbey and through the buildings of the prestigious Benedictine nunnery, where 45 abbesses succeeded one after the other from 1132 to 1792. At the time of the Revolution the Abbey was broken up into parcels and sold. Today its buildings, some of them altered in the 19th century, are spread over more than seven properties. Those on the right were incorporated into a private estate known in the 20th century as "Le Val Ombré" and those on the left into a private property, which at the turn of the century was called "les Vallées."

The trees are part of the Abbey's ancient gardens. These gardens were watered by canals that the abbesses created by diverting the course of the Réveillon brook. Antoine Franconi had them redesigned by the landscape architect J. Lalo, a pupil of I. M. Berthault, who wrote De la composition des parcs et jardins pittoresques, *Paris, 1824. Franconi acquired some of the Abbey's buildings and altered them for his family's gymkhanas, the Cirque d'Astley, later called the Cirque Olympique, Hippodrome de l'Etoile à Paris.*

The miracle of Saint Fiacre, patron saint of gardeners, engraving by Sadeler, after Martin de Vos

In 1734 Louis XV declared the fair at Yerres to be Saint Fiacre's Day and that Saint Fiacre be honored at the parish church, which in the fourteenth century had been dedicated to Saint Honest.[25]

In Provins on Saint Fiacre's Day festivities began with an election of the King of Roses, whose one-year reign began with a coronation during the Magnificat at the Vespers service, with flaring torches and crowns of roses. Provins is renowned for cultivation of the dark red rose carried back from the Crusades in the thirteenth century by Count Thibaud the Great.

In the nineteenth century the Commission for the Inventory of Art Treasures posted the following notice in the church at Yerres in the district of Boissy-Saint-Leger[26]: "In the niche formed by the enlargement of the nave a sixth picture represents the village's patron, Saint Fiacre, life-size, in a religious costume consisting of a white robe and black cowl. On a nearby table covered with red carpeting lies a crown and scepter." This latter detail symbolizes a visit made to the saint by Scottish ambassadors on the occasion of his father's death. The visitors presented him with the Crown's respects whereupon he implored God to give him leprosy. He was miraculously cured, once the messengers had departed.

In the painting Saint Fiacre holds a spade in his left hand, reminding us that while at the monastery at Meaux he requested and obtained from Saint Faron permission to

retire to a hermitage not far from town. The town granted him as many acres as he could clear in a day, so long as he had dug a ditch all around it. The hermit traced with his spade the boundaries of his domain and the ground opened of itself, and of themselves trees fell and the ditch was dug. In the background of the picture, on the right at the edge of a wood, we see a church and monastery. This work, measuring 2.50 meters in height by 1.30 meters wide, was destroyed in the second half of the twentieth century. We have taken our iconographic information from the engraving after Martin De Vos, which is reproduced here and which should be compared to Gustave Caillebotte's *Yerres, in the Kitchen Garden, Gardeners Watering the Plants*.

In Brie at this period and especially in the Yerres Valley[27] gardeners working on estates were grouped together in such organizations as the Brotherhood of Saint Fiacre at Brie-Comte-Robert, which was disbanded in 1862; the Union of Yerres Gardeners; and the Fraternal Order of the Gardeners of Brunoy and Its Environs, which ceased to exist in the second half of the twentieth century.[28] These institutions were, to a degree, provident societies intended to ensure the welfare and retirement benefits of their members and to underwrite a social program for their families. In order to raise money, an annual festival was organized for Saint Fiacre's Day and each member took his turn at running the event.

First, a floral work called the Bouquet was created by arranging flowers, vegetables, moss, and foliage on the horizontal shafts of a carriage in such a way that they composed a closely worked carpet-like design. Such work was extremely popular at the time of Queen Victoria and required the most competent gardeners and skillfully run hothouses to produce. On this carpet a statue of Saint Fiacre was displayed against a vertical armature on which foliage, flowers, and vegetables were attached topiary-fashion and according to individual taste and to the possibilities that the

YERRES (S.-&-O.) — Vue d'une Propriété - Rue de Paris

A gardener at work, Yerres

gardening year afforded, in such a way as to suggest a mill, waterfall, gigantic vase of flowers, ship, or hot-air balloon. Paraded through the village streets, the Bouquet was greatly admired.

The order of the procession was usually as follows: first, the musicians; then the saint's relics followed by the procession's emblem or baton and the Society's banner. Then came the gardener members of the Society, the Bouquet, and two lines of marchers. The public followed. Flower girls, or "Daughters of Flora" (Flora being the goddess of flowers and gardens), dressed all in white and carrying baskets, tossed petals over the spectators.[29]

In the morning the procession's participants assembled at the parish church for the celebration of a High Mass and to have the Bouquet blessed. On leaving the church the gardeners left offerings of brioches and the marchers proceeded to a reception at one of the town's hotels. Weather permitting, this was held outdoors in the hotel garden. Then the Society's members and local persons of rank attended a banquet. The afternoon was devoted to a regional floral and horticultural exhibition and competition in which individual gardeners entered products which they had grown and of which they were most proud, and a jury awarded prizes. This encounter among skilled workers promoted professional ties.

The Corporation of Master Gardeners was organized into categories of merit according to special skills, such as individuals in charge of public gardens or responsible for the care of small, enclosed, family-size gardens, those caring for fields or small meadows, keepers of orchards or officers of the Inland Waters and Forestry Commission, men skilled at trellis work and at training plants into hedges or on arbors or as espaliers, and market gardeners responsible for the wholesale cultivation of vegetables. At Yerres the "path of the trellis workers," which begins at the boundary of Limeil near the Château de Brevannes and ends at the Etoile de Bellevue near the Château de la Grange du Milieu and the Château de Grosbois, keeps the memory of one category of these workers alive in these woods.[30]

The Daughters of Flora were not members of the Corporation.

It does not appear that "La Becnaude" who, according to tradition, is an envious, Devil-possessed, evil-tongued woman sometimes depicted as wearing a Brie headdress, attended the festival at Yerres.

According to imaginative interpretations of legend, the peach tree has come to be associated with the saint who, when tempted by Satan, planted a peach stone, which grew into a tree bursting with flowers and fruit. The ash tree with its spade-shaped heartwood is also linked to Saint Fiacre.

Landscape near Yerres (*also known as* View of the Yerres
Valley and the Garden of the Artist's Family Property),
c. 1877
Oil on canvas, 48 × 65 cm.
*A garden at Yerres with a distant view on the left, beyond the river
and the meadow, and beyond Concy, of the Yerres uplands known
as the Godeaux and Taillis hills. Toward the right are the hills of
Montgeron, referred to as Chalandray and La Garenne.*

G. Caillebotte 1875

The Park of the Caillebotte Estate at Yerres
Oil on canvas, 65 × 92 cm.
Signed and dated lower right "G. Caillebotte, 1875"
Along this path a man and a little girl, the artist's niece
Zoë Caillebotte, walk from the flower garden and the
kitchen garden toward the "casin," which we see on the
other side of the lawn, in the eastern section of the park.
Note the brilliant circular flower beds. The central
plantings in the bed in the foreground seem to be red
impatiens and, in the bed on the left, white impatiens.
The greenery on the left screens the water garden and the
pond. On the right, the southern part of the landscape is
wooded.

IN THE FOOTSTEPS OF GUSTAVE CAILLEBOTTE

This section is intended to serve as an aide-mémoire, or small walking guide. It has been prepared with a view to efficiency, to direct the reader along an ideal route, but should not be substituted for the real excursion, which one should undertake at one's own pace from one clump of trees to another, from one garden structure to the next according to a prescribed order detailed and analyzed below, following the original design of the park.

Our walk, taking in only those places in Yerres that Gustave Caillebotte painted, will reveal the great diversity of subjects that inspired the artist during the period of ten or so years in which he worked there.

Aside from those haunts of his formative years, some sites were of greater importance to Caillebotte than others. These survive in masterworks, which he showed from 1876 to 1880 at the exhibitions of Impressionist paintings and are the only ones which he personally titled.

The titles are important; see the section called "The Yerres Valley in Impressionist Exhibitions." The italic numbers refer to sites on the map which follows.

Taking as a point of departure an area downstream of the bridge over the Yerres, above the communal washhouse *1,* look carefully at the river *2* "of a deep blue-black, frigid, asleep under high shade" (Alphonse Daudet). On the left bank is the property's ornamental farm *49* to *51* and the aviary *52.*

Return to the Rue de Concy, along the fronts of the property's buildings, to the Meadow Cul-de-Sac. The gates seen from the other side of the Rue de Concy are those of the old Brault property. Maurice Brault, friend of Gustave and Martial Caillebotte, appears in the following paintings, *The Card Game, The Man on the Balcony;* and *Game of Bezique.*

Enter the park by the small gate situated at the intersection of the Rue de Concy and the Meadow Cul-de-Sac. Admire the southern façade of the "casin" or main house. Sometime before 1879 Caillebotte painted the magnificent cedar from the other side, in *Yerres, Part of the South Façade of the "Casin," 1.*

Follow the perimeter road and the Flower Garden Path *16.* In this wooded southern part of the landscape park the following were painted:

Yerres, Colonnade of the "Casin", c. 1870, *2;*

The Park at Yerres, 1877, *3*—this is the edge of the lawn;

Yerres, Path Through the Woods in the Park, painted before 1879, *4;* and,

Yerres, Path Through the Old Growth Woods in the Park, painted before 1879, *5.*

Since these various works have an east-west orientation, it is a good idea during the course of the walk to turn around several times to discover the different points from which the artist viewed the landscape.

Probably the following were also painted here:

Yerres, Soldiers in the Woods, c. 1870, *6;*

Self-Portrait Wearing a Summer Hat, done before 1879, *7;* and

Yerres, Camille Daurelle under an Oak Tree, done before 1879, *8.*

The Flower Garden Path leads us first to the Rose Garden *19* where Gustave Caillebotte painted *The Kitchen Garden,* c. 1877, *13,* and, perhaps also c. 1877, *A Garden, Yerres,* in which one can make out arches used to support climbing roses *13.*

Cross the Rose Garden toward the west wall *20* of the Flower Garden *22.* Different canvases painted here testify to Caillebotte's fascination from this time on with flowers and flower colors, flower beds and flower borders, and sculpted masses of blooming plants, as well as with movement and the juxtaposition of color and brilliant effects. The gardener's palette and the artist's palette become one. Paintings which were done here are:

Wall of the Kitchen Garden, Yerres, c. 1877, looking south, *9;* and

Wall of the Kitchen Garden, Yerres, 1877, looking north, *15.*

Inside the blue washed door *21* in the Flower Garden *22 The Gardener* was painted in 1877, *10.* This painting looks east and shows one of the Flower Garden's greenhouses *241* and the back of the blue washed door *21.*

Also painted in the fruit and vegetable garden *26-30* were:

The Kitchen Garden, Yerres, c. 1877, *11,* focusing on the basin in the axis of the flower-bordered paths *27;* and

Self-Portrait in the Park at Yerres, *before 1879* *Oil on canvas, 64 × 48 cm. Done after* Self-Portrait Wearing a Summer Hat, *this was painted at the far end of the lawn looking southeast, near the first circular flower bed and the tree, which we also see, on the right, in* The Park of the Caillebotte Estate at Yerres. *The artist's position and facial expression closely resemble those in a pencil drawing said to have been executed near the end of his life,* Self-Portrait in a Hat *(pencil, 49 × 31 cm.) This work, like the self-portrait done about 1892, is supposed to have belonged to Joseph Kerbratt with whom the artist sailed.*

Yerres, in the Kitchen Garden, Gardeners Watering the Plants, painted c. 1876–77, looking northeast, *12*.

Turning east and retracing our steps, re-enter the path separating the Rose Garden *19* from the lawn *10* and look at the Italianate house or, as Caillebotte called it, the "casin." Here was where he painted

The Park of the Caillebotte Estate at Yerres, 1875, looking east toward the eastern colonnade of the Italianate house, *16*.

Proceed toward the river by the path planted with plane trees *36*. Before reaching the riverbank *2* we should consider works Caillebotte painted in the Meadow on its left bank, facing more or less west. Both the Meadow, which belongs to the property *31*, and the communal or Great Meadow *3* are involved here:

The Nap, 1877, *17*;

The Meadow at Yerres, 1878, *18*;

Riverbank, before 1879, *19*;

Woman Seated under a Tree, c. 1874, *20*; and

The Meadow at Yerres, c. 1875, *21*.

The last four works were done in the Great Meadow *3*. The following were painted on the river where it flows by the Meadow or the Great Meadow *3*:

Oarsman in a Top Hat, c. 1878, *25*. Here we are looking downstream.

Proceed east along the river, *37* in the direction of the conservatory *41*. This side of the river appears in:

The Yerres, Effect of Rain, 1875, *22*; and

The Yerres, Effect of Light, painted before 1879, *23*. In both these works we are looking upstream.

Opposite, on the river's right bank, the Buet property, whose park was created in the eighteenth century (*4* and *5*) is the probable site of *Luncheon of the Boaters Beside the Yerres*, c. 1876, *24*.

We continue our stroll along the Yerres where the following paintings were done on the river not far from the end of the pond:

Fishermen on the Banks of the Yerres, c. 1876, *27*; and

Fishing, 1878, *28*. In these canvases we are looking upstream.

On the river where it borders the property of the park were painted:

Oarsmen on the Yerres, 1877, *29*

Boaters on the Yerres, 1877, *30*;

Périssoires on the Yerres I, 1878, *31*;

Périssoires on the Yerres II, c. 1878, *32*—here we look upstream;

Boater Fishing on the Yerres;

Sailing Dinghy on the Yerres, 1878, *34*, in which we look downstream under conditions of an east wind; and

Périssoire on the Yerres, c. 1878, *35*, looking upstream not far from the public washhouse *1* and the bridge over the river, where our walk started.

On the river's left bank in the park looking east we have *Boater Pulling in His Périssoire, Banks of the Yerres*, *36*.

From the property's diving board we have four works facing east:

Bathers, Banks of the Yerres I, 1877, 37;

Bathers, Banks of the Yerres II, 1878, 38; and

Bather Preparing to Dive, Banks of the Yerres, c. 1878, 39.

Walk the length of the Conservatory's west side *41*, then head immediately south of the pond *38* to the wooded area where, in about 1878, Caillebotte painted *Landscape, Banks of the Yerres, 41*. The pond itself is featured in *Yerres, on the Pond, Water Lilies, 40*.

Come back to the Conservatory *4*. Admire its neoclassical façade, tilted so as to allow the rays of the sun to enter. Proceed toward the Italianate house. On the left of the path Caillebotte painted *Yerres, Through the Grove, the Ornamental Farm*, c. 1879, *44*.

We now arrive at the "Casin," or Italianate house, which is the property's main house. Pause before the colonnade and look north. This is the site of *Garden at Yerres*, painted c. 1876, *45* a work that features the Swiss House *43* and is the only known painting we have of this structure.

Turning west to face the lawn *10* and the flower beds *44* at the end, and turning our backs on the colonnade, we will see where the following pictures were painted:

Camille Daurelle in the Park at Yerres, 1877, 47;

Yerres, the Lawn in the Park, Sunset Number Two, before 1879, 48;

Yerres, the Lawn in the Park, Sunset Number Three, before 1879, 49;

Yerres, the Lawn in the Park, Sunset Number Four, before 1879, 50; and

Yerres, the Lawn in the Park: Sunset Number Five, before 1879, 51.

Changing direction slightly to look from west to southwest toward the path leading to the ice cellar *11* we find ourselves confronting the site of:

The Orange Trees, 1878, 53;

Yerres, the Lawn in the Park, Seen from a Path, before 1879; 54;

Yerres, the Lawn in the Park, Seen from a Path, Sunset Number One, before 1879, 55;

Yerres, the Lawn in the Park, Seen from a Path, Sunset Number Six, before 1879, 56; and

Yerres, Woman with a Parasol on a Path, before 1879, 57.

Here was probably where Caillebotte painted *Portrait of Camille Daurelle*, c. 1877, 47.

On the lawn *10* near its east end he painted *Yerres, on the Grass*, before 1879, 52.

Turning to face the southwest corner of the "Casin" we find the site of *Portraits in the Country*, 1876, 58.

The three French windows on the ground floor behind the colonnade *8.1* are those of a drawing room where Gustave Caillebotte painted:

Billiards, c. 1875, 59.

In a small adjoining sitting room in the angle of the house looking north toward the Exhedra *45* he painted:

Madame Boissière Knitting, 1877, 60;

Portrait of Zoë Caillebotte, 1877, 61; and

Portrait of Madame Charles Caillebotte, 1878, 62.

North of the Italianate house, behind the Exhedra *45* in the stables of the ornamental farm Caillebotte painted:

Horses in the Stable, c. 1874, *65;*

Yerres, Reddish Bay Horse in the Stable, before 1879, *66;*

Yerres, Dark Bay Horse in the Stable, before 1879, *67;* and

Yerres, the Aviary in the Ornamental Farm, before 1879, *63.* The Aviary's north side is shown *52.*

Probably not far from here Caillebotte painted *Yerres, the Ornamental Farm, Interior of a Storeroom,* before 1879, *64.*

Proceed to the park gate *7* near the gardener's house *9.*

After crossing the Rue de Concy, return to the bridge and look upstream to where the river flows near the seventeenth century structure known as the Budé Fountain.

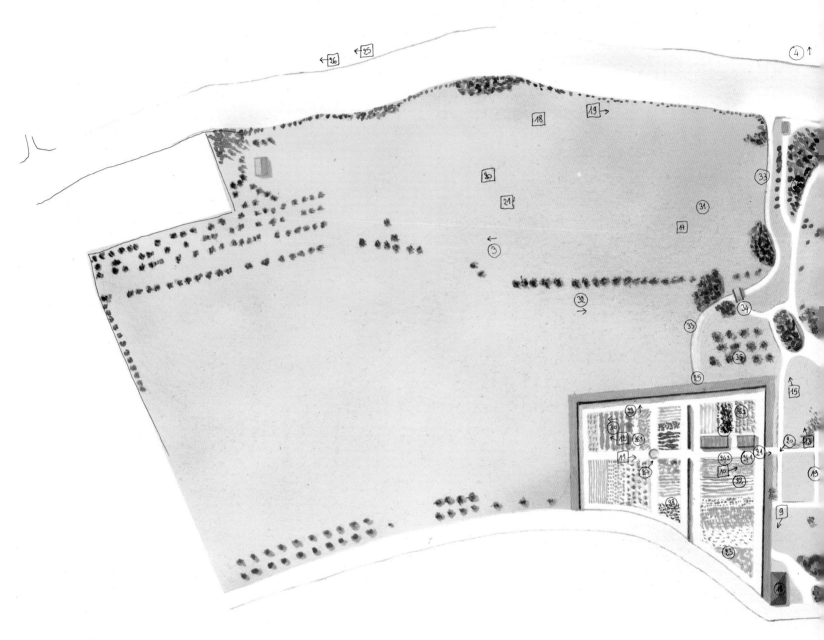

LEGEND
Circled numbers designate places.

Numbers inscribed within a square refer to paintings.

Arrows point in the direction the painter faced while executing a specific work.

Numbers placed above the river identify paintings having boats as a subject.

C. DALISSON

Matching the Paintings to the Sites

I. Works that were certainly executed on the sites and at the dates we have indicated:

1. *Yerres, Part of the South Façade of the "Casin"*, before 1879
2. *Yerres, Colonnade of the "Casin"*, c. 1870
3. *The Park at Yerres*, 1877
4. *Yerres, Path Through the Woods in the Park*, before 1879
5. *Yerres, Path Through the Old-Growth Woods in the Park*, before 1879
9. *Wall of the Kitchen Garden, Yerres*, c. 1877
10. *The Gardener*, 1877
11. *The Kitchen Garden, Yerres* c. 1877
12. *Yerres, in the Kitchen Garden, Gardeners Watering the Plants*, before 1879 (c. 1876–77)
13. *The Kitchen Garden, Yerres* c. 1877
15. *Wall of the Kitchen Garden, Yerres*, 1877
16. *Park of the Caillebotte Estate at Yerres*, 1875
17. *The Nap*, 1877
18. *The Meadow at Yerres*, 1878
19. *Riverbank*, before 1879
20. *Woman Seated under a Tree*, c. 1874
21. *The Meadow at Yerres*, c. 1875
22. *The Yerres, Effect of Rain*, 1875
23. *The Yerres, Effect of Light*, before 1879
25. *Oarsman in a Top Hat*, c. 1878
26. *Périssoires on the Yerres*, 1877
27. *Fishermen on the Banks of the Yerres*, c. 1876
28. *Fishing*, 1878
29. *Oarsmen on the Yerres*, 1877
30. *Boaters on the Yerres*, 1877
31. *Périssoires on the Yerres I*, 1878
32. *Périssoires on the Yerres II*, 1878
33. *Boaters Fishing on the Yerres*, 1877
34. *Sailing Dinghy on the Yerres*, 1878
35. *Périssore on the Yerres*, c. 1878
36. *Boater Pulling in His Périssoire, Banks of the Yerres*, 1878
37. *Bathers, Banks of the Yerres I*, 1877
38. *Bathers, Banks of the Yerres II*, 1878
39. *Bather Preparing to Dive, Banks of the Yerres*, c. 1878
41. *Landscape, Banks of the Yerres*, c. 1875
42. *Yerres, on the Pond, Water Lilies*, before 1879
43. *Zoë Caillebotte in the Garden, Yerres*, 1877
44. *Yerres, Through the Grove, the Ornamental Farm*, before 1879
45. *Garden at Yerres*, c. 1876

46. *Camille Daurelle in the Park at Yerres*, 1877
48. *Yerres, the Lawn in the Park, Sunset Number Two*, before 1879
49. *Yerres, the Lawn in the Park, Sunset Number Three*, before 1879
50. *Yerres, the Lawn in the Park, Sunset Number Four*, before 1879
51. *Yerres, the Lawn in the Park, Sunset Number Five*, before 1879
53. *The Orange Trees*, 1878
54. *Yerres, Lawn in the Park Seen from a Path*, before 1879
55. *Yerres, Lawn in the Park Seen from a Path, Sunset Number One*, before 1879
56. *Yerres, Lawn in the Park Seen from a Path, Sunset Number Six*, before 1879
57. *Yerres, Woman with a Parasol on a Path*, before 1879
58. *Portraits in the Country*, 1876
59. *Billiards*, c. 1875
60. *Madame Boissière Knitting*, 1877
61. *Portrait of Zoë Caillebotte*, 1877
62. *Portrait of Madame Charles Caillebotte*, 1878
63. *Yerres, the Aviary in the Ornamental Farm*, before 1879
65. *Horses in the Stable*, c. 1874
66. *Yerres, Reddish Bay Horse in the Stable*, before 1879
67. *Yerres, Dark Bay Horse in the Stable*, before 1879
71. *Self-Portrait in the Park at Yerres*, before 1879

II. Works probably painted on the sites and at the dates we have indicated:

6. *Yerres, Soldiers in the Woods*, c. 1870
7. *Self-Portrait Wearing a Summer Hat*, before 1879
8. *Yerres, Camille Daurelle under an Oak Tree*, before 1879
40. *The Painter under His Parasol*, c. 1878
47. *Portrait of Camille Daurelle*, c. 1877
52. *Yerres, on the Grass*, before 1879
64. *Yerres, the Ornamental Farm, Interior of a Storeroom*, before 1879
72. *Banks of the Yerres*, c. 1878

III. Works perhaps executed on the sites and at the dates we have indicated:

14. *A Garden, Yerres*, c. 1877
24. *Luncheon of the Boaters Beside the Yerres*, c. 1872

IV. Sites that inspire memories of Caillebotte or that were possible sources of inspiration to him:

68. The bridge may have inspired *Le pont de l'Europe*, c. 1877
69. *The Medicis Venus*
70. *Study of Paving Stones* may have served for *Paris Street: Rainy Weather*, 1877

The Sites

APPROACHES TO THE PROPERTY

1. Public washhouse
2. The Yerres River
3. The Great Meadow
4. Le Buet "L'Isle de Virginie" (eighteenth century)
5. Le Buet grotto (eighteenth century)

THE PROPERTY ITSELF

6. Main Gate
7. Small Gate
8. "Casin"
8.1. Colonnade of the "casin"
9. Gardener's house, reservoir and well
10. Lawn
11. Belvedere or Gazebo, ice cellar
12. Thatched cottage
13. Grille gate
14. Chapel
15. Natural rocks
16. Flower garden path
17. Site of statue
18. Another thatched cottage
19. Modern symmetrical garden (nineteenth century)
    Rose Garden or Rosarium
20. Path edged with flower beds bordering the garden wall
    Flower garden
    Fruit and vegetable garden
21. Blue gate to these gardens
22. Flower garden
23. Flower garden gazebo
24. Greenhouses
24.1. Main greenhouse
24.2. Another greenhouse
24.3. Another greenhouse
25. Water pump
26. Kitchen garden
27. Basin at the intersection of the kitchen garden paths
28. Small-fruit garden
29. Espalier walls
30. Site of cold frames
31. The property's meadow
32. Row of poplars
33. Canal (supplied with water from the river)

34. Stone bridge
35. Orchard
36. Path bordered with plane trees
37. Path along the river
38. Pond
39. Lower end of the pond
40. Site of the diving board
41. Conservatory or orangery
42. Well
43. Swiss house: dairy
44. Flower beds
45. Exhedra
46. Basin
47. Washhouse on the property
48. Bridge of timbers and worked wood
49. Entrance to the ornamental farm
50. Cowsheds
51. Stables
52. Aviary
53. Other paths

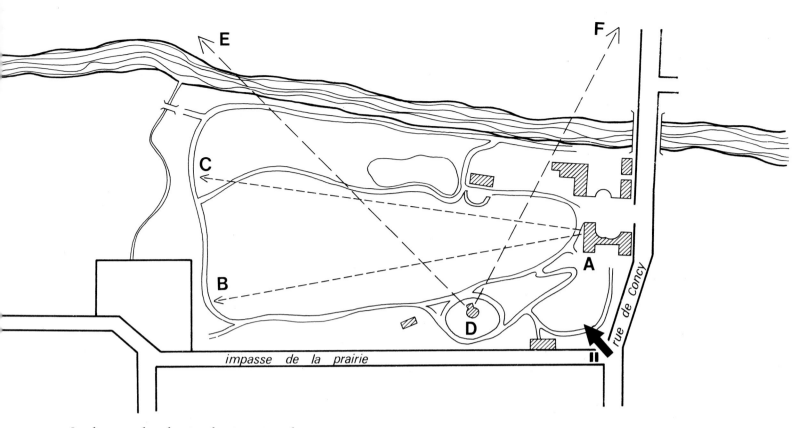

Landscape garden, drawing showing points of view

THE LANDSCAPE GARDEN

"When planning a landscape garden one must first of all take into account the contours of the land and establish vistas in keeping with them. After considering the terrain and what will best suit its physiognomy, a plan should be devised to direct the eye of a person looking out from the house's windows to views created in the composition itself and the beauties of the surrounding landscape. Enclosing walls must be hidden, as they limit the imagination and have a deadening effect."[31]

"The walls having been carefully dissimulated, then, by hedgerows, slopes, and various plantings, the eye should be stopped only by objects specifically designed to attract it, and it must not be able to gauge the property's true extent.

"The designer should only begin drawing after judicious reflection. Like a painter, he must subordinate everything to rules of perspective, and he will trace those curves that most harmonize with the natural form of the land. He will take into account the effect of the placement of each object. He will soften distance by boldly emphasizing foregrounds in such a way that, through the use of broken lines, backgrounds appear to recede. He will avoid angles. His design will have no triangular, square, oblong, or rhomboid forms, or parallel lines that could have the effect of giving his plan a geometric character or making it seem stiff. Sections of his composition set aside for ornamental planting will, above all, be exempt from such mistakes. A good garden

The colonnade of the "casin" today.

design should not include zigzag paths. The only permissible use of the zigzag is on a steep slope and then it must be camouflaged by shrubberies and trees placed between the turnings. Curved lines are pleasing only on a large scale and even then contours should be gradual and not abrupt, never seeming to be on the verge of making an about-face.

"Large roads running in straight lines have no place in the composition unless they define a main avenue leading to a house with a geometrical, severe, or antique character, or to a temple, church, or triumphal arch.

"If a composition requires a rather long avenue by which carriages and horses are intended to arrive, it should be laid out in smooth curves, as the eye will be shocked if a line, no matter how far away, appears to double back on itself as it will seem to do if the curve is too acute.

"Where space is limited, care should be taken to use only trees whose height is in proportion to the available area . . . In the same way, medium-size trees should be used liberally if the object is to continue the pattern of a grove or shrubbery and the eye of a spectator looking out of the house's windows toward a selected view will pass over and above this grove or shrubbery."

In support of the above, we list here a few of Gabriel Thouin's rules:[32]

1. The principal building should command pleasant views over the garden and excite the beholder's curiosity and desire to stroll about the sights, which themselves will provide vistas of the countryside or of some other structures.

2. Trees with green and darker foliage should be planted near the house so as to set off the foreground strongly. Smaller trees with paler foliage should occupy the middle ground. Trees of still lesser stature and with silvery leaf color are placed in the background, much as a painter uses the same effects.

3. The path or road around the property should be as long as possible and, unlike those endlessly and pointlessly twisting paths of the so-called English garden, should be pleasantly and simply contoured so that pedestrians, riders, and persons arriving by carriage should experience no difficulty.[33]

4. All paths leading off from this perimeter road should have a destination, whether to different buildings or to restful stops or scenic views, each of which should have the character of a tableau.

5. "Specimen trees should be isolated in the meadow in groups of an uneven number."

We add to this last rule of Thouin's that such trees should never obscure a view but be placed in such a way rather to emphasize and enhance it.

OPPOSITE:
Yerres, Colonnade of the
"Casin," *before 1879*
(c. 1870)
Oil on canvas, 43 × 30 cm.
Stamped lower left

The Gardener's House

"The gardener's house will take on the character of its garden. In a rustic setting this dwelling might take the form of a farmhouse. Under certain circumstances it may be placed at the entrance to the property . . . If the design is pastoral, it can assume that character . . ."

Portraits in the Country, *1876*
This is a detail showing the park from the west side of the
"casin" and, to the south, the gardener's house.

The Woods

"A wood differs from a forest in that the trees which compose it are not as tall and include both young specimens and mature growth. For this reason the view cannot be very extensive. A wood is often used where space is limited, in order to conceal this fact and give the illusion of a sweep more vast than really exists. A wood is planted informally without preconceived purpose or design. Its character does not aspire to the majesty and grandeur of a forest but is, rather, picturesque, pastoral, or wild. In a wood, ornamental structures need not be severe in style. In such a setting the woodcutter's thatched hut, the charcoal burner's cabin, the hermit-saint's retreat will fit in perfectly."

Yerres, Path Through the Woods in the Park, *before*
1879
Oil on canvas, 23 × 39 cm.
Stamped lower right
The colonnade of the "casin," ornamented with Medici
vases, is lighted by the sun.

An Old-Growth Forest
"A wood may consist of mature trees standing so close together that there is no space between their branches, in which case it is called an 'old-growth forest.'"

A Copse
"If trees are too far apart, they may be made to seem closer by adding a copse, which can be no more than the close planting of shrubs or small trees only a few feet tall. On a small property this alone without any mixture of tall trees produces effects that are often more agreeable than any other. When, on the contrary, such an arrangement covers a large stretch of land, the artist will need to resort to every ruse at his command to relieve its monotony. A wood draws much of its charm from its outer contour. If the latter extends up to the summit of a hill, the indentations and outward bulges of this line will produce a mixture of light and shade that is particularly effective and preferable to a more uniform edge with even shading.

"Such indentations when composed of different plantings can be extremely agreeable. Isolated trees will lighten and vary the outline of the wood and, in places where the indentations are large, a few open groupings may be placed at the entrance. If a definite sweep is wanted, it should be built up to the top of the hill, for if the summit is bare, it will seem too small and lose its most important character. A wood is more attractive and charming in such a situation than in any other. There one finds shade and coolness without humidity. Vistas can be arranged advantageously because the planting in the form of an amphitheater allows the artist to direct the eye as he wishes over and above the masses of greenery.

"The charms of a wood are not limited to its surface and contours. The interior provides a setting for charming scenes. Intersecting paths allow for delightful walks but should not cover too much distance without opening out or else boredom will set in. In steep places paths are not raked, instead grass is used to hold the earth. Skillfully contrived glades, grassy banks, and other resting places situated at points commanding picturesque views will further enhance a landscape. Care must be taken in choosing the entrance. If two small hills happen to form a hollow between them near the house, then that is where the road would most favorably be placed. Viart[34] has said that rows of trees can from the beginning follow the twistings and turnings of such an access road, advancing in company with it toward the middle of a grassy opening surrounded on all sides by dense woods. These outer contours will be interrupted by large masses separated at intervals, each one less extensive than the clearing to which the path leads, so as not to distract the eye from the principal line.

Yerres, Path Through the Old-Growth Woods in the Park, before 1879 Oil on canvas, 43 × 31 cm. Stamped lower left The characteristically sloping lawn was lighted on the right by the morning sun and, on the left, by the sun in the afternoon.

As one advances, and as the woods begin to draw closer, the bordering row of trees will melt into these woods, which for some distance will serve as a framework for the avenue leading to the house. Imperceptibly, the space will open out and give way to successive clearings leading off, now on one side, and now on the other, into the dense growth, their entrances separated either by small shrubberies or by trees leaning inward over the path. This should always be handled in such a way as not to interrupt but to emphasize the sweep of the road, especially if it is meant as a main avenue. As the way opens out further, groups of trees on one side and, on the other, an isolated specimen having some singularity that draws the eye may be made to stand out gracefully against the grass and serve to mark the road's continuity.

"Observation of the sun's movement throughout the day is more important than that of its annual declination. As the light from its rising and setting strikes the horizons of the landscape, the interior of large masses will be brightly illuminated, while deep shadows are projected on the other side. Such effects cannot be attained

Model of a bench suitable for use in the woods

11

by a north-south orientation. From this observation we also derive our theory about the laying-out of paths intended for pedestrian use. Shade is perhaps the most desirable commodity in a garden, above all in the season when gardens are most used. The well-planned landscape garden is nothing more than a harmonious sequence of different views, enjoyable only if the spectator stands outside their framework—for the wooded masses that compose or ornament them are always at and not above his eye level. All these fine perspectives and optical effects calculated to enchant him are lost if he walks continually under dense foliage or through heavy thickets. Since it is from broad allées and resting places that we admire the principal views, footpaths must necessarily be open and treeless in proportion to the scenic views to be admired. This is why in laying out our landscape garden it is difficult to allow room for those long, regularly shaded avenues that Académus[35] recommended for meditation and the leisurely contemplation of human wisdom. It is possible to guard against the great heat of the day by giving our footpaths a generally northeast-to-southeast direction."

Groundcovers

"Groundcovers differ from the carpeting we are used to seeing in pastures, lawns, and greenswards in that they are for the most part composed of plants with obvious flowers and are employed to ornament the ground in the shade of trees and shrubs, in copses, groves, and woods. We juxtapose them to areas of grass in such a way that they seem to be the work of nature, and they should contain no exotic plant, or at least none distracting to the eye. The artist should go into the fields and observe how carpeting plants occur in nature and which kinds are most attractive. Enchanter's nightshade, with its silvery petals, will glitter in the cool shade of an ancient forest oak and hold its own among the ferns and moss that crowd the base of an ivy-covered trunk. Sagittaria, rushes, and varieties of iris add interest to wooded places where a brook's clear waters meander. Ranunculus, lesser celandine, and the charming primrose spring up on the edges of fields. Wild orchids, centaureas, and a thousand other plants, each lovelier than the last, will cover the hilly places of a wood.

"Charming carpets of flowers may be created by sowing together seeds of morning

OPPOSITE:
Yerres, Soldiers in the Woods, *before 1879*
(about 1870)
Oil on canvas glued on cardboard, 40 × 30 cm.
Stamped lower left
Target practice near a path in the southern part of the park calls to mind the following comment by Edmond de Goncourt in 1871: "Amid the young greenery and flowering spring shrubs, here some National Guardsmen lie beside their rifles gleaming in the sun, there a blond serving girl pours a soldier's drink with charming Parisian grace, and in every corner and under all the leafy shelter, on the cloth of the military uniforms, streaks, zigzags, stripes of color à la Diaz."

glory, Virginia creeper, nigella, thlaspi, petunia, catchfly, and dwarf china aster. Nature's groundcovers are nothing more than devices for spangling the ground with the most brilliant color, and nature does this only in those places where they are needed to vary pleasantly the effect of green and woody plants. In a meadow nature appears to have limited herself in order not to reveal all at once all she is capable of lavishing on her other compositions. The gardener must take care to hide all traces of the hand that has planted his carpet. If he leaves any clue to betray cultivation, the mind will demand more and these graceful field flowers will lose all the charms of their simple natures, since there will be no reason not to believe that they could be replaced by others more rare and consequently more valued..."

Ivy

"Ivy can also be used as an evergreen carpet... Easy to maintain, it contributes an effect all its own to bedding designs. It has been in wide use for some time."

Writers argue that the name of the small town of Yerres, formerly written as Edera, Hedera, Hierra, Irria and Yeres, is derived from the Latin *hedera*, or ivy— *lierre* in the French—a decorative, densely foliaged plant whose woody stems and green shoots put out abundant short roots, which enable it to cling, crampon-like, to any support. Ivy leaves and the wood of mature plants are used in the herb trade for their hemolytic properties and as vasoconstrictors and antispasmodics. The leaves are chiefly taken internally for persistent coughs and for asthma. The wood's antispasmodic properties formerly made it a popular material in fashioning wooden cups to be used by children afflicted by whooping cough. Because of its hemolytic properties—that is, it destroys red blood cells—ivy should always be used internally with great caution.

Among the Celts the "calendar tree" formed the basis of initiatory knowledge. The Ogham, over which the god Ogmios presided, consisted of thirteen months of twenty days each corresponding to the lunar year. In this calendar ivy represented the period from September 30 to October 27. The consonant "g" for Gort in the Irish alphabet corresponds to it.

THE PERIMETER ROAD

"The shade of nearby trees will cast their shadows during a great part of the day, and this must be taken into account when laying out the road that encircles the park. The indispensable and characteristic nature of such a road is that it is developed around the whole and brings the sightseer by slow degrees, without detour or shock and without retracing his steps, and by a route opposite to that from which he started, to the manor house. The road's usefulness and beauty lie in making it possible for the arriving traveler to contemplate and admire successively all the park's details, and the

Yerres, Woman with a Parasol on a Path, *before 1879*
Oil on canvas, 39 × 25 cm.
Stamped lower left
The artist used the right side of this canvas for a study of buildings in the Briard style of architecture.

most common mistake in designing such a road is to allow it to pass too close to boundaries or fences, which must, above all, be concealed from the conscious eye.

"This will be achieved if the manor house is favorably situated, either through the positioning and broad design of interior lawns, which, stretching out irregularly between wooded areas, will seem to extend far into the distance and dissolve there into vast open space [this is why the "Meadow" is located to the west of our park] or else through the positioning of plantings, which, as they approach some neighboring forest, will connect the latter so closely to the garden that it will appear to be its setting."

The neighboring forest in our case is Mont Griffon, to the north.[36] We are looking at a very handsome example of the integration of a garden with its surroundings.

Elements of a construction at Yerres:
—artificial rocks
—a grotto: the ice cellar
—on either side in the rock formations staircases and stone benches
—on top, a belvedere or gazebo roofed with overlapping slates cut to resemble scales

Rock Formations
"Most landowners, unless prepared to spend vast sums, are not in a position to imitate nature by creating imitation boulders.[37] All the resources of art and all the means that fortune can place in the hands of the artist will fail, however, if he cannot also reproduce the simplest effects that natural rocks give a landscape. Their character, nearly always picturesque, majestic, wild, and imposing, derives from their essential roughness and from the sheer size of their masses. A boulder rarely exists in isolation and is almost never found except in mountainous places exposed to a thousand

assaults by the elements, on naturally rocky terrain, where it rises among other boulders and only there produces picturesque effects. If we should happen to stumble onto an isolated crag in the midst of some sandy plain, we would feel no pleasure because it would not be in harmony with its landscape. It could not call up in our minds any suitable references and, far from inspiring a picture, would instead distract from its setting and receive nothing from it. From this we conclude that in a flat place, on ground that is neither hilly nor irregular, the artist, no matter what his pretext, should never attempt to install any rock formation, even if he has the means to do so.

"A boulder is, however, the ornament most commonly sought by amateurs for their gardens, and few understand its effect. Either they construct a shape whose masonry betrays its origin or they pile up rocks with no character or harmony. This unfortunate counterfeiting of nature usually results in little more than a hole or two in the ground, which the gardener may find handy for summering houseplants. In vain such productions are given the name of 'rock' or 'crag.' The least-sophisticated eye, even one unaccustomed to nature's wilder beauties, detects the fraud and marks it as absurd.

"The gardener who finds himself with hilly or mountainous terrain on his hands is, however, permitted to create boulders where none exist. All he need do is take borings on some high point where, almost certainly, he will find close under the soil's surface rock underpinnings whose grayish complexion wind and rain will soon obligingly sweep clean for him. This is how nature has revealed, little by little, the secondary rock masses of all our mountains, and this is the reason why, unless one can imagine some ancient natural upheaval, a boulder placed arbitrarily in the middle of a plain looks ridiculous. In uncovering such ledges, the artist merely reveals in a moment what nature would eventually produce, and so the exposed rock faces will be in harmony with the landscape.

"When stones occur naturally, before deciding too narrowly the form of his design the artist should judge whether with a little work he can adapt them to its character, or whether, should they prove intractable, he might rather fit his picture to them. In the first case, Morel[38] advised that 'strengthening and accenting are all that one can do with rocks; one should be satisfied if, with all the means available from art, one succeeds in making their effects stronger and more dramatic.'

"In the second case the artist 'will refrain from undertakings beyond the scope of art; he will leave it to nature to produce what great upheavals she will to embellish his tableaux.'"

A glass-enclosed gazebo or cabinet vitré such as was used at Yerres

Imitation Rocks

"Despite the foregoing remarks, cases will occur where stones can serve as material, in which event they cease to play a principal role in the picture but become subsidiary—for example, where they are used to create a waterfall or some other unusual effect, and then we only glimpse parts of them and the less detailed these parts are the more natural they will seem. Or the artist may wish to extend the height of a hill in such a way as to emphasize something placed between it and a remarkable vista: if the character of the scene does not allow for a tower (which would be most desirable), a rock outcropping may be constructed and a gazebo or summerhouse placed on top of it. The artist who does this is advised to make an exact copy of a model chosen from nature. He should scout around the countryside for such rocks as can be transported and conserve carefully their deep, rugged crevices and, in placing them, give them the same relative position they had in their old setting. Where nature serves as a model an essential point to bear in mind is that the stones used should all be of the same type. We show here some models of this sort of artifice, and we repeat, they should only be used when absolutely necessary and where the rocky character of the site establishes suitability and need."

A Grotto

"The grotto has also to do with rocks but is of a completely different character. Caves are believed to be mankind's first habitation. Access to a grotto should be easy, the entrance sufficiently broad to allow light to penetrate its innermost reaches. The interior may be furnished, but with a simplicity that should call to mind our species' earliest days when, coming fresh from our creator's hands, we had no notion of art. A stone chip may serve as a seat, heaped moss and dried leaves covered with an animal skin can make a bed, housewares may consist of coarse matting, large shells, and the husks of colocynth or coconut.

"In a tamer and more pastoral setting the grotto can be more picturesque and may imitate the lair of one of those underground-dwelling families we find commonly along the banks of the Loire, mainly in the city of Angers. To achieve such an effect, seal off the grotto's entrance with a wall pierced by a door, a small window, and in the upper part, a hole to allow smoke to escape. Such a habitation may be furnished rustically or even, if one wishes a pleasant surprise, may include a richly and elegantly fitted-out salon. The more simple and rude the exterior, the more delightful such a contrast will be. The Paris architect, if he takes the trouble, will find examples of this kind of thing in a stroll around the outskirts of the pretty village of Nanterre.

"A few fruit trees and a small vegetable garden can be planted in front of such a dwelling. An arbor can provide a curtain of greenery before the façade.

"At the end of a dark path the stroller will enjoy coming upon an obscure grotto transformed into an enchanting resting place. More than one such site has served as a trysting spot for lovers.

Tapestry of trees and foliage with peacock; 18th-century Aubusson; private collection.
Here we see a combination of rocks, gazebo, and stairs in a work that could have inspired the construction at Yerres. Woven after a design by Jean Pillement of Lyons, an artist known for his travels, his taste for the exotic, and for his chinoiseries. Pillement worked particularly for Stanislaus Leszczynski I, King of Poland, from 1704 to 1709 and then from 1733 to 1736. Stanislaus was overthrown by the Russians and replaced by August III; after 1738 he devoted himself to the embellishment of Lunéville and Nancy. Pillement also worked for Queen Marie Antoinette. The central motif here is a gazebo inspired by the "peoples of Asia" and built on rocks over a sort of grotto under which a small boat might pass. Such a construction recalls "the Rock" straddling the small streams in the English garden at Chantilly, built in 1772–74 by Prince Louis-Joseph de Bourbon Condé on the site of the meadow at Candie. At the "piroque landing" visitors to the garden boarded small vessels painted blue or red and equipped with sails striped with colors matching their masts. Three boats carried musicians. During the voyage the boat's passengers discovered the "cave" formed by the enormous arch of rocks high above the stream, reminiscent of the interior of stone quarries in Syracuse. The second motif here brings to mind the pagoda at Chanteloup near Amboise, built as a monument to friendship by the Duke de Choiseul in 1775 and inspired by the 1762 pagoda in the royal gardens of Kew near London.

"From this it can be seen that a grotto may be excavated on a site offering the proper characteristics. However, the artist will avoid giving the entrance too regular a shape. He will remember that a grotto should always appear to be the work of nature. It need not have the appearance of a dwelling; it may be no more than an accidental irregularity in a rock face and still achieve a very considerable effect. Ivy, bignonia, Virginia creeper, or some other vine may not only be used to adorn the entrance but may be encouraged to twine as far into the interior as light and air are available for growth. If by a lucky chance the artist is able to direct a trickle of water from an underground source toward the bottom of his rocky cave, and cause it to cascade from a height of several feet into a basin and thence flow on in the form of a clear stream, he might then screen the entrance with the cool shade of massed tall and picturesque trees and thus create a delightful resting place in which to meditate during summer's burning heat."

The ice cellar, constructed in the old way, which is to say of stone, and in existence at Yerres in 1810. Around 1859 it was considered to be a "heat conductor," since the ice was not insulated by straw and wood according to the so-called American method advocated by Pierre Boitard-Louis Verardi.

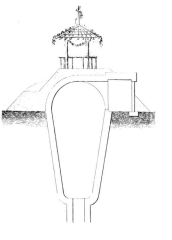

The Ice Cellar

"The ice cellar has a place here because of its use as a domestic adjunct.[39] Not only was ice kept in it but, during summer months, it was also used to store food that would spoil in a warmer place.

"Fruit wrapped in two thicknesses of paper and enclosed to the number of fifteen or twenty each in tin or zinc containers and lined up on three shelves or planks was thus kept fresh a very long time.

"In a gay pastoral setting an ice cellar excavated under a knoll and surmounted by a small summerhouse accented with decorative trees and shrubbery will not only be beautiful but will also afford shade to maintain the earth's coolness and solidity. Where the ice cellar's door must harmonize with the architecture of an elegant house, a monument resembling the entrance to an Indian or Egyptian temple might be considered."

In the above remarks we glimpse the preoccupation of the time with the conservation of food.

Display of Fruit, *1881*

Oil on canvas, 75 × 100 cm.

Signed lower right (by Martial Caillebotte) "G. Caillebotte"

In this composition, intended to hang in the dining room of the artist's friend Albert Courtier, notary at Meaux, plums, perhaps damson or greengage, are shown wrapped and resting in tin or zinc containers, in keeping with the way of conserving food at that time. When this painting was shown at the seventh exhibition of Independent Artists in 1882, Joris-Karl Huysmans wrote, "Unlike most of his colleagues, [Gustave Caillebotte] gets better. Adopting no special line, he avoids repeating himself and thus the inevitable falling off that accompanies repetition. His fruits, standing out from their beds of white paper, are extraordinary. We can feel the juice beneath the skin of his pears, whose pale gold surface he mottles with great slashes of green and pink. Condensation mists and moistens his grapes. This is a strictly true representation, of an absolute fidelity of color, a still life exempt from the usual flaws, which signals the end of those swollen hollow fruits with impermeable epidermises on the usual rubbery gray and sooty-black backgrounds. We find the same integrity in a sunny pastel seascape and in a view of Villers-sur-Mer flaunting its raw colors in the Japanese way."

The French name "Reine Claude" for the greengage plum dates from the 17th century when such plums were introduced in France, at Blois, by Queen Claude, daughter of Louis XII and Anne de Bretagne and wife of François I. Queen Claude concerned herself with reform of the Benedictine Abbey Notre Dame d'Yerres, as well as that of the Abbey Royale Notre Dame de Jarcy, farther up the river at Varennes-Jarcy.

Gazebo roof (detail). The shape of the slates here is called "scalloped." In Alsace, tiles cut in this form are referred to as "beaver tailed" or, in German, Biberschwanz. Slate came from Fumay in the Ardennes. Pierre Boitard-Louis Verardi wrote on the subject of slates cut for roofing, "We have succeeded in treating them with oil, which not only improves their appearance but contributes to prolonging the life of the stone."

OPPOSITE:
Returning from the flower garden in the dahlia season: close by on the right is the thatched cottage.

Use of bamboo in the design of a pavilion or gazebo attests to the early-19th-century infatuation with things Japanese.

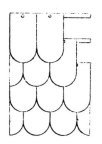

A Belvedere or Gazebo

"Among Asian people gazebos are nothing more than pavilions commonly used in the evening as places to eat ices and enjoy the cool air, and to contemplate the day's dying fire.

"We in the West give this name to small, light, gracefully shaped structures designed to take advantage of an unusual view, at a specified elevation."

Detail of an interior design, which inspired the glazing of the windows

HABITATIONS ET MONUMENTS CHINOIS.

A *Thatched Cottage*

"Thatched cottages are the pleasantest and commonest ornaments in landscape gardens. They should conform absolutely with their surroundings, otherwise they will seem shabby and look out of place. When such structures are large enough, they may be used as dwellings, or they may serve as storehouses for gardening or agricultural equipment. Different characteristics will fit them to various settings. Some, in the English style, may accomodate small households...

"If the property owner is tapping his wood resources, such cottages or huts may be used to house woodcutters or charcoal makers. Remote corners, clearings, and the edges of woods offer suitable sites. A small kitchen garden can vary the foreground, and a few fruit trees chosen from species requiring minimum care may shade the roof. In building such a structure thought should be given to clean simplicity of line. Above all, avoid an appearance of poverty, since this is hardly the condition of workingmen. The cottage's appearance should be spotless and cheerful, attesting to the care given it by its inhabitants.

"Thatched cottages may be used in less wild or more pastoral settings; for instance, we might imagine them to be inhabited by modestly prosperous small farmowners proud of their independence. Ornamentation in such a case will give the impression that the residents, beside cultivating a few acres of land, operate some small business that keeps them from poverty. The little garden will commonly include a few flowers, nearby will be an orchard of fruit trees of good quality, and grapes trained up the posts of the portico may stretch along the walls and frame the windows. Some small clue may indicate that hospitality is available for a sum of money, for example, two wooden benches under a thatched shelter may invite the tired traveler to rest a moment; however here the illusion is over..."

The grille gate: looking from the park toward the Great Meadow Cul-de-Sac

Thatched Cottage, Trouville, *c. 1882*
Oil on canvas, 54 × 65 cm.
Signed lower left (by P. A. Renoir) "G. Caillebotte"
The angle from which this cottage was painted reminds
us of one of the cottages in the park at Yerres.

A Grille Gate

"An openwork iron gate can easily take on the character of the setting it frames, and even render that setting more striking.

"One can make it Gothic, rustic, pastoral, or simply ornamental."

Example of a chapel

The Chapel

"Some chapels are modest structures, which derive importance from their effect, others are veritable monuments intended to quicken our souls to memory or to inspire divine piety. Their pictorial effect leads us to place them in large gardens among natural surroundings, with sufficient space to allow them to be isolated.

"Chapels and oratories in the styles of different countries may be adapted to the character of any setting in which one wishes to place them. However, if the architecture is severe, such a building should always be relegated to a remote, tranquil spot."

The estate's chapel is in the English style, a mixture of Romanesque and Gothic.

"Where such a chapel is shaded by groupings of ancient trees, it will never fail to awaken some stirring of religious piety."

Self-Portrait, c. 1889
Oil on canvas, 55 × 46 cm.

A *Statue*

In Gustave Caillebotte's day a statue that no longer exists was situated at the intersection of the path leading, on the left, to a thatched cottage and another path, which veered, on the right, toward the Rose Garden. A boulder has been placed on the site. Other statues may be seen in the Exhedra.

"In fine, the statue of an ancient gallant knight... erected in a corner of a forest, on the spot where, the old chronicle tells us, he fell a victim of black treachery, to the spear of an infamous knight."

In this sacred wood might not such a statue honor rather the Gallic god Ogmios? If we are to judge by still-extant shards of sculpture lying among the ivy, it may even have been a likeness of the Roman god Mercury, protector throughout all times and all places of travelers and merchants, placed at the intersection of the traveler's route.

"In a landscape garden statues are anomalies that, though they can be agreeable enough, must be used with restraint. Yet who can resist a glimpse from the windows of a luxurious house of a distant statue rising out of dark foliage? The appearance, at the end of a straight path, of a statue's head and shoulders will produce a fine effect. Elevation of the pedestal will make it visible above the treetops..."

Gates, Trellis Work, Fences, and Hedges
"Gates, trellis work, fences, and hedges would seem at first glance to offer little interest; however, when used prudently, they offer pictorial advantages not always achieved by larger efforts. Seen through masses of greenery, their uniform tone and regular shape contrast pleasantly with the differing forms and brilliant coloration of foliage."

OPPOSITE:
Wall of the Kitchen Garden, Yerres, *c. 1877*
Oil on canvas, 27 × 41 cm.
The wall of the flower and kitchen gardens, side facing the landscape garden, looking from a path leading to the rose garden. Petunias were planted in the long bed. J. J. Decaisne and C. Naudin give us the following on crimson and white petunias: "These two kinds, particularly the crimson one, are known throughout the world for the richness and brilliance of their flowering. Left to themselves and kept at a distance from each other they do not seem to vary much. On the other hand, they interbreed easily and produce hybrid forms, which, by cross fertilization, create an infinite number of new types in multiple combinations of white, pink, crimson, ruby-red, and purple. Some flowers are notable for the unusual breadth of the corolla, others are circled in green, still others have become double or very full. Preference for one or the other of these varieties is a question of taste. To us, however, it seems that single medium-size flowers reticulated with crimson on a background of pink or clear rose are the best of all. These variations, which occur in individual plants, do not breed true but must be multiplied by cuttings. Except for this one case, propagation of petunias is exclusively by seed. Petunias demand so little that one might say they grow on their own. Sometimes, if the winter has not been too rigorous, they escape from gardens and appear freely on the outskirts of towns, and this is generally the case in the South of France, where they often survive and their stems become semiwoody. As bedding plants, they form wide, vigorous tufts that send branches sprawling along the ground and must be cut back often in order not to monopolize all the space. Apart from this slight inconvenience, few plants are as agreeable to grow or repay better the care they require. Their flowering begins in June and continues without interruption, increasing until the first frost. Aside from the major role they play as bedding plants, petunias do well in pots and, since their stems tend to lengthen indefinitely, they can be attached to different kinds of trellises, which will soon be covered with their flowers. Petunias can be trained on walls, or grouped broadly in the landscape garden."

Bignonias, which enjoy warmth and sunlight, will carpet a wall. In Caillebotte's time, the variety most prized by lovers of these rampant-growing climbers with composite, pinnate, deciduous leaves and brilliant summer flowers, was the Virginia trumpet vine, or trumpet creeper (bignonia or tecoma radicans), a large vine native to the southern United States, with clusters of long tubular flowers of a vivid scarlet or, in some varieties, dark red. Half-hardy in the Ile de France, it will survive the winter if given light protection. Bignonia used to be considered one of the most beautiful of outdoor climbing plants. The Chinese bignonia (bignonia or tecoma grandiflora) from east Asia is also semihardy in northern France and has red flowers, which resemble somewhat those of the preceding variety, though the tube of the corolla is shorter and the lamina more widely open.

Bignonia, or Virginia
Trumpet Vine

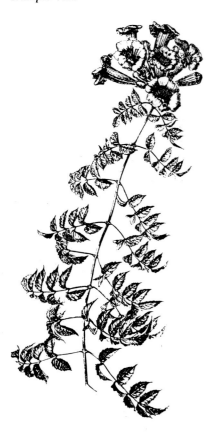

[Caillebotte] loved flowers which brightened and perfumed the air. [He was] our wise connoisseur of gardens.

GUSTAVE GEFFROY, *Monet*, 1924

FLOWER GARDENS

"In some sense there is not and cannot be a kitchen garden without fruit trees; it can also be said that no garden of any kind exists without flowers. One cannot even find a market garden where Flora has not sown a few of her gifts. In the modest vegetable garden of the poor one will always find a flower sparkling like a lost jewel.

"Only in a small number of city plots does one find gardening limited to flowers. Searches in other places yield only scattered examples here and there and this only since the vogue for landscape gardening has become as popular as the art of Le Nôtre used to be. Flowers are and will always be our great garden ornaments. They shine everywhere, among woody plants, in beds in the centers of lawns, on the edges of green groundcovers, and around the bases of hillsides. It is not our wish to change all this. We can hardly disapprove of something nature herself has inspired, for she is the guide on whom we rely to save us from ridiculous mistakes.

"However, our own personal inclination has always been to create a different and pleasant outlook for each side of the house, and with this in mind we strive to include in our designs the decoration of one part of the grounds within sight of the house with a flower bed whose form is in harmony with the rest of our composition."

In Caillebotte's day the cultivation of ornamental flowering plants at Yerres tended to be confined to the flower garden and to borders and decorative beds near the main house and its lawn rather than being included in a landscape garden.

"Since horticulture, now become an art, has been inundated by plants from all over the world—with endless numbers of large bedding specimens and other new acquisitions arriving in profusion to take their places within view of the house—and since we do not wish to deprive ourselves of the visual pleasures such material provides, we have designed new forms of borders and, in effect, created different kinds of flower beds.

"The flower garden itself may take the form of a single plot occupying an entire small property or it may turn out that, because of its dimensions or some obstacle, it cannot be placed in such a way as even to be seen from the house. We shall try to give an idea of such an out-of-sight garden.

"Let us say that for some reason our flower garden cannot be near the house, still

The Gardener, *1877*
Oil on canvas, 60 × 73 cm.
Signed and dated lower left, "G. Caillebotte 1877"
On the left, in the flower garden, is a greenhouse, at the
back the gate to the landscape garden. Did the artist
remember this work when he painted, around 1882, the
bent figure of a gardener in The Kitchen Garden,
Petit Gennevilliers?

we must do something to make it possible for our eyes to discover some part of it; an attempt must be made to keep it from being too remote, since the pleasure it gives is ever new, while the care it demands is ever necessary. The preferred exposure is southeast, the desired form a square or somewhat lengthened parallelogram. The soil must be light, loose, deeply worked, screened, and enriched with successive applications of rotted manure. In some locations the different plants to be grown will require made earth. Many bulbs demand sandy soil mixed with compost. Other plants need heavy soil or leaf mold or pond muck and so on.

"Diversity in the nature of plants and in their requirements will also necessitate the designing of different special sections of the garden, making it difficult to bring the whole into harmony. One cannot grow in the same beds with equal success shrubs, herbaceous plants, and bulbs. The latter come up every year and, if one is to enjoy them over a long period, must be kept to themselves and be given some protection from the sun. Screens designed to serve this purpose may be permanent plantings such as arborvitae or vines, or they may be made of cloth.

"Similar obstacles to the harmony of the whole oblige us to compose our flower garden of tableaux leading smoothly one into the other and to place on the edges of each bed some screen that will stop the eye. It is difficult to list materials for such gardens, since gardeners rarely agree on the choice of plants. One will grow a vast quantity of roses, another will prefer lilies, a third dahlias.[40] Yet another will fill his beds with exotics from the Cape or from the tropics and will build a greenhouse to supply these from one end of the season to the other, in pots that he sets directly into the ground and takes out later...

"Fashion and new technologies also from time to time alter a garden's plan.

"A pergola or gazebo can be part of a flower garden, in a location where it will be possible to enjoy the most complete view of the whole. Greenhouses and frames used in the growing on and holding of some of the plants will be included within its walls."

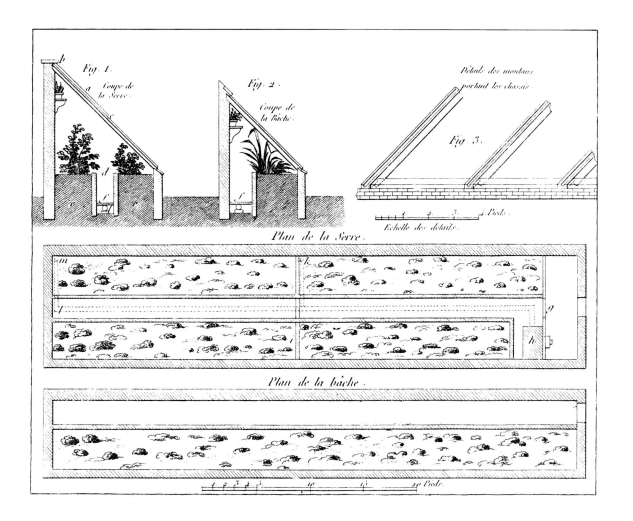

A Greenhouse in the Flower Garden

The diagram here shows in cross section an ordinary working greenhouse. "Such an unadorned, utilitarian building can only be placed in a flower garden, where its looks will not be objectionable. "Assiduous upkeep, perfect cleanliness, and coats of tinted oil paint renewed at the least sign of need are required to keep it attractive.

"Such a greenhouse is covered by two rows of glazed sashes, the upper ones, *a*, opening by means of hinges attached as at *b*. The lower sashes are simply fixed and held in place by hooks or may be hinged at *c*, as described. A walkway, *d*, is excavated lengthwise through the center of the greenhouse. On either side, low brick walls contain soil and bark beds, *c* and *e*. The heating duct, *t*, is laid under the walkway. On the diagram can be seen a small box, *g*, installed in the entrance. Here the stove is lighted, *h*, and smoke prevented from injuring the plants inside.

"Shelves may be installed for pots containing such hardy plants as aloes, cacti, and other succulents. One can use the same construction to make a house that is both heated and cool, by simply adding a glass partition as in *i*, and shortening the heat duct so that it ends at *k* rather than continuing to *l* and *m*.

"Figure 2 shows a smaller house or forcing frame containing only one bench, which is usually filled with leaf mold for growing delicate plants directly in the soil. Since its width scarcely exceeds two meters it requires only a single row of sashes."

Doors of the dining room at Petit Gennevilliers. These views of the greenhouse at Petit Gennevilliers were painted by Gustave Caillebotte in about 1893 and were photographed by his brother, Martial. The numbers refer to Martial Caillebotte's plates:

Upper left (D.1.G.B.): Orchids; *oil on canvas, 108 × 42 cm.*

Lower left (D.1.G.B.): White Orchids; *oil on canvas, 75 × 42 cm.*

Upper right (D.1.D.H.): Yellow orchids; *oil on canvas, 108 × 42 cm.*

Lower right (D.1.D.B.): Orchids and Plants with Red Flowers; *oil on canvas, 73 × 42 cm.*

OPPOSITE:
Upper left (D.2.G.H.): Orchids; *oil on canvas, 108 × 42 cm.*

Lower left (D.2.G.B.): White and Pink Flowers; *oil on canvas, 75 × 42 cm.*

Upper right (D.2.D.H.): Orchids; *oil on canvas, 108 × 42 cm.*

Lower right (D.2.D.B.): Begonias; *oil on canvas, 75 × 42 cm.*

At Petit Gennevilliers near Gustave Caillebotte's house the artist was to build a greenhouse in which he would raise orchids, then newly fashionable in the Ile de France, and around 1893 orchids became the subject of a dozen or so of his works.

In 1986 we sent Marcel Lecoufle, an orchid specialist at Boissy-Saint-Léger, black-and-white photographs taken by the artist's brother Martial Caillebotte at Petit Gennevilliers of four canvases and eight dining-room door panels. The following is Monsieur Lecoufle's reply (the numbers refer to Martial Caillebotte's photographs):

"Here are identifications I can give you offhand, in spite of the lack of color in the photographs:

Cattleya Trianae or *Cattleya Schroderme* at the top, various *Paphiopedilum* on the left (including *P. Purpuratum*?). *Odontoglossum Rossili* bottom right

Dendrobium Phalaenopsis (or similar) at the top *Zygopetalum* in the center and *Odontoglossum* (*crispum* or hybrid) at the bottom

Dendrobium Nobile var. *Sanderianum*

Stanhopea Tigrina

D1DH: *Oncidium Macranthum* at the top, *Cattleya Dowiana?*

Odontoglossum (= *Rossioglossum*) big one at the bottom

D1GH: *Stanhopea Bucephalus* or similar at the top and *Dendrobium Dalhousianum* (or similar) at the bottom

D1GB: *Laelia Purpurata* and *Paphiopedilum Callosum*

D2GH: *Zygopetalum Mackayi* at the top and *Odontoglossum Harrisianum?* at the bottom

D2DH: *Cattleya Citrina*, *Odontoglossum Insleayi*, *Phalaenopsis Amabilis*, *Dendrobium Infundibulum?*

D1DB: *Cattleya* in the center and probably *Odontoglossum* at the top and *Dendrobium Superbiens* at the bottom?

D2GB: *Lycaste Skinneri Candida* and some rex begonia

D2DB: Some *Paphiopedilum*, a *Phragmipedium* and Rex Begonia President Carnot."[41]

ON THE IMPORTANCE OF THE DESIGN

EXEMPLE DE PLANTATION, PRIS A FROMONT, CHEZ M. SOULANGE BODIN.

The restoration of the Château de Fromont property by Solange Bodin. This example of a garden is particularly interesting. A 17th-century estate with magnificently laid out French—style gardens lay neglected for more than a century, during which time, taste, and fashion changed. In the first half of the 19th century its owner ordered a new, more natural design. Many parks evolved in this way at that time.

"Plants are easier to care for when grouped together in regular or irregular geometric shapes . . . Flowers of similar color, whether long flowering varieties sown directly into the soil or potted specimens set in at the peak of their bloom, can be massed in parallel plots or beds. A small pool or basin is often placed at the center of such an arrangement . . ."

The well-known amateur horticulturist Soulange Bodin wrote, "The layout of the flower garden depends in equal measure on the nature and kind of flowers to be grown, the space one wishes to allot to each variety, and the frequency with which they must be renewed throughout the season. Some will be planted directly in place, while others will be brought in almost full grown. In whatever state, the quantity should be such that the entire bed never seems too bare. Detailed preparations leading to this effect demand much in the way of taste, foresight, and horticultural knowledge on the part of the garden's creator, who cannot indulge himself in too much fantasy; the law of proportion and suitability arises from a sense of beauty in general. It is essential that within a large garden there not be too many changes or the effect will seem patchy; conversely, in a small space too-large borders will appear heavy. The different groupings of flowers should also balance each other. They should compete for the viewer's attention so that the eye does not become stranded in, say, a border devoted entirely to tulips, which are slow to bloom and quick to fade, but find rather

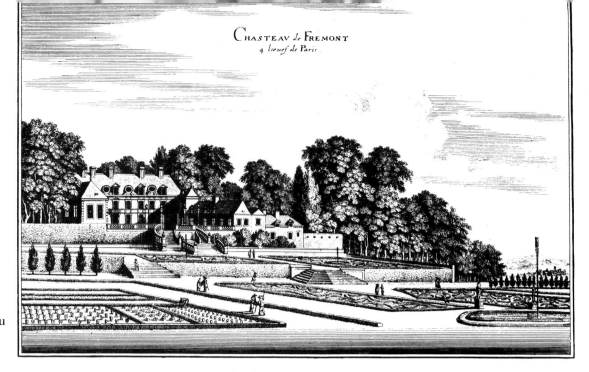

Gaspar Merian
View from the Château
de Fromont 4 Leagues
from Paris, *c. 1655*

some nearby diversions and delights to console it for those frequent empty spaces that occur in a flower bed, and for the successive fading of its more ephemeral charms. Skill in the pleasant art of dealing with too-obvious gaps comes with work and practice."

Soulange, quoted above by Pierre Boitard and Louis Verardi, redesigned the property of Jérôme Nouveau, Secretary of the Postal Services from 1639 to 1665, at Fromont, today in the commune of Ris Orangis, in the Department of Essone. Fromont overlooked the Seine and the Sénart forest near Draveil-Champrosay on the river's right bank, and in the seventeenth century its gardens were such that an impressed John Evelyn listed them, along with those of the Château de Richelieu, in his 1657 roster of French gardens, which he intended to incorporate into a book on gardening history. Alphonse Daudet, who, as we know, stayed at Draveil-Champrosay, called one of his works, published in 1894, *Fromont jeune et Risler ainé.*

Of Soulange Bodin, Boitard and Verardi wrote in the sixth edition (1859) of *A Treatise on the Design and Decoration of Gardens,* "Among the printed plans we have described, we wish fervently that we had been able to include the design of one of the best French landscape gardens we know, that created by the late Soulange Bodin at Fromont. The composition of this park of roughly two hundred arpents united simplicity of layout and richness of arrangement of rare plants in perfect harmony with the art of establishing scenic views. Alas for landscape gardeners, no pre-established scale plan was made. Rather, Soulange, who was a genius, plotted everything on the spot. With his unerring eye, and without the aid of a compass, he created it all. He looked, he meditated . . . he commanded too-regular terraces to be moved and softened into gentle slopes, he made harmonious hillsides rise up as if by magic, and the result was charming.

"In our fifth edition, in 1838, we wrote that the Fromont garden, situated in the commune of Ris on the road to Fontainebleau, extends from the main road to the Seine over land sloping east and north, and overlooking the large, fertile river valley toward the forest of Sénart. It has beautiful plantings of trees and shrubbery, both native and exotic; buttressed by the forest crowning the hills on either side and perfectly harmonious with all the great scene surrounding it, it forms a single magnificent landscape without apparent limit other than the vast horizon. Soulange anticipated this effect, he planned this fusion of artifice and nature, which we can still see perfectly today. The application to his work of this principle of adaptation, this strength he has made so clear in his writings and which stamps the character and merit of this beautiful and graceful composition survive to our time. Everywhere the simple and natural interior scenes of his garden disappear into rich and extensive vistas outside it, the countryside round about melting all the more subtly into Soulange's design in proportion as the most distant parts reproduce far off the aspects of plantings incorporated into the garden itself.

"The house stands on the site of an ancient château whose gardens were planted by Le Nôtre. The merest vestiges of one of the most beautiful compositions of this great master were visible when Soulange undertook to bring back to its natural state, to refashion, in a word, a site disfigured by ruined terraces and crumbling slopes, creating in their place beautiful and apparently random (though, in fact, artfully arranged) plantings. The gardens at Fromont expressed a principle of harmony and of enjoyment never attained even in its grandest period by the formal garden.

"Le Nôtre's vast terraces, statues, and flowers, with the Seine and the broad hillside rising on the opposite bank must have formed a beautiful spectacle. Still, the elevation of his terraces' symmetrical ornaments was inadequate to frame distances. They failed to provide the strong plays of light that the irregular masses of dense trees bring into relief, so that the continuous line of the hill and the houses on it at the time merely produced a chill monotony. What was needed to animate and perfect this beautiful composition? A few clumps of tall trees in the foreground, which, by interrupting the continuous lines, multiplied the number of tableaux and allowed only the hillside's most picturesque scenes to be glimpsed. The deep shadows these trees cast heightened the effect.

"We have tried to make clear this trick of emphasizing objects in the foreground, called *repoussoirs*. Soulange designed the long line of buildings spread across the hill, then accented or, in effect, superimposed groupings of trees like curtains to hide the monotonous repetition of walls and less picturesque objects and to force the eye to concentrate instead on brighter and more interesting views."

The deciduous hybrid magnolia soulangeana, which grows to a height of 6 to 8 meters and whose white flowers are tinged purplish-red on the outside, is named for Soulange.

In his diary, Eugène Delacroix, living at Draveil-Champrosay in 1849, wrote, "Wednesday, September 6, at Fromont. Saw Madame Soulange. Spoke for a long while with the gardener, who is extraordinary looking. Came back for dinner." Delacroix was to return later to Fromont.

The Gardener, *1877*
(detail)
South-facing bed running
the length of the wall.

According to Boitard and Verardi, the head gardener at Fromont was a Monsieur Keteleer who wrote in *Encyclopédie du jardinage,* on the subject of "The Variable Flower Garden," "The essential character of such a garden lies in the possibility of changing its composition and in consequence its appearance at will so that any plant or group of plants that is beginning to fade can be removed and replaced immediately by others starting into bloom. In order to keep up such a garden satisfactorily it is necessary to have a reserve nursery where material can be grown along in pots, to be plunged into the beds as needed . . ."

"Flowering plants belong as much in the landscape garden as in the formal garden but are much more numerous in the latter, where they fill up borders and rectangular and circular and odd-shaped beds and are used as edgings."

The following celebration of border, bed, and parterre is from Emile Zola's *La Faute de l'Abbé Mouret:*

"Thus Albine and Serge walked in the sun for the first time. They gave off an alluring scent. They made the path shiver with excitement while the sun rolled out a golden carpet under their feet. Seductively, they advanced among the large flowering bushes, so desirable that the distant bypaths called out to them with a murmur of admiration, just as crowds salute their long awaited kings . . . The flowers dropped their heads in adoration.

"In the border there was much emotion. The old flower bed acted as an escort. In a vast field gone wild over a century, a corner of paradise where the wind scattered the rarest flowers and the happy peace of Paradou, sleeping beneath the big sun, prevented the degeneration of the species, the temperature was even and the earth, long fertilized by each plant in return for the privilege of living in its silent strength, the vegetation was enormous, superb, powerfully savage, full of nature's accidents, displaying monstrous flowerings unknown to the spades and watering cans of gardeners. Left to itself, free to grow shamelessly, deep down in that solitude, nature became each spring increasingly unconstrained, gaily gadded, amused itself by offering itself strange bouquets which no hand would reach out to gather. And it seemed in a rage to destroy Man's efforts. It rebelled, tossed masses of flowers into the centers of paths, attacked the rockery with rising tides of moss, strangled by the neck and brought down with the flexible cords of its vines the marble statues. Its powerful shrubberies broke the stones of pools, stairs, and terraces, and crept along until it overpowered all cultivated places, moulding them at will, planting there as a flag of rebellion seeds picked up en route, humble flora which it changed into monstrous greenery. In the past the parterre, maintained for an owner with a passion for flowers displayed in beds and borders, contained a marvelous choice of plants. Now the same plants were perpetuated, multiplied into such countless families and spreading so to the four corners of the garden that it had become no more than a hodgepodge of hookey-playing shrubbery beating against the walls, a suspect place where drunken nature hiccupped verbena and carnation."

Wall of the Kitchen Garden, Yerres, 1877
Pastel, 44 × 49 cm.
Signed and dated lower left
"G. Caillebotte 77"
Bed along the wall of the flower garden
and the kitchen garden in the landscape
park, looking north toward the river
  Diagram of a kitchen garden by P.
Boitard and L. Verardi similar to the one
at Yerres:

The Parterre

"The parterre, a component of the flower garden, may make up the whole or form only a part, and is still used in the large formal gardens of châteaus and palaces.

  "The choice of plants, their rarity, the brilliance of their flowers, their singularity and the way they blend together give the parterre its visual charm and makes the spectator oblivious of its scale..."

The Border

"In the past the border was the one element most generally in use by landscape gardeners. Then it had a straight edge. Today it is given curves and tends to follow the line of the plantings in the composition of which it forms a part, and is of uniform width, not exceeding 2 meters, and never less than 1.3. The edges, finished in boxwood, bricks, stones, or even with wooden planks, rise 6 to 8 centimeters above the ground and the center forms a 15- to 25-centimeter-high crown. Borders show to best advantage along the edges of lawns, shrubbery, paths, and so on. From time to time the soil is excavated to a depth of 30 to 50 centimeters and replaced with leaf mold so as to accommodate shrubs and plants that will not thrive under ordinary conditions..."

The Rectangular Bed

"Rectangular beds are shaped like straight-sided parallelograms and are separated by 40-centimeter-wide paths. Their width varies from 1 to 1.6 meters, and they may be any length. They are planted with such attractive material as tulips, ranunculus, or hyacinths in a succession of kinds, or sown with annuals intended for eventual transplanting to ornamental beds or other places. Rectangular beds do not ordinarily enter into garden design because it is necessary to make them afresh in several locations as the soil becomes impoverished through overplanting."

Some of Gustave Caillebotte's works owe their perspectives to the use of garden twine, which, fitted out at both ends with stakes, was used to lay out such beds. Much of Caillebotte's originality comes from the influence on his compositions of illustrations from garden guides and treatises.

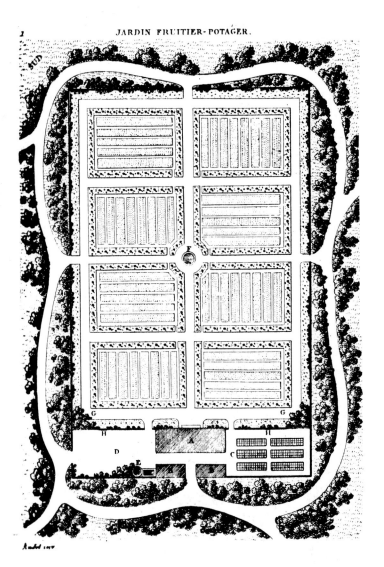

JARDIN FRUITIER-POTAGER.

A KITCHEN GARDEN

Model of a kitchen garden from Boitard and Verardi similar to the one at Yerres.

"A. *Gardener's house;* B. *Sheds;* C. *Starting frames;* D. *Courtyard;* E. *Well and trough from which a pipe may convey water to the basin or pool and possibly, where needed, to buried butts;* F. *Garden basin or pool;* G. *Fig trees;* H. *Five-foot-high walls.*

"*This kitchen garden is enclosed inside a landscape garden and is entirely hidden, nevertheless it is connected to the paths of the landscape garden. In such a design great care must be taken that surrounding shrubbery not be higher than the walls and that their roots not be invasive. Since shrubs attract insects and pests, they should ideally come no nearer than 4 meters. This walled garden measures a third of a hectare and cannot include large vegetables. A more extensive plot might contain more square meters but the proportions would be the same.*" At Yerres the fruit and vegetable garden covers 2 hectares.

The Kitchen Garden, Yerres, *c. 1877*
Oil on canvas, 60 × 73 cm.
The pool or basin at the intersection of the main paths in the fruit and vegetable garden. The painter placed himself in front of the blue door leading to the landscape park, facing west. According to P. Boitard, "The two main paths that intersect at the basin are wide enough to permit a cart to transport manure where it is needed."

At the age of 16, Salvador Dali painted The Kitchen Garden at Llané-Petit, 1920. *Of this youthful landscape, which could have been inspired by Caillebotte, Dali wrote, "Cadaquès, from earliest childhood I adored it almost fanatically . . . The walls were covered with paintings and etchings by Ramon-Pichot, then in Paris, so my breakfasts introduced me to Impressionism. Indeed, this school is the one which in all my life affected me the most."*

Caillebotte's recently discovered major work, *Yerres, in the Kitchen Garden, Gardeners Watering the Plants,* pays homage to garden labor and to gardeners. It depicts the northwest part of the kitchen garden at Yerres. The river, flowing from right to left, is hidden by poplars planted beyond the meadow. In the distance on the right is Mont Griffon. This picture is characteristic of Caillebotte's experimentation at this time; in its bold, outspoken naturalism, its concern for composition and for ways of framing a scene, in its sense of the value and precision of detail, use of space, symmetry, exaggeration of foreground elements, respect for truth, and the radiating or star-shaped lines of the axes of the composition, which have been analyzed in other works by other art historians, it succeeds in dramatizing for us a moment in the daily life at Yerres.

The subject is treated with great frankness and a certain humor characteristic of Caillebotte. It is free of convention and has an unusual spontaneity, which adds to our pleasure. The gardeners, got up in the traditional blue apron, also, amusingly, wear Panama hats and have bare feet. Probably they are the artist's brothers who have been given the duty of watering vegetables at the end of a summer day, after an afternoon of boating. The plants being watered by these two strapping young men are beans, which are usually sown one seed every 10 or 12 centimeters, either in a furrow or in the flat bottom of a trench spaced form 40 to 50 centimeters from the next row. Beans are also planted in hills of five to six seeds per hill, spaced 40 centimeters in all directions.

"Except in market gardens, fruit trees are always planted with vegetables, therefore we will discuss these two subjects together . . .

"The condition of a fruit-and-vegetable garden depends on the finances and tastes of its owner, and on the tastes of his landscape gardener. Proprietors who can afford only this one kind of garden locate it near the house, and lay it out so as to look attractive and to be easily accessible. Care has to be taken to prevent surrounding trees from casting shadows and to keep out their roots. The kitchen gardens of people of modest means are always close at hand and ornamental; to this end they are given the best possible sites, and the owners' tastes, interests, and judgment play their part.

"On rich properties where the designer cannot bend to his elaborate design the simple, regular shape and unchanging nature of this kind of garden, he tends to ignore it entirely or, if obliged to include it, to place it far from the house and hide it behind dense plantings. Obviously, a kitchen garden should not be placed under the windows of a palace. Still it must be given sunlight and good, well-worked soil, and be properly oriented. If absolutely necessary that its walls be hidden, shrubs that do not exceed the walls' height and that have noninvasive roots should be used. Shrubbery growing close to walls will always harbor insects, slugs, and small quadrupeds, which will continually invade the garden and play havoc there. For this reason space must be left between the shrubs and the wall they are meant to screen.

"A low-lying site or one deep in a narrow valley will contribute little to the quality of a garden's produce. Fog, late-spring and early-autumn frosts are to be feared. A very high site will warm up late in spring and cool off prematurely in autumn, resulting in a shortening of the growing season, a fact not to be disregarded. If we add the inconvenience of exposure to wind, often to storms, and lack of water, it is easy to see that the best fruit-and-vegetable garden will be found at a median elevation sheltered form the north wind by a hill, woods, or buildings. It is not always possible to overcome the difficulties that prevent a kitchen garden from being perfect, yet a common fault, due to ignorance, is simply bad location, with its attendant greater or lesser disadvantages . . .

"The size of the kitchen garden depends on the number of persons living in the house, the amount of land available, and other variable factors we cannot foresee. Only the gardener responsible for furnishing vegetables to the kitchen and fruit to the pantry can judge exactly how big the garden should be in order to produce what is needed. Unfortunately, few landscape architects consult gardeners on this point or any other. By inclination or design some families consume more and others fewer fruits and vegetables. Owners of average means whose judgment is sufficiently enlightened may have gardens that provide both fruits and vegetables and are ornamental as well; in the latter case the gardens will be larger than the absolute minimum. We have no hard rule for the size of this kind of garden except that it must never be so small that the sun cannot shine everywhere on it or air be prevented from circulating freely. Assuming these two points, form is closely linked to size. A long, narrow parallelogram, whatever its orientation, makes an extremely bad garden whose produce will be mostly of poor quality due to lack of sun and air.

"The depth of soil should be at least 60 centimeters, since few fruits or vegetables require less than this for full growth. A meter or more is still better. If one will examine carefully the roots of mature peas, spinach, beans, lettuces, and so on, it will be seen that in their search for nourishment they have penetrated, where the earth permits, as deep as sixty centimeters. If possible, a garden should not be situated over springs, else it will need to be drained. Soil well prepared for fruit growing by deep digging, manuring, and trenching will be sufficiently open to allow the passage and retention of rain water. It must not dry out too quickly in summer or retain too much water in winter but should be friable, the texture loose enough that it can be cultivated easily in all seasons. If the surface is uneven, do not try to level it. Unevenness coupled with slight differences in the nature of the soil will allow greater latitude for growing a variety of crops. The best soil for a garden is rich and loose, the worst is stiff clay, and light sand is no better.

"Greenhouses and frames are arranged in rows to save work, and face due south or slightly east. It is essential that they have the choicest exposure in the garden.

"Taste and common sense have resulted in the honorable kitchen-garden custom of planting trees along the walls and in beds surrounding plots devoted to vegetables. In the first case the trees are espaliered and attached to the wall itself, which provides shelter from wind and cold so that their fruits ripen better than if they were exposed to the open air. Trees planted in beds surrounding vegetable plots used to be trained in the shapes of stemmed goblets or fans and can still be seen in these two forms in some gardens, though the shapes generally preferred now are the *quenouille* and the pyramid because they are less contrary to nature and do not obstruct the view so much.

Peaches, Nectarines and Apricots, *before 1879*
Oil on canvas, 17 × 27 cm.
Stamped lower right
The peach, which originated in Asia, only prospers in the Paris
area if planted in a protected site, or is espaliered, preferably with a
southern exposure.

"Assuming that the ground to be used has first been suitably ploughed, improved, manured, leveled, divided into partitions suited to its size, provided with paths whose width is in proportion to the entire design, and that utility and attractiveness have also been taken into consideration, then around each plot a border of appropriate fruit trees can be planted and lastly a bed will be provided along the walls for espaliering.

"As for actual planting, imagine first the height and spread that ten- or twelve-year-old trees might attain, subject to the form to which they are to be trained. Even an inexperienced gardener will assume that the comparative size of trees depends not only on age but that each species and variety will have its own characteristics. A mirabelle plum will not reach the height of a Monsieur plum, the doyenné pear is never as tall, all things being equal, as the Saint Germain. Nevertheless, since regularity and symmetry are musts in a fruit and vegetable garden, as a general rule all trees are planted an equal distance apart and the resulting disadvantage lessened by mixing the different kinds. Here we come to two important questions, first what is the ideal spacing of the trees and then how many and what varieties..."

In discussing the general principles of gardening and its practical applications, and after having dealt with the problem of exposure, Descaisne and Naudin write on the subject of artificial heat as follows: "... A proper exposure will assure a garden an amount of natural warmth appreciably higher than that which would result from the general climate of the surrounding area, but such increase is not always sufficient even for the cultivation of ordinary vegetables in common use. Air and soil temperature may be raised by such different means as hot beds and espaliering the plants on walls..."

"Espaliering plants on walls may be said to come under the heading of exposure, but since walls are constructed by the hand of man, it is suitable to speak of them here. Their purpose is generally to concentrate the sun's heat on the trees attached to them and which they serve to support. A tree is referred to as "espaliered" when it is planted at the base of a wall and its branches, pruned and controlled according to rules, are fixed to the wall's surface by clamps, nails, and so on. The wall provides the tree with protection against wind and bad weather.

"In well-kept gardens fruits such as grapes, pears, peaches, and apricots are customarily espaliered on every exterior surface of the house and its enclosing walls, where exposure warrants. In some special orchards the entire terrain is given over to walls solely constructed to support trees. Examples of such orchards can be seen in many countries, but none is so striking as those devoted almost exclusively to the cultivation of peaches at Montreuil-aux-Pêches, known today as Montreuil-sous-Bois, near Paris. The construction of these low but (given the size of the terrain) numerous walls demands a relatively large investment, which the gardener will only risk if he is assured—by the existence of a large nearby town—of earning a reasonable profit from the sale of his produce.

"Depending on location, elevation, and exposure, espalier walls increase heat as much as would be achieved by an additional three, four, or even five or six degrees of latitude south. The same advantages cannot be enjoyed in all countries and under all climates. Where the sky is habitually overcast and the sun's radiation almost nonexistent, as along the Brittany coast and in western England, walls offer little help in stimulating growth. The opposite is true in inland countries that enjoy a continental climate and where the sky is brilliant. In such places espalier walls protect the trees from the rigors of winter and even more from spring's intemperate weather, and in the fine days of summer and fall they focus all the heat necessary for the development and the ripening of fruit.

"In northern and central France, Germany, England, and countries with similar climates, espalier walls are commonly built to a height of 2 to 2.5 meters. In more northern latitudes it is advantageous to build them higher. Thickness will depend on height. For a wall 2 meters high 40 to 45 centimeters is an adequate width; the width of walls measuring 3 to 3.5 meters should be increased to 50 centimeters or slightly more. In all cases the greater expense in building thicker walls is offset by the advantage gained in greater solidity and heat retention. Walls not only store up heat and release it during the day but throughout the night continue to give it off gradually, and the benefit they produce in this way is in proportion to their thickness.

"Horticulturists debate whether it is better to stucco and thereby lighten the color of espalier walls, or to leave the stone exposed. Certainly stone that has become darkened by prolonged exposure to light and air absorbs solar heat more rapidly and in greater quantity than when coated with white, and gives off heat faster into the circulating air after the sun has set. These are advantages; however, uncoated walls, unless built of cut stone, which is rare, or of bricks so perfectly joined that they form an extremely uniform surface, have the great inconvenience of harboring in their crevices a multitude of destructive insects such as snails, caterpillars, and earwigs, which in some years cause great damage. If, on the other hand, we take into account the fact that white surfaces, by absorbing the sun's warmth more slowly, reflect it with greater intensity and cool off more slowly during the night, we will not hesitate to choose pargeted and whitened walls, not only on the sides the trees are trained on but on the backs of the walls as well.

"An enhancement of espalier walls that should not be overlooked consists in providing them with a cap or sort of roof which projects out over the wall's face by several centimeters. Such a cap can be permanent or removable. Its purpose is to keep off rain and snow, which can injure the flower buds. It also serves to prevent nocturnal loss of heat and protect against hoarfrosts, which may succeed it on windless spring nights.

"The permanent capstone is made of bricks or slates laid flat and set into the wall. Its advantages are balanced by one flaw, which is that, by diminishing the amount of light reaching the top of the tree, it interferes with the ripening of fruit. For this reason it must not be too wide. On a wall 2 meters high it should not exceed 6 to 8 centimeters in width. A wall 3 meters high can take a capstone of 10 centimeters. A removable cap is made of straw matting or thin planks fixed to the wall's top with the

Peaches, Apples and Grapes on a Vine Leaf, *before 1879*
Oil on canvas, 21 × 31 cm.
Stamped upper right
According to P. Boitard
*L. Verardi, "Our late peaches and muscat grapes would not ripen
in Paris if they were not grown against a wall with a southern
exposure. Other varieties of peach and grape need morning and
afternoon sun. If the winter bon-chrétien, the Saint-Germain, or
the crassane cannot ripen fully in a southern exposure, at least they
attain a size that they would not obtain elsewhere, and qualities
that improve later in storage."*

aid of suitable supports and slightly tilted so as to shed rain. This kind of protection, which is essentially a screen, is much used around Paris, especially for peaches, and while the trees flower, serves as an important protection against late and sometimes deadly spring frosts. It is taken away as soon as all such danger has passed. Canvas stretched above the trees would have about the same effect . . ."

Peach Trees Espaliered in Fan Shapes with Oblique Branches
Along the espalier wall on the right in Gustave Caillebotte's painting a type of peach-tree espalier called "fan shape with oblique branches" can be clearly seen, while other espalier-trained forms seem to be "fans à la diable." This latter method, used in Montreuil-sous-Bois near Paris, consists of controlling the tree's main branches in such a way that they can cover a great surface of the wall. According to Pierre Boitard and Louis Verardi, "Since the so-called Montreuil method has long been considered a classic, its fundamental premise must be discussed here." A number of famous painters have been said to be unaware of "clashing colors." With equal justice it can be claimed the inhabitants of Montreuil are oblivious of "wrong exposures," since they plant their peach trees in the teeth of the north wind where no other gardens will succeed. Since the principal business of the people of Montreuil is to harvest abundant peaches and early vegetables and since they depend solely on the heat of the sun, it is interesting to learn that their success in their objective comes as a result of dividing their gardens into parts surrounded by walls, forming as many smaller gardens whose walls break the wind and whose interiors hold the sun's heat. Each plot or small garden usually measures 24 by 36 meters; some may be smaller. All the walls are built very roughly by the farmers themselves of quarry stones bonded by mortar, set directly on the ground and covered with a layer of stucco. Before placing the capstone, they fasten at a distance of 1.3 meters jutting, slightly tilted, 60-centimeter-long laths on which are laid small straw mats to protect the blossoms from spring frosts and inclement weather.[42]

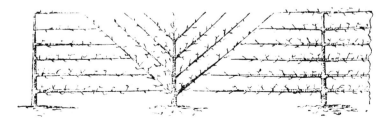

*Espaliered peaches trained
horizontally and fan shaped,
grown together*

Warmth of the soil

Up to this point we have been concerned only with the warmth of the air, and no one will doubt that necessity for successful plant growth. What is less generally known, and what is essential to understand, is that the warmth of the soil, subterranean warmth—or, in general terms, the warmth of the environment into which the roots are planted—is hardly less necessary than warm air in encouraging and sustaining the life of plants.

Ignoring this principle has led and still leads every day to numerous failures in the work of inexperienced gardeners.

Gardening has two means of increasing the temperature of the soil beyond that which it would naturally get from the climate. These means are hot beds and the warming of air by means of fires.

Hot Beds

"Hot beds are made of fermenting organic matter arranged in layers over or near which are set the plants whose growth is to be induced or activated. As the matter decays, it ferments, thus heating up and passing on its warmth to the soil. To avoid losing the heat thus obtained and in order to protect the plants from intemperate weather, the beds or frames are usually covered with glass sashes or with bell jars.

J. Decaisne and C. Naudin give us information on the composition of the compost and on the building or installation of the frames as follows: "Commonly their width varies from 1 to 2 meters, with a depth of 50 to 80 centimeters or even a meter and they may be any length, buried in trenches or simply set directly on the ground." As for the fermentation, "Experienced gardeners know when they place their hands in the soil and find its temperature to be about equal to that of the body—28 to 32 degrees centigrade—it has reached the proper warmth. When the temperature has risen to the desired level, sowing or planting is done directly into the earth or in pots sunk to their rims in the frame. In the south or where the season is advanced and the weather settled, the surface is left exposed and is only covered with matting cloth at

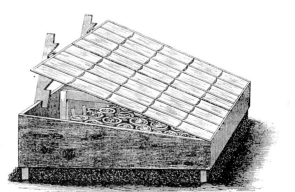

Frame

night to protect it from nocturnal drops in temperature. In the latitude of Paris and similar climates, especially in winter, it is indispensable that the frame be covered by glass sashes. These serve as portable roofing for the wooden frames. Higher on one side than on the other so that when closed they shed rain, they are placed on the frame in such a way as to cover it completely. The higher side is on the north; the sash itself slants toward the south. The illustration on page 131 shows a frame with its sash half open. Where the season permits, it is possible to replace the sashes by simple bell jars, but the loss of heat is much greater..."

Watering Cans

Gustave Caillebotte's attention to detail gives us an idea of the reality of the kitchen garden as it existed in his time. This *analytical* preoccupation is as evident in the artist's rendering of watering cans as in descriptions of these objects by authors of specialized treatises. Decaisne and Naudin describe watering cans as follows:

Professional watering can

"Receptacles of diverse forms are used to water plants. The size varies, depending on the strength of the person using them. The most common form is that of the market-garden watering pot, enlarged in the middle and equipped with two handles, one curved, the other straight and attached to the spout. This spout emerges from the base of the can and ends in an enlargement closed by a thin plate pierced with holes through which water is discharged in the form of rain. In many cases the spout is detachable so that it can be removed or replaced, depending on whether plants are to be watered one by one or collectively...

"The shapes of watering cans have been much modified. In recent years their sides have been flattened, making them easier to carry." The second person in the painting *Yerres, in the Kitchen Garden, Gardeners Watering the Plants* is using two cans of this type.

"A watering can has also been designed with a single circular handle emerging from the rear of the can and ending at the spout, a shape that is less tiring for the worker to tilt or raise." The first gardener in the painting is using a pair of such cans, so shiny that they seem to be new.

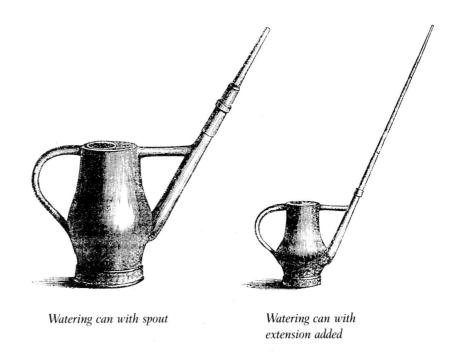

Watering can with spout

Watering can with extension added

"Watering cans are made of oiled tin, or of zinc or copper. The latter are much more expensive but last better, and when no longer usable their metal retains some value."

Market-Garden Cloches

"On the subject of "propagation by seed, cuttings, and grafts and the use of forcing frames and cloches to hasten growth or facilitate germination" Decaisne and Naudin wrote, in the work previously cited, "Not only are frames with glazed sashes used to conserve heat around seedlings but glass cloches as well. The latter keep out cold air and allow the sun's rays to reach the soil. The effect of a cloche is only slightly less than that of glazed sashes; however, because of their relative narrowness and their round or polygonal shape, they leave an appreciable area of soil uncovered, resulting in a certain loss of heat. This defect is compensated for by the ease with which they are moved from place to place. In gardens in northern and central France and to a degree in the south, cloches play an essential and even indispensable role in

Market garden cloche

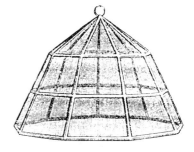

Faceted cloche

gardening, serving not only to assure successful starts but to protect mature plants against intemperate weather.

"Cloches manufactured in one piece are called 'market-garden cloches' and are widely used in Paris. A second type, with a lead or tin coated iron frame fitted with glass panes, is referred to as a *verrine* and has the advantage that broken panes are easily replaced. Cracked whole cloches may still be used; if broken into two or three pieces they are almost totally useless. One may attempt to mend them be securing the fragments with cloth strips treated with white lead diluted with drying oil. Such cloches cost less than *verrines*.

"Cloches not only stimulate seed to germinate and protect delicate plants against cold but are widely used in starting cuttings..."

Yerres, in the Kitchen Garden, Gardeners Watering
the Plants, *before 1879 (detail)*

Paul Chevrier's Bean

Beginning in 1826, Paul Gabriel Chevrier lived at Bretigny-sur-Orge along with the many rural gardeners and farmers who raised vegetables for the Paris market. In 1872 Chevrier planted a late crop of white flageolet beans, widely grown in that region, and because of early frost was forced to harvest it prematurely. On a September night he pulled up his plants with their pods not fully ripened and hung them to dry in a shed. When he and his family sampled a few they observed three new differences: the beans had retained their green color and only a small percentage had shriveled, they were easier to cook than dried beans, and they tasted as if freshly harvested. Chevrier, noting that a fully ripened and normally handled hulled bean was white, deduced that his prematurely harvested crop had probably retained its ability to germinate. He sorted out and planted the greenest and plumpest beans. The resulting plants developed normally until harvested at the proper time. Chevrier tested his beans for six years and in 1878 received a prize at the Versailles Exhibition.

His discovery of a new way to harvest and dry flageolet beans while still green was of considerable economic interest to his entire region and resulted in the prosperity of the local commerce in this vegetable, which is sold at the Arpajon Fair. Chevrier's bean was christened "flageolet Chevrier d'Arpajon," a name later shortened to "Arpajon bean." Long and painstaking work using genetic and phytopathological information has led to a proliferation of varieties.

Antique varieties of flageolets. Upper right: Very early flageolets d'Etampes. Etampes is in the name of a town in the present-day department of Essone. Lower left: Dwarf flageolets, "first triumph."

Nettle-leaf flageolet

An Orchard

"An orchard consists of a parcel of land that cannot be enclosed except by a hedge and in which fruit trees larger than those in a garden are grown. The trees, planted in quincunxes, so shade the ground that vegetables will only thrive among them while the trees are young. Once grown, they deprive lower plants of air. When planting orchard trees, it is worthwhile to pay attention to the nature of their roots and to alternate those having tap roots with trees whose roots spread. If the orchard's owner possesses a kitchen garden sufficient for his needs, he might use the spaces between his orchard trees to plant short-lived early-bearing fruits."

Such was the case at Yerres, in one of the orchards seen southeast of the kitchen garden in the photographic plan reproduced in "A History of the Property." A second orchard of large trees was located to the north of the kitchen gardens between the canal and the periphery road of the landscape park.

"Of all gardens orchards demand the least care, especially if the trees' principal limbs are properly shaped. An annual tilling, a little manure every five or six years, and a winter's visit, if growth indicates, to prune the branches, destroy moss and lichen, and remove dead wood will be all it requires. In other seasons the most it will need is thinning, where absolutely necessary, of overabundant fruit. Such are the important points for a productive orchard . . .

"Nurserymen who grow worthwhile new varieties of fruit are well known. They advertise in catalogues that can be useful to the gardener wishing to make knowledgeable choices."

A MODERN FORMAL GARDEN
IN THE NINETEENTH CENTURY

"All about them the roses bloomed amorously, smiling feverish red and white smiles, opening out as though baring themselves, garments falling open to reveal the riches of lovely breasts. Yellow roses like barbarian girls shed their golden petals, wheatstraw in color, citron, the hue of the sun, all the shades of napes ambered under hot skies. A tenderer flesh of tea roses, adorably moist, displayed silken parts hitherto modestly hidden, finely traced by a network of blue veins. The roses laughing existence grew: barely tinted white roses snowy as a virgin's foot thrust forward to test a spring, pale roses more discreetly warm and creamy than a glimpsed knee or than the flash of a bright young arm inside a wide sleeve, bold roses showing warm blood through their satin-like bared shoulders, like naked hips, like all the nakedness of women caressed by light; bright corsage roses with petals half-open like lips, exhaling whispers of perfume like warm breath. And the climbing rose with her rain of white flowers cloaking all these other roses, all this flesh, with her lacy clusters and innocence of

Painters' rose

airy mousseline while, here and there, bloody, nearly black roses like the lees of wine pierced this bridal purity as if with a passionate wound. Fragrant woodland marriage drawing May's virgins onward toward the fecundity of July and August; the first unskilled kiss plucked like a nosegay in the wedding dawn. In the grass, moss roses in high-necked green wool dresses awaited the approach of love. Along the path striped by the sun's rays flowers prowled, thrusting their faces forward, soliciting the light, passing breezes. Under the clearing's tent smiles gleamed, each one different, each rose making love after her fashion, some timidly with blushing hearts only consenting to open their buds half way, others panting and untidy, corsets unlaced, wide-open to the point of dying. Some small, gay, lively roses all in a row wore knots of ribbon in their bonnets; some were enormous, bursting, round as fattened sultanesses; some, impudent and wanton as young girls, showed off petals whitened with rice powder. Honest women were there with correct bourgeois necklines, and permissably original aristocrats of supple elegance who invented their déshabillés. Full, cup-shaped roses held out perfume as if in precious crystal, roses with heads thrown back released it, urnlike, drop by drop, roses round as cabbages exhaled with the even breath of sleepers, tightly clasped buds held their petals close and yielded only faint virginal sighs."

EMILE ZOLA, *La Faute de l'Abbé Mouret,* 1875

"The formal garden, like architecture, has rules and laws of proportion, and although this kind of garden is far removed from the naturalness of the plants that adorn it, one must admit that, on a grand scale, its geometrical symmetry affords the eye great pleasure... Its perfect harmony with the architecture of a rich, formally designed residence gives an overall effect of majesty and grandeur worthy of the power of wealth... This type of garden is so involved with architectural art that by itself it yields designs that call for the profoundest study.

"Printed plans exist of parterres compartmented in the so-called French manner. Here we discuss parterres divided in the 'English' style. In such designs some relationship with the old method survives, though they offer much more variety. Edgings still consist of dwarf box, and the beds are filled with ornamental plants. Usually in each compartment a plant of a different color is used and care taken that it harmonize pleasantly with those in neighboring sections. The same system can be applied to a collection of roses."

A Rose Garden, or Rosarium

"The rosarium, which is a space especially devoted to growing roses, will be where the amateur reckons up his true wealth. In this charming nursery he will invest all his pride and receive all his satisfaction, it is where a handsome collection of flowers salutes the return of the season and where a new rose repays him for the care he has given it.

"A rosarium is a school of roses set up as one sets up a school of botany. Ordinarily the area is divided into beds 1.3 meters wide and of any desired length, edged with thick, round-edged wooden planks painted green and set on the ground, rising no higher than 15 centimeters. Planks make better edgings than boxwood since the roots of the latter will eat up the roses' sustenance. Paths between beds should be 1.3 meters wide... A design for a rosarium that includes a circular section will have its own elegance.

"Standard roses are planted 1.5 meters apart and between them a bush on its own stock, perhaps of the same species as its grafted neighbor, so that the gardener can compare the yield resulting from the two methods. On either side of this row, a row of plants on their own roots is placed, making a total of three rows. In a planting of this kind one can exert all the order one desires and have room to study and enjoy the roses in the most complete and agreeable way. The number of beds can be increased, in which case some other means of edging must be found."

Gustave Caillebotte's *The Kitchen Garden,* painted around 1877, shows a rosarium. In *A Garden, Yerres,* painted around the same date, the same garden is shown, with hoops covered with climbing roses. (These two paintings are not reproduced.)

Concerning a "School of Roses"
"As I was leaving the studio, I paused before some sketches of roses. Renoir told me he was doing some studies of flesh tints for a nude."

AMBROISE VOLLARD[44]

It is useful to remember that until recently, when the geneticist C. C. Hurst did work at Cambridge, no one was aware of the early hybridizing of the eglantine, which resulted in the deep red and old pink roses of nineteenth-century European gardens. A cross of eglantine with two distinctly different races of climbing musk roses and the bright red, perfumed Rosa Gallica, which dates to 1200 B.C., produced a range of Damask, Gallica, and Alba roses in all shades ranging from white to crimson. The high period of hybridization in this color range, which has relatively limited genetic possibilities, was reached in Holland in the seventeenth century. After repeated crosses between Albas and Damasks, the Dutch obtained a rose with one hundred petals, known as the "cabbage rose," "rose of Provence," or "painter's rose."

At the end of the eighteenth century cultivated roses resulting from centuries of selection were introduced from China. These were derived from two wild species, Rosa Gigantea, whose flowers had a fragrance of tea, and Rosa Chinensis, a once-blooming red or pink climber. At an unknown date a sport of Rosa Chinensis produced a dwarf rose having the great virtue of repeated flowering. Since 1792 all roses have descended from Rosa Chinensis and three hybrids of Rosa Gigantea.

Cultivation of roses developed at the end of the same century in French Brie at Grisy-Suisnes. When on July 26, 1800, Admiral de Bougainville acquired the Château de Suisnes his gardener, Christophe Cochet, actively participated in this movement and by September 14, 1875, the Society of Rose Growers of Grisy had thirty-two members. In 1876 Scipion Cochet founded the *Journal des Roses,*[45] which ceased publication in 1914. In 1868 the following note appeared in the *Guide Bleu*: "... Today fields of roses contribute to the richness and beauty of the entire Brie region from Villecresnes to Coubert and Soisnolles, but the township of Grisy-Suisnes remains the center of this enterprise, which, thanks to 'forcing' techniques, furnishes cut flowers for the Paris market almost year round."

After citing different works published between 1800 and 1863, J. Decaisne and C. Naudin wore in *Manuel de l'amateur de jardin,* "Great uncertainty still exists about the limits of botanical species of roses... The best guide seems to us to be Dr. Lindley's monograph[46] written forty years ago but to which subsequent botanical works have added little." Apropos of Rosa Centifolia Decaisne and Naudin wrote,

Rose with Purple Iris, Garden at Petit
Gennevilliers, *c. 1892*
Oil on canvas, 79 × 36 cm.
Signed lower right
Did this scene remind the artist of the
Rose Garden at Yerres?

"Gardening catalogues mention several hundred varieties of hundred-petaled roses with or without qualifying them as hybrid. We have pointed out that the arbitrary classifications of these catalogues, whose ends are purely commercial, have no scientific value... It would benefit rose lovers greatly if the catalogues were rigorously expurgated and only truly first class roses left. If such a thing were done many ancient varieties almost abandoned today would be included and at the top of the list."

In rounding out our remarks on roses we should like to point out that when Gustave Caillebotte lived at Yerres the following kinds were in general cultivation:

For more than 3000 years:
   Rosa gallica
Since the sixteenth century:
   Rosa centifolia
   Rosa Eglanteria
   Rosa foetida
   Rosa foetida 'Bicolor'
Since the seventeenth century:
   Rosa spinosissima
   Rosa Sulphurea
Since the eighteenth century:
   Rosa centifolia 'Muscosa'
   Rosa alba Semi Plena
   Rosa arvensis
   Rosa pendolina
   Rosa chinensis (Old Blush)
   Rosa alba (Cuisse de Nymphe)
   Rosa alba (Celestial)
Dating from before 1830:
   Rosa centifolia minor (Petite de Hollande)
   Rosa Banksiae 'Alba Plena'
   Rosa nitida
   Rosa virginiana
   Rosa Noisettiana (Champney's Pink Cluster)
   Rosa rubrifolia
   Rosa dupontii
   Portland Rose Crimson King
   Rosa gallica (Jenny Duval)
   Rosa Brunoni
   Rosa gallica (La Belle Sultane)
   Rosa Banksiae Lutea
   Rosa borboniana
   Sempervirens hybrid (Adélaide d'Orléans)

Moss rose cristata

Moss rose Zoë

Garden Rose and Blue Forget-Me-Nots in a Vase,
before 1879
Oil on canvas, 34 × 26 cm.
Stamped upper right

Tea rose Mélanie Willermoz

Bengal rose

Bourbon island rose Guillaume le Conquérant

Multiflower rose

Rosa alba (Konigen von Danemark)

Rosa carolina

Rosa Macounii

Sempervirens hybrid (Felicitie et Perpetue)

Rosa centifolia 'Cristata'

Rosa Noisettiana 'Aimée Vibert'

Dating from 1830 to 1850:

Rosa damascena (Madame Hardy)

Sempervirens hybrid (Reine des Belges)

Rosa chinensis 'Viridiflora'

Rosa borboniana (Queen of Bourbons)

Rosa alba (Madame Plantier)

Rosa gallica (Président de Séze)

Rosa foetida 'Persiana'

Rosa bourboniana (Coupe d'Hébé)

Rosa bourboniana (Prince Charles)

Rosa alba (Madame Legras de Saint-Germain)

Rosa Noisettiana (Caroline Marniesse)

Rosa damascena (La Ville de Bruxelles)

Rosa gallica (Charles Mills)

Dating from 1850 to 1860:

Tea Rose Sombreuil

Rosa borboniana (Louise Odier)

Rosa centifolia 'Muscosa' (Nuits de Young)

Rosa Centifolia Muscosa (Salet)

Tea Rose (Gloire de Dijon)

Rosa rugosa

Rosa centifolia 'Muscosa' (Julie de Mersan)

Rosa centifolia 'Muscosa' (William Lobb)

Portland Rose (Marbrée)

Climbing Tea Rose (De Voniensis Olg)

Portland Rose (Comte de Chambord)

Remontant hybrid climber (Enfant de France)

Dating from 1864:

Climbing Tea Rose (Maréchal Niel)

Rosa centifolia 'Muscosa' (Eugénie Guinoisseau)

Dating from 1865:

Remontant hybrid climber (Souvenir du Docteur Jamain)

Dating from 1867:

Rosa borboniana (Boule de Neige)

Tea Rose hybrid (France)

Dating from 1868:

Rosa borboniana (Zephirine Drouhin)

Portland Rose (Jacques Cartier)

144

Dating from 1869:
    Everblooming hybrid climber (Paul Neyron)
    Rosa Noisettiana (Rêve d'Or)
Dating from 1870:
    Rosa Virginiana 'Plena'
    Rosa Watsoniana
Dating from 1872: *Rosa borboniana* (La Reine Victoria)
Dating from 1874: *Rosa borsaultiana* (Madame Sancy de Parabere)
Dating from 1876: *Rosa nutkana*
Dating from 1878: *Rosa borboniana* (Madame Pierre Oger)
Dating from 1879: *Rosa noisettiana* (Madame Alfred Carrière)
Dating from 1880: *Rosa centifolia 'Muscosa'* (Blanche Moreau)

Capucine rose

Edgings

"In formal gardens edgings add precision and neatness to the contours of the gardens' different compartments. For many years edgings were luxuries kept up at the expense of the flower beds and other garden parts, which they defined, and consisted of large boxwoods permitted to grow to a height of 60 centimeters. At intervals, and especially at corners, some of these were clipped in the shapes of globes, pyramids, chess pieces, benches, even armchairs. Aside from the serious problem of exhausting the soil well into the flower beds, these large boxwoods overwhelmed low and delicate plants.

"Today's edgings serve their intended purpose. Allowed to grow no more than 8 to 10 centimeters, they are kept cleanly trimmed, neat, full, and of an agreeable green color. So far, dwarf box is the only material found to offer all the qualities needed to make an attractive border. Fashion, which delights in change, has tried in vain to substitute other plants. In vast compositions whose contours have little need of rectification some have been more or less successful, but the dwarf box will always be best for the small garden where grace and neatness are valued. The only attention an edging requires is clipping two or three times a year with the greatest possible precision, which is to say that no least twig or tiny branch should exceed the length of any other. Height should always be twice width. Gaps should be refilled promptly. We have seen box edgings in the shapes of stars, rosettes, and other designs, even mottoes and emblematic devices. This is not in the best taste, yet it can have its charm, and if the artist has a useful end in view, he should include it in his composition. If we come upon a small kitchen garden and a few flowers at the entrance to some secluded retreat it would not seem unsuitable; if at the end of this same garden a needle-shaped yew cast its shadow on a sundial whose divisions were marked in small boxwoods, would that be unsuitable? We do not think so, given the composition's usefulness. The same would be true in many circumstances impossible to foresee here; the amateur will decide for himself . . . "

The Park at Yerres, *1877*
Oil on canvas, 81 × 59 cm.
Signed and dated lower right
"G. Caillebotte 77"
An example of accent edging, here consisting of rows of begonias, impatiens, and pelargonium. On the lawn at left, a blue cedar, in the background the colonnade of the "casin," and on the left of the colonnade, a potted orange tree.

Accent Edgings

"An accent, or facing, edging consists of a row of flowers intended to provide a vivid effect. Generally it follows the contours of a flower bed, bit of lawn or some other small composition. Intended for ephemeral effect only, the plants are sown in place, in furrows. Two sowings per year of fast-growing annuals will produce a succession of bloom, the first planting sown in place as we have said, the second made up of plants grown elsewhere and transplanted into the row."

Stone bridge, elevation

Bridges

"Since bridges tend to be in keeping with the composition as a whole and with the architecture of the main house, they will take precedence in this treatise over rustic houses and cottages, which are of secondary importance.

"Bridges are perhaps the most interesting of all decorative garden structures both for their utility and their pictorial effect, and their use has much increased. We list them among utilitarian features and do not include them in any design whatever unless they serve an obvious purpose or appear to do so. Under all other circumstances and despite any visual charm they may have, we consider them not only in bad taste but even absurd. If, however, it appears that a landscape would profit by the addition of a bridge, an attempt might be made to introduce one even where not absolutely indispensable, provided it appears to serve a need.

"A bridge should be situated over running water and care taken to conceal each end, whether by bringing it onto the scene above the low arch of a wall assumed to enclose a neighboring property, or by making it seem to disappear into a distant landscape that cannot be entered but where the eye can follow briefly, or in any number of other ways suggested by the terrain."

On the Canal
By means of a pump this canal makes use of river water, which is then used to water the flower garden and the kitchen garden.

A Stone Bridge
"Subject to architectural laws, constructed in severe or graceful style, regular or eccentric in shape, harmonizing with the main house and costing much more than other kinds, [stone] bridges are especially suited to the properties of the rich. They fit in with extensive vistas; if built too closely together, as in a small property, they will seem too massive.

"The positioning of a stone bridge should be such that during the greater part of the day the sun will shine on the side facing the direction from which it will most often be seen [this is the case at Yerres], for if its bulk is constantly in shadow, it will appear flattened and give a gloomy and even disagreeable impression. A bridge of dressed stone in a bold, regular shape embellished by an iron railing, lanterns, vases, and so on will make a fine addition to a noble prospect whose central focus is a luxuriously appointed castle or a villa. Where the landscape demands less richness, where the architecture of the house, however majestic, leans more toward elegance than severe formality, the bridge's ornaments should be in a lighter style."

This postcard from the turn of the century recalls Caillebotte's Woman Seated under a Tree *and* The Meadow at Yerres.

OPPOSITE
Woman Seated under a Tree *c. 1874*
Oil on canvas, 46 × 38 cm.
Signed lower left "G. Caillebotte"
Caillebotte was not the only painter who depicted this humid swampy area, a sort of small scale "Amazon forest" within the climate of the Ile de France, not far from Montgeron. At different times toward the end of his life Jean-Baptiste Camille Corot lived and worked in the Yerres Valley. Between 1855 and 1860 he painted Plain with Cows; *in 1868,* Montgeron, Willow Grove at the Water's Edge; *around the same date,* Montgeron, Pond with Cow and Peasant Woman Carrying a Pail; *and* Brunoy, Meadow on the Bank of the Yerres, *works whose titles remind us of the commonality of interests of Caillebotte and Corot both of whom treated the same themes and were equally drawn to the landscapes and atmosphere of the Yerres Valley. These works foreshadowed the nascent Impressionist movement.*

YERRES (S.-et-O.)
La Prairie

The Meadow at Yerres, *c. 1875*
Oil on canvas, 73 × 92 cm.
This can have been painted either in the meadow of the Caillebotte property, accessible by the stone bridge over the canal, or farther west in the Great Meadow.

THE MEADOW

"A meadow is one of the most common features of the large landscape garden and also one of its most charming, yet attractiveness is not enough, it must also serve some purpose. Meadows occur naturally on valley floors and along the banks of streams; they extend into all the twistings and turnings and all the detours of the edges of woods and groves.

"Bailly[47] says that a meadow should not be covered with a single species of plant, nor should it be smooth as a sheet of water. Irregularities produced by a variety of plants will not distort the overall design and the plants themselves will add—in the multitude of their tints and colors through the changing seasons and in various forms of their flowers, leaves, and stems—a thousand amenities to the landscape as a whole and in its details. In order to understand the superiority of meadows spangled with flowers and a great diversity of plants, we need only glance at one in springtime to see how, in a single plant, the green color changes from shade to shade or is pleasantly variegated with white, yellow, blue, or red. Instead of rejecting the adventitious plants that appear among meadow grasses, instead of weeding them out in the name of beautification, we should multiply them by sowing seed of kinds we esteem for their virtues and, above all, for their flowers. Then we shall not only have replaced the earth's brown color with an extensive green, but shall have turned it into a natural parterre, into a meadow and a flower garden which at every stage will give us bouquets of flowers less rare and less precious than those in real parterres yet not less pretty and sweet smelling."

A meadow requires little upkeep. Moisture can be maintained by natural irrigation. Mowing should be done once or twice a year. As for creating it, that is something else, demanding care and close observation and some knowledge of botany. Below we offer some recommendations.

The Nap, *1877*
Pastel, 36 × 53 cm.
Signed and dated top left "G. C. 77"
The posture of the person at the foot of the tree in the
meadow at Yerres is the same as one of the figures in the
Flemish Pieter Brueghel the Elder's Land of Milk and
Honey, *1567, in the Munich Pinakothek. The utopian*
idea of a country where laziness is a virtue goes back to
Antiquity. The French fable of the Land of Plenty
appeared in Germany in 16th century, in a rhymed
version at Nuremberg in 1536, then in a prose version in
Antwerp in 1546. In about 1885 Cézanne's son Paul
was to pose for his father's painting, The Nap, *executed*
in a manner that foretold the arrival of Cubism.

Grasses, in varieties dependent on the nature and quality of the soil, form the basis of all natural meadows. Our first advice is to observe what species grow spontaneously on the spot one wishes to convert to a meadow and to add plants from the lists below.

"For a marshy place, water fescue, meadow foxtail, geniculate-stemmed foxtail, timothy, sweet holcus, blue melica, water bluegrass, swamp speargrass, dog's tail grass, geniculate-stemmed bent, giant bromus, wild barley, water hairgrass, false hairgrass.

"In dry and sandy soil, meadow oats, yellow oats, sheep fescue, recumbent fescue, tough fescue, wild foxtail, soft holcus, nodding melica, ciliate melica, rough meadow grass, bulbed meadow grass, compressed meadow grass, bromus, inermous bromus, flexuous hairgrass, white hairgrass, foliated hairgrass, creeping bent.

"In average soil, downy oats, sweet vernal grass, orchard grass, bluegrass, annual meadow grass, speargrass, rye grass, quaking grass, comose bent, red bent, dog bent."

The "Bocage"

"Poets in France use the word 'bocage' to describe a natural woodland of moderate size containing both shade and open grassy spaces. The French word *bocage*, which comes from the Italian *bosco*, or woods, denotes in landscape gardening a romantic place far from the house, formed by a unity of irregularly spaced groups of trees separated by distinct gaps. These groups will vary greatly in width and height but together will form a single composition sprinkled with clearings intersecting in all directions and producing a multitude of vistas. In order to bring closer sections that seem too distant or to fill up a too large empty space, a solitary tree may be planted, chosen from a species whose form or leaf is in some way remarkable; otherwise, lost against mass foliage it would not be effective. For the same reason, however, specimen trees are rarely used in this kind of planting.

"A bocage must be both light and graceful. To this end, increase the distance between clumps of trees and plant in the gaps a number of groupings of smaller trees unconnected with each other and separated by considerable distances. In some situations planting will be absolutely necessary, in others it will suffice to thin out existing trees and enlarge clearings to provide a more open feeling. A further word: trees used to create this pleasing genre of landscape should be chosen among species that most resemble each other in habit, leaf, and green color so that they form a unity; anything which might in any way jar the general effect should be removed. The visitor strolling through such a woodland will be guided not by roads but by simple footpaths, which wind across the clearings and end up always at some place that offers stimulation to the eye or to the imagination."

To the artist who considers converting a natural woodland into a bocage we could not give better advice than that of M. de Viart when he wrote, "It is only after much

*Small house near the pond, in the bocage
in the time of Madame Dubois*

research, work and care, then, that he will succeed in producing the effect expected in a bocage composed according to the rules. In the space of a few springtimes the trees will fill out and reward him with a pleasure that ususally comes only after a long wait. First, attention will be given to the trees that make up the original woodland and to the paths that cross it. The largest trees with the most voluminous branches will be felled, especially those located on the edges of clearings, taking care not to damage specimens intended to remain and that the artist will select from among the medium-size and the youngest. Once this first operation is carried out, groups must be formed within the remaining trees according to general or specific rules of designing a bocage and depending on what is required by the site, culling unwanted growth or, where necessary to shape the groups appropriately, moving others young enough or of a species capable of successful transplanting. Two or three well-designed groups will suffice to break up a straight line of open spaces, especially if the edges have been thinned. These empty areas will fall easily into the structure of clearings that, stretching from one side to the other of the total area, will erase the original forms completely. A bocage is an uncultivated woodland that preserves the simplicity of nature."

The Yerres, Effect of Light, *before 1879*
Oil on cardboard,
28 × 49 cm.
Stamped lower right
In the foreground, trees in the family park—we are looking upstream

WATER

*The Yerres today, seen from
the property*

"Plants are not everything in the ornamentation of gardens. Water has a powerful effect, too."

Kirk Varnedoe wrote on this subject, "Water is one of the favorite themes of Impressionist painting and often refers by analogy to the activity of the painter, for it unifies and smooths out the image it reflects while at the same time fragmenting it into small shimmering bits."

Bodies of water and springs, objects of a cult going back to earliest antiquity, served traditional villages as places of communal contact and social exchange. In gardens of

The Yerres today

OPPOSITE:
The Yerres, Effect of Rain (*also known as* Riverbank in the Rain), *1875*
Oil on canvas, 81 × 59 cm.
Stamped lower right
Rainfall is a climatic factor indispensable to the growth of plants. Abundant winter rains replenish the soil with much needed water. Summer rains are beneficial in proportion to their intensity. According to statistics of the National Office of Meteorology, the average number of rainy days per year in the department of the Essonne over a period of 15 years was 150 and the average amount of rainfall in millemeters per year over a period of 40 years was 604. The amount of water that falls during the growing period of many plants is not sufficient. If better growth and yield are desired, irrigation and overhead watering (see Yerres, in the Kitchen Garden, Gardeners Watering the Plants) *are indispensable.*

The Norwegian landscape painter Fritz Thaulow, who arrived in France in about 1880 and became a resident of Dieppe, revealed a kinship to Gustave Caillebotte when he painted Reflections.

the Ile de France as early as the sixteenth century water became an aesthetic element. In parks fountain builders and water professionals enjoyed a wide reputation for their fountains, pools, water tournaments, waterside buffets, canals, grottoes, shrines to nymphs, waterfalls, and rockeries. Everything became a pretext to cause water to spring forth from the earth, to give pleasure.

In the nineteenth century Boitard made it possible for us to picture water fêtes in the Valois tradition as they were conceived and enjoyed on the pond of the Fontainebleau gardens, at the time of Naturalism and Impressionism.

Water is an important feature in much of the work Gustave Caillebotte did at Yerres. We see this in the reproductions of his paintings and pastels as we stroll through his family's park. The very high level of some of these works, with their enormous strength and intensity, puts them in the category of masterpieces and reminds us that we must reassess this original and unique artist.

In the second half of the nineteenth century, boaters, canoists, yachtsmen, swimmers, and fishermen participated in a return to water pleasures as in the time of

A view upstream, Brunoy

Riverbank, *before 1879*
Oil on canvas, 28 × 41 cm.
Signed lower right "Gustave
Caillebotte"
From the meadow, the right
bank of the Yerres and Mont
Griffon—we are looking
east, and upstream

OPPOSITE
Brunoy, the Soulins
Bridge, *before 1879*
Oil on canvas, 30 × 22 cm.
Stamped lower right
This was painted at Brunoy,
above Yerres, from the left
bank of the river. Looking
downstream we see two or
three arches of a bridge built
in 1746 on the initiative of
Brunoy nobleman Jean
Paris de Monmartel so that
the town's inhabitants could
reach Soulins by a route
skirting the parks and
gardens of his château.
Behind the artist on the
other side of the Soulins
road, which ran along the
left bank of the river, the
Château de Soulins stood in
the second half of the 19th
century. At one time the
château was owned by the
goldsmith Charles
Christofle.

Banks of the Yerres,
c. 1878
Oil on wood, 15 × 22 cm.

Watteau. A new phenomenon, the advent of water sports as we know them today, brought about a certain democratization of these activities. From a diversion reserved for an aristocratic few the pleasures of water became little by little available to society at large. Yerres, Argenteuil, and Bougival played their roles in this. So did Gustave Caillebotte, as much in his life as in his work.

"You have sometimes run across a painting that has seemed right yet also somehow lacking. You found it satisfactory but wished it were more 'finished.' You studied it and realized that what it needed was the final brushstroke, the artist's conclusive idea, which brings a masterpiece to life. We are affected in the same way by a

Périssoires on the Yerres, 1877
Oil on canvas, 103 × 156 cm.
Signed and dated lower left "G. Caillebotte 1877"
The river as it flows past the Great Meadow. In the
background are the hills of Montgeron, where the painter
Carolus-Duran's property Le Moutier and the collector
Ernest Hoschedé's Château de Rottembourg were
situated.

landscape without water. Water is a natural, vivifying part of a beautiful garden. Its effect is both magical and indispensable, and its absence will engender a feeling of such incompleteness that we will rack our brains to discover what can be missing in what seems otherwise a splendid picture.

"So many•different sensations result from the sight of a lake in a garden! We never tire of its mysterious charm. As we wander along its banks the shadows of trees flicker on its surface and the sun's bright gold breaks through. A cloud passing slowly by on a light breeze suddenly obscures a star, then for an instant ruffles and darkens the transparent water. A flock browses on the fresh green grass of its banks. What delight we feel when the moon illuminates all this with her uncertain light and the silence is

Sailing Dinghy on the Yerres, *1878*
Oil on canvas, dimensions unknown
Signed and dated lower right "G. Caillebotte 1878"
In 1859, according to the treatise on gardens, recreational vessels of the time were gondolas and Chinese junks. The small boats designed to visit romantic grottoes became more utilitarian, turning into rowboats and fishing skiffs, and the single-seater canoe with its agile paddler was more often used for sailing. The first centerboard sailboats appeared on the river. Boating was a favorite activity of Caillebotte.

broken by the nightingale, the faint clatter of a fish seizing an unwary insect, the murmur of a wavelet reflecting somberly moonlit foliage! The artist should go to every length to add this delightful accessory to the landscape garden.

"In deciding where to locate a body of water, the designer should remember to keep it at a reasonable distance from the house, to save the residents from the discomforts of early morning fog, especially in autumn.

"Like air and land, water needs inhabitants. Brightly colored fish will add a pleasant note but will not always be easy to see, unless the spectator comes near. The surface should be populated with waterfowl such as curlew, wild duck, moorhen, and so on. Water birds are easily lured to the artificial lake or pond if its banks include some bushes or plants that thrive in such places. Flocks migrating inland from the chilly seacoast will arrive in countless flocks, sometimes finding your property by following the river that irrigates it. Graceful swans with rounded streamlined breasts will cut through the water like the hulls of boats, whether you live in a castle with an ornamental lake or have added a pond to an ordinary garden.

"Natural bodies of water fit into landscape parks and gardens and into woods and irregularly shaped grounds. Artificial bodies of water suit the sumptuously designed formal garden. We divide natural bodies of water into those in which the water is still and those where it is moving. Natural lakes and ponds, 'English' rivers, some man-made lakes, rock pools, and wetlands contain still waters. Fountains, natural rivers, mountain streams, and waterfalls are in motion. Whether the water extends outward in long motionless sheets or runs murmuring across a meadow or rushes headlong downhill in crashing, boiling cascades, it is sure to please even persons insensitive to nature's beauty, as long as the hand and art behind the scene remain hidden. If, because of some incident of the terrain, the direction of the water's flow has had to be altered, the signs of this interference should not be apparent even to the most penetrating eye. The current must appear to be carried along by the natural slope."

"The Yerres is a charming and temperamental river that does not like to flow

Boaters on the Yerres, *1877*
Pastel, 52 × 86 cm.
Signed and dated lower right "G. Caillebotte 1877"
"I met Lautier during a pike-fishing outing at
Villeneuve-Saint-Georges. A mutual friend, Paul
Matout, was rowing and Lautier was handling the line at
the end of which revolved the glittering trolling spoon.
When I spoke to Renoir about Lautier, the painter said,
'Introduce us . . .' and so I did, at lunch . . ." Ambroise
Vollard, 1937

*Périssoire on the Yerres,
c. 1878
Oil on canvas, 65 × 82 cm.
Signed lower left "G.
Caillebotte" by the hand of
P. A. Renoir
In the background is the
bridge over the Yerres. On
the river's right bank are the
shower-bath establishment
built by the municipality,
the communal washhouse
near the watering place and
the ancient ford, and a
landing stage on the property
called "Le Manoir" or "Les
Charmilles." The type of
hat one finds in ten or more
of Caillebotte's paintings
and which the artist, his
friends and members of his
family wore at Yerres was
woven of an American
palm called* bonbanaxa *in
Panama. These hats had
different shapes. During the
Second Empire one of the
manufacturers of Panama
hats was the Kampmann
Firm at Strasbourg. In
1874 Edouard Manet
painted a person in
profile wearing such a
hat, canoeing in the
Argenteuil basin off Petit
Gennevilliers:* Monet at
Work in His Studio.

straight on but amuses itself in wandering. It winds and twists and sweeps along in sinuous curves and wide bends that double back on themselves, and in some places it disappears into mysterious clefts and seems to have dried up, then is discovered running on in full flood. Sometimes, exposed to the open sky, it idles along among fields or between rows of airy willows. Then it plunges suddenly under a canopy of trees with shade so dense the green waters turn black and sunlight can scarcely penetrate."

VICTOR CHERBULIEZ,[48] *La Ferme du Choquard*, 1882

YERRES (S.-&-O.) -- Les Bords de la Rivière. - La Prairie.

The River

"A river is made up of streams that flow together and mingle in the same bed. Abundance of water makes it easy for a river to overcome obstacles so that its banks are less irregular and tend to be more parallel than those of brooks. The wider the river the less winding its course."

Périssoires on the Yerres, *1878*
Oil on canvas, 157 × 113 cm.
Signed and dated on the right
"Gustave Caillebotte 78"

Boater Pulling in His Périssoire, Banks of the Yerres, *1878*
Oil on canvas, 73 × 91 cm.
Signed and dated lower right "G. Caillebotte 1878"
Beginning around this time the river, like the street that begins at the beach in the seaside town, was a meeting place where ties were formed and a special life peculiar to the Yerres was carried on. According to descendants of families who summered on properties at Epinay-sous-Sénart, Brunoy, and Yerres, whose park bordered the river, people visited each other by way of the Yerres, which served as a pretext for introductions and played the role of matchmaker. This was also true of the upstream villages of Varennes-Jarcy and Boussy-Saint Antoine, and of Crosne and Montgeron downstream.

Oarsmen on the Yerres, *1877*
Oil on canvas, 81 × 116 cm.
Signed and dated on the right "Gustave Caillebotte
1877"
The oarsman in the foreground is smoking a pipe. In
1881, Caillebotte would paint his brother Martial and
A. Casabois smoking pipes in Game of Bezique.

167

De Viart writes, "If the valley floor is not quite flat, if it does not form a level meadow, and if the slopes continue straight down on each side and meet in the middle, then the river will take its direction from the base of the hill having the steepest pitch and, by passing alternately from one side to the other, will follow the foot of those hillsides, usually where the terrain is lowest. The wider the river the greater this effect will be, as can be observed in the basins of large rivers. The artist should keep these natural principles in mind if he wishes to give his composition the rare verisimilitude that can make art as attractive as nature.

"Often an obstacle will disturb the continuity of the river's course and the water will be forced to spread out on either side to encircle an island and the banks will cease to be parallel. Then each fork will have two parallel banks, from the point where they separate and up to their junction. The island thus formed by an accretion of sand and alluvial deposits will vary in shape, especially if located in a bend or loop of the river. Usually its length will measure three or four times its width and each end will be rounded, the one exposed to the current being the more eroded.

"When we say that the two banks of a river should be parallel, we do not intend this as a principle to be applied without exception. Currents attack one bank more than the other, and a very solid shore or a boulder or even tree roots will cause irregularities without which there would be no variety but only a humdrum sameness like that which settles gloomily over the imagination of the traveler passing along a canal. Riverbanks should be ornamented with the same vegetation as those of lakes and ponds. Structures such as mills, buildings that house machinery, fishermen's huts, and so on will take their character from the setting."

The Yerres river

Boats

"We classify boats, which vary the pleasure of our tour, as garden 'structures,' since they add to the charm of settings•fortunate enough to have water.

"It is less important to adapt boats to the character of their settings than it is to key them to other structures in the garden; still their form should be beautiful. Gondolas[49] and Chinese junks charm us because their lines are light and graceful. Boats should be equipped with awnings to protect their passengers from the sun. If the setting is Italian, the vessel can take its form from the Rialto's classic gondolas . . . and for a few moments we can believe we are in Venice. If we prefer the French rowing boat, then we will need to be skillful with oars and sail in order to navigate through reefs and past islands, while our passengers are busy with net and line."

Giverny, September 14, 1891

Dear friend,

Your boat would be very useful to me at this time. I am working on a number of canvases of the Epte and am very ill at ease in my round-stemmed Norwegian rowboat. If you actually have no need of your craft, ship it to me by a boat which can drop it off at Vernon or at the canal lock at Port-Villé. The train might be more practical. Let me hear from you.

Best wishes,
Claude Monet

P.S. If your boat is stable and of a good size it will be a great help to me.

Figure number 1 as listed by P. Boitard, although of Asiatic inspiration, irresistably calls to mind Claude Monet's water-bound studio, referred to in the letter to Gustave Caillebotte when the latter was living at Petit Gennevilliers.

Oarsman in a Top Hat, *c. 1878*
Oil on canvas, 90 × 117 cm.
Signed lower left "G. Caillebotte," also stamped lower right
This painting was shown as number 8, Boating, *at the fourth painting exhibition April 10 to May 11, 1879. Can it be that this Parisian, who at the sight of a boat off the Great Meadow cannot resist taking off his coat and picking up the oars, is Edouard Manet? Compare his head with the "man in a top hat" detail of Eugène Delacroix's "July Twenty-Eighth," also known as* Liberty Leading the People *or* The Barricades, *shown in the Salon of 1831. Although the image here is reversed, Gustave Caillebotte or his model may have intended homage to Delacroix, unless this was purely an unconscious memory.*

Recreation on the River: The Diving Board
A springboard was set up for diving at the place where the riverbank was converted into a bathing site.[50] This board can be seen in one of the views taken by Cautin and Berger, photographers, for Madame Dubois and reproduced on the preceding page. A custom of the day was to offer a glass of port to bathers as they emerged from the Yerres.

Bather Preparing to Dive, Banks of
the Yerres, *c. 1878*
Oil on canvas, 117 × 89 cm.
Signed lower right
*"Do you remember the pine tree that
stretched out its woolly head over the
ravine on the bank of the Arc? That pine
whose needles protected our bodies from
the sun's heat, ah! may the gods preserve
it from the woodman's axe!"*
Paul Cézanne to Emile Zola

OPPOSITE:

*The Yerres river seen from the park,
looking upstream. From left to right,
the watering place, the ancient ford, the
public washhouse and shower baths,
the bridge. In the right foreground, the
property's diving board.*

Bathers, Banks of the
Yerres, *1877*
*Pastel, 75 × 95 cm.
Signed and dated lower
left "G. Caillebotte 77"*
*This diver must have
enjoyed a certain success
for the originality of his
bathing costume. In
1908 Le Douanier
Rousseau dressed in
similar suits four
"football-rugby" players
training in the autumnal
landscape of the Bois de
Boulogne in Paris. In
Rousseau's painting two
very dark men wear blue
and white stripes, and
two strawberry-blond
men wear red and white
stripes.*

Sketch for Bathers, Banks of the Yerres, *1878*
Pencil, (paper) 40 × 26 cm. (drawing)
28 × 21 cm.
This sheet was reproduced as Paris in Summer, at the Bathing Place *in the July 17, 1880 issue of* La Vie Moderne *and also served as an illustration for the article "Painters in the Country" in the September 1, 1921,* Bulletin de la Vie Artistique.

OPPOSITE:
Bathers, Banks of the Yerres, *1878*
Oil on canvas, 157 x 117 cm.
Signed and dated lower right: "G. Caillebotte 78."

. . . a laundress at the washhouse beating her linens steadily and vigorously.

PAUL VERLAINE, *Dédicaces IV*

The property's washhouse today

A Utilitarian Structure: The Washhouse

Some designers exclude structures from their plans, others tastelessly pile them up.
Both extremes should be avoided. Such elements should be used as a painter does,
discreetly and only where the site and its surroundings call for them. Then the effect
will be pleasant and will add interest and a pictorial accent. Before discussing
individual constructions and the valid and rigorous rules that apply to dealing with
them, we should like to quote de Viart's instructions for his ingenious method of

envisioning a structure beforehand: "Draw a picture of the building under consideration to a large scale and from its most attractive angle. Color the drawing and shade it realistically, attach it solidly to a strong piece of cardboard, then cut it out along its outer edges. At the construction site drive two conspicuous stakes into the ground at a distance from each other equal to the width of the planned edifice, then, holding the drawing to which you will have attached a third stake, stand on the spot from which you intend the building to be viewed most often and, extending the drawing toward the two stakes, move it by slow degrees away from the eye until the two extremities of its base seem to touch the foot of the two stakes. Drive the third stake, with the drawing attached, into the ground. You will be able to study and judge the effect the building will have after its construction. The drawing must be shaded in accordance with the average natural light of the construction site."

The small private washhouse, built of wood in a style matching the Swiss house (see below), sits almost opposite the public washhouse and is equipped with a "floating washboard" which consists, at each end, of a horizontal wooden winch, a chain, and a toothed rack for raising or lowering the platform according to the level of the river's water. Wooden rails served as clotheslines. The picture gives us an idea of the importance of cleanliness in Caillebotte's day and the care devoted to domestic linens, which were often embroidered.

Laundry Drying,
Petit Gennevilliers, *c. 1888*
Oil on canvas, 54 × 65 cm.

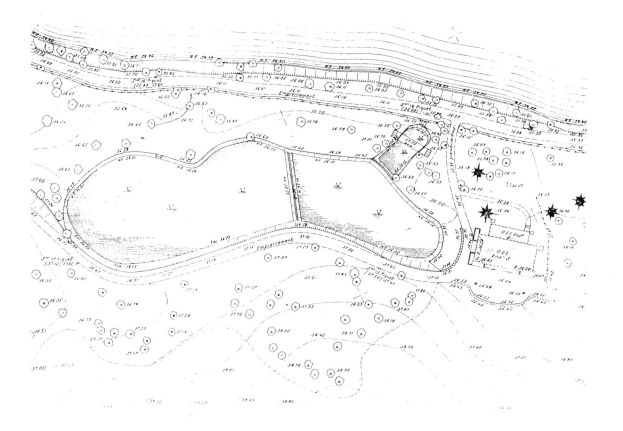

Diagram of the pond. To the north, the river (top of the drawing); on the right, the pond's tail end. The bridge is constructed of timber and worked wood. On the far right is the orangery with its west façade facing the pond.

THE POND

"We give the name 'pond' to an artificial body of water formed by a dam or embankment that stems the flow of a small brook or river and forces its waters to rise and cover a greater or lesser area. A pond's main characteristic will be irregular contours, including the pleasantest and most varied loops and bends, which must result from natural influences. Although a pond's water is still, it is influenced by wind. Whipped-up waves will beat against the shore and attempt to flow outward in all directions but be deterred by elements offering varying degrees of resistance. In some places the water will spread out over sandy flats. In others, rocks and solid high ground will present invincible obstacles. The result will produce coves cutting into the land and small, steep, banked promontories jutting into the water. The landscape gardener should imitate these phenomena if he wishes his work to be pleasing...

"Although a pond that owes its existence to man cannot, properly speaking, be a work of nature, we class it among natural waters because no excavation is needed to produce it and because a rock fall, by closing a stream's channel, can create one naturally. By imitating these rock falls, we can provide charming natural-looking pools, but the physiognomy of the site must lend itself to the change and be perfectly in harmony with it. Such a pool belongs in a wild and romantic setting. If you cannot

Landscape, Banks of the
Yerres, *c. 1875*
Oil on wood, 40×49 cm.
The property's pond

create a lifelike imitation of the natural accident that supposedly formed it, then you
should avoid aiming at its usual severe character and allow your dam to show—then
you will have an ordinary pond of a kind which adds charm to settings of all other
types." This is the case at Yerres.

"It may happen that you wish to turn a pond of sufficient size into a small lake.
Then you must disguise your dam or embankment by making its contours irregular
and varying its height and by camouflaging its width with plantings. Breadth can be
increased by gently sloping the two sides. Sluices for lowering the water level for

fishing can be hidden in a fisherman's house or similar building in another style, which may introduce a new motif. Enlarge the part of the lake where the stream enters. Ordinarily very long and narrow, this is referred to as the 'tail.' Take care to artfully plant the banks of the pond or lake if you wish to achieve the inexpressible charm these bodies of water arouse in all of us who love nature's simple and pure pleasures.

"The flexible osier will bend its long branches with glints of gold and coral over the water, the weeping willow will trail across the transparent surface, silvery poplar and dark-leafed alder will contrast against the blue sky or reflect in the clear water, large trees will shade the bank. In places the shore will join a meadow and be ornamented by it with plants remarkable for bright color and beautiful flowers. Flowering rushes whose roots extend along the muddy bottom will lift umbels of pink and lilac, sword flags and water lilies and many other pretty indigenous plants will splash the banks of your artificial body of water with their brightness without ever betraying the existence of the hand that planted them there. In some places water chestnut, reeds, rushes, and other aquatic plants will carpet the water's surface with green and give shelter to the water hen and the teal duck and their families. Variety and grace are the two notes we count on to ensure the attractiveness of the pond and its plantings."

Around 1985 Claude Monet's grandnephew Jean-Marie Toulgouat designed a pond in the water garden that the artist created around 1893 as an extension of Le Clos Normand, his flower garden at Giverny. A striking resemblance will be seen if we compare the pond at Giverny, which turns its back on the Epte and looks from east to west on a diagram that has north at the top, with the part of the pond at Yerres situated west of the dam, which turns its back on the Yerres and looks from east to west on a diagram having south at the top. The small promontory formed by the town of Yerres corresponds to the pier at Giverny.

Yellow pond lily

FAR RIGHT:
Common water lily

On the Lily Pond

... I have seen, my dear, a pond covered with water lilies with broad wide-spread leaves or small slender ones...

HONORÉ DE BALZAC, *Les Paysans*

Yerres, on the Pond,
Water Lilies, *before 1879*
Oil on cardboard
19 × 28 cm.
Stamped lower left

". . . herbaceous and essentially aquatic plants having a perennial rhizome and large, lengthily petiolated, smooth, round or oval leaves ordinarily split at the base as far as the insertion of the petiole, intact or denticulate, floating on the surface of the water; flowers often very large, always solitary, very regular, either white, yellow, red or blue, supported by a cylindrical stem equal in length to the depth of the water and blooming above the surface." Such is Decaisne and Naudin's description of water lilies in their treatise, which appeared while Gustave Caillebotte lived at Yerres. According to these authorities, water lilies are the adornment of fresh water, whether moving or still, in all climates. France possesses two species, the yellow pond lily, or *lutheum*, and the white water lily, or *nymphaea*, whose large snowy flowers are graceful works of art. Both species are found in lowland rivers and ponds. The authors add, "Antiaphrodisiac properties commonly attributed to them do not appear to be justified . . . ," also that these beautiful plants, long neglected by horticulture, have recovered their place of honor in gardens, where pools are built expressly for them either outdoors or in heated greenhouses, depending on the species. In Caillebotte's day a number of European greenhouses were famous for their luxurious tepid pools vast enough to contain all known varieties of tropical water lilies, including the most gigantic.

Gustave Caillebotte executed this painting of water lilies long before the theme became important in Impressionist painting. He seems to have led the way here.

Natural Rock Formations

We have discussed rock formations arranged by man. Some of the natural ones near the tail end of the pond on the Caillebotte property have characteristics that in general would fit them only for a wild, austere, and solitary place. Grouped in sheer powerful masses, cut so as to rear up abruptly and reveal deep precipices, their effect is both majestic and grand. Smaller stones scattered across the face of a hillside seem merely picturesque and would fit almost any setting.

Plantings add to the character of stones. Towering mature trees with dark foliage such as most conifers complement romantic crags. Too large spaces between rocks can be filled with dense planting to trick the eye into assuming more is hidden. Too many boulders in small masses can be thinned out by blasting, or can be removed, buried, or covered over by creeping plants.

The choice of trees, shrubs, and other plants is important. To appear natural, only material that thrives in dry sterile places should be used. Laburnums do well in rock clefts. Their growth will be stunted, their trunks will bend picturesquely and whole small trees may even seem to hang by their roots. Toward the end of May or early June their beautiful and highly decorative golden yellow wisteria-like flowers appear in drooping lateral clusters 20 to 30 centimeters long.

A Bridge in Timber and Worked Wood
This bridge spans the tail end of the pond.

"Wooden and other rustic bridges blend into wild, rural, or pastoral landscapes and will sometimes fit an imposing one... They are best seen at close range, in gardens that are not too large.

"A wooden bridge should have something of grace, lightness, and wit in its design. It should be ingenious not only in its details but in the whole and give the air of having won out over conventional architecture in solidity and pictorial charm. If such a bridge is in some way eccentric and daring, it will enhance a nearby simple or rustic house and will seem to be attached to it by several contact points..."

Alphonse Daudet wrote in 1873, "I read a bit, I even tried to paint. The other morning there was a beautiful red sunrise with dense fog. In the shed a pile of apples attracted me with their colors shading from the soft green of new leaves to the fiery tints of dead ones. But I could not work long. In a moment the sky turned black and rain came down in torrents. And great flocks of wild geese in full flight with their necks stretched out passed over the house, announcing by the scattering of white down from their wings, winter and snows to come..."[51]

THE ORANGERY

The orangery today.

"An orangery [is] built in such a way that the plants in it are exposed to the sun's benefits for a longer part of the day than in other kinds of greenhouses. The advantages are obvious. Its architecture should be both simple and noble. If only oranges and other material that do not become dormant in winter are to be grown the roof need not be glass . . ."

As early as 1700 Father Maumenet, on the occasion of a visit to the Yerres Valley, praised the Brunoy property of Minister of the Royal Treasury Jean-Baptiste Brunet:

I cross the courtyard where a luxurious greenhouse
Displays its treasures.
Scarcely has the breeze's amorous breath
Dispelled winter's rime
Than a thousand orange trees
Perfume the house's every cranny.
Their sweet scent spreads far
And quickens my soul.

At that time the delicately scented white orange blossom was a symbol of the Immaculate Virgin's purity and chastity, and brides wore orange blossoms as emblems of fertility.

In his canvas *The Orange Trees* Caillebotte shows a summer pastime in the country, reading, in the shade of orange trees. In 1876 in *Portraits in the Country* he painted his mother reading.

In several of Caillebotte's works, including *The Orange Trees*, he painted dogs. He also included this animal in his life, as we see in the photograph taken at the Place du Carrousel in Paris.

In *L'Anneau d'Amethyste* Anatole France wrote, "The dog is a religious animal. Wild, he adores the moon and its reflections on the water. These are his gods and he prays to them with howls in the night. Domesticated, he makes himself affectionate and agreeable to the powerful spirit who dispenses the good things in life, man."

Caillebotte also painted dogs in *Le Pont d'Europe*, 1876; *The Painter under His Parasol*, 1878; and *Roses, Garden at Petit Gennevilliers*, 1886. These highly matter-of-fact portrayals of man's best friend are very different from his humorous 1885 painting of his brother Martial's greyhound, Paul, a work strongly reminiscent of Jean-Baptiste Oudry's 1725 painting of Louis XV's two English greyhounds, Misse and Turlu, in which Oudry gave the dogs a near-human quality, in the edginess peculiar to their breed, the choice of postures, and recognition of their beauty, as if the artist intended them to be society portraits. It is possible that Caillebotte admired Oudry's work, which hung in the Louvre and which later, in 1890, was sent to Fontainebleau. Some opulent Caillebotte still lifes also hint at a debt to Oudry.

The Orange Trees, *1878*
Oil on canvas,
157 × 117 cm.
Signed and dated lower left
"G. Caillebotte 78"
The individual in the
foreground is reading near
the colonnade of the
"casin."

A Grove

"A grove is less extensive and more artfully arranged than other kinds of woods and may be placed close to the house. Groves belong in all kinds of gardens . . ."

OPPOSITE:
Yerres, Through the
Grove, the Ornamental
Farm, *before 1879*
Oil on canvas, 32×25 cm.
Stamped lower left

A Well

"We have said that artificial uses of water are appropriate in ordinary as well as fancy gardens. What distinguishes their forms from natural water sources is that in general they provide excuses for the use of sculpture and architectural ornament and are subject to the rules of art rather than nature. What understanding of hydraulics is behind the shining column of water that shoots up from its marble prison, only to fall back in rains of diamonds, behind the brilliant sheets jetting from the shell the sea nymph holds, from the sea god's urn, from the gaping mouths of dolphins so realistic we almost hear them groan!

"Individuals who have only very deep wells and do not wish the expense of hydraulic machinery can use ordinary methods of bringing up water, but the design of the well must fit its setting. The example illustrated here could be placed near an ornate house."

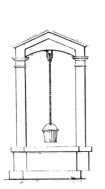

Example of a well

The traditional architecture of wells in the Brie region varies. Some Briard wells are round with peaked tile roofs, and the opening covered by a wooden shutter. Others consist of simple wooden lids to protect the water. Still others have conical, often exaggeratedly pointed, tops. The most unusual, in the form of bishops' miters, still exist in the village of Yerres, often attached to buildings, and are rarely beautiful.

"A truly magnificent house . . . the drawing was made in the Oberhasli."

"Among residential styles of architecture the wooden Swiss house, which we might also call the mountain house, should be given the place of honor. A faithful reproduction of such a dwelling perched against a slope or crowning a knoll or hill where it will most stand out is sure to stir strong emotion in travelers who have had the great good fortune to visit Switzerland, that land where nature is so impressive that she may be said to have outdone herself. The property owner who has pines, poplars, beeches, and other straight-grained forest trees will be able to build one at little expense.

"Houses in the Canton of Bern, because their structure is varied and graceful, are the best known, most popular, and most imitated, though rarely with exactitude. We

". . . the interior of such a house and its rustic furnishings. The chalet, used in Switzerland as a barn, should not be confused with the Swiss house, built for human inhabitants of all classes, rich or poor."

The Swiss house at Yerres today

include drawings of several and will describe them and attempt to explain the extraordinary simplicity of their construction.

"During Swiss winters both mountain and valley are snow covered, therefore the ground-floor walls of their houses are made of masonry, and the building, though wooden, rests on stone. Farm animals are kept in the interior of this ground floor. Ordinarily the back part of it, which is fitted with open-work timbers, serves as hayloft... The rest of the structure, with the exception of door and window hardware, is entirely of wood, and the construction is mortise-and-tenon fastened with wooden pegs...

"The roof consists of small planks, 16 by 60 centimeters, overlapped so that five or six thicknesses at a time ensure protection from cold, the whole secured by battens pegged through to the rafters, then by stones placed on top of the battens so that the entire construction is anchored against wind... This method of roofing, very economical for anyone who has access to inexpensive wood, can be prohibitive for others. Property owners who can afford tiles substitute them or use wide, very heavy slates. A roof of planks or slates is easy to construct; however, we prefer curved tiles if the structure will support their weight, since the roof projects quite a lot.

"The special character of the Bernese house comes from the ornamental wooden balcony that runs around its four sides, often decked with pots of flowers. These balconies protect the lower part of the house in the same way that the overhanging roof protects the upper part. Tools are kept there and linen hung to dry, and the inhabitants are able to step outside to enjoy the air without wetting their feet with snow or mud. The designs of these balconies varies...

Milking, *before 1879*
Two pencil drawings on one sheet of paper, 31 × 80 cm. (drawing on left 9 × 8 cm., drawing on right 8 × 9 cm.)

G. Caillebotte.

Garden at Yerres, *c. 1876*
Oil on canvas, 59 × 81 cm.
The Swiss house near the "casin" or main house. In the
foreground circular flower beds mark the edges of the
lawn. A pine or possibly spruce tree between the two
buildings denoted the transition between the different
motifs, one evoking Switzerland, the other Italy.

"Plans can be modified and the house made smaller by building it only one room deep. For the best effect it is essential that the proportion be longer than wide . . . All these buildings, constructed of pine, last for centuries, even in Switzerland's humid valleys. Neither the interior nor the exterior is painted. Ornamental motifs and biblical quotations are carved into the wood of the façade . . .

"Since the publication of the above illustrations and remarks, fashion has adopted Swiss houses, which it refers to as 'chalets,' and they have come to be used as ornaments in large and small gardens and for low-cost housing, and are even brought prefabricated into towns where the price of land continually increases. Time will show whether they fill their purpose. They have been the object of some minor criticism. It is said that their wooden walls are too thin to afford adequate protection from extreme heat or, in winter, to shield against cold, and it is true that Bern, their native canton, is not in the heart of Switzerland's snows and glaciers. The Bernese people are not only inured to cold but know how to dispel it with wonderful thick stone stoves. Where we live, central heating replaces Bern's pine trees. We have

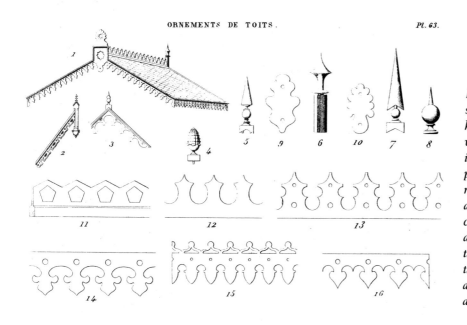

ORNEMENTS DE TOITS.   PL. 63.

Examples of lambrequin motifs for the eaves of a Swiss–style house. Compare these with those on the Swiss house at Yerres. Figure 1 represents an entire roof with various ornaments. The designs in Figures 2 and 3 are intended for gables. Figures 4–8 are finials to accent the peaks, as in Figure 1. Compare Figures 4 and 8 with the roof ornament of the property's aviary. Figures 9 and 10 are escutcheons to mask the ends of the framework, as can also be seen in Figure 1. Figures 11, 12, and 13 are designs to be made of wood or zinc and placed on top of the ridge, as in Figure 1. Some beautiful examples of these last are cast in iron. The motifs in Figures 14, 15, and 16 are made of wood or zinc and used at lower levels as shown in Figure 1.

personally visited several of these houses during hot weather and found nothing to complain of . . .[52]

"Whatever the case, 'chalets' are a happy addition to our collection of different picturesque buildings. French architects have already learned new tricks to decorate them . . ."

At Yerres the Swiss house served as a dairy and was located at the far end of the group of farm buildings used as stables.

"The dairy is a delightful accessory with its charming white stone brackets, . . . its wide round table, and great white porcelain milk pans."

THE "CASIN"—AN ITALIANATE HOUSE

The colonnade of the "casin," today

Yerres, Part of the South
Façade of the "Casin",
before 1879
Oil on canvas, 81 × 65 cm.
Stamped lower left

"In Latin as in Italian the word 'villa' signifies a 'house in the country.' In Italy it is common to use the word for a very large and luxurious country house not far from a city, equipped with attractive pleasure gardens decorated with all the amenities art can offer—in short, what in France would be called a 'château.' It is an error to

Examples of "casins," or Italianate houses. On this page we see four different versions of this sort of country house, examples of which were built in the Yerres Valley in the mid-19th century. One can be seen at the intersection of the Avenue de la Grange du Milieu and the Rue de Villecresnes (today the Rue René Coty). Another survives at Brunoy at the junction of the Brunoy Road and the Pyramid Road, a designation describing a perspective from La Folie, Brunoy's great château, once the property of Louis Stanislas Xavier, Count of Provence, the future Louis XVIII. Today these roads, situated where the La Garenne and Beausserons neighborhoods meet, are called the Avenue General Leclerc and the Rue Talma.

designate, as is often done in France and England, the least pokey little house as a 'villa.'[53]

"In Italy a 'casin' is commonly a small country house. However the word includes extremely large and splendid examples, which in France would readily be given the name 'château.'"

Picturesque Houses in Different Styles

The decorative elements we will describe here are those of the "casin" at Yerres in Caillebotte's time.

"Instead of following the usual unvarying regular design of country houses, today's architects diversify them by designing two or three small groups of related buildings... In order for us to enjoy the effect of these attractive dwellings, we

Portraits in the Country, *1876*
Oil on canvas, 95 × 111 cm.
Signed and dated lower left "G. Caillebotte 1876"
We are looking from the west side of the "casin" toward
the park. The gardener's house is to the south. Note the
tubbed orange trees, the pattern of the awning, and the
garden furniture.

Yerres, the south side of the "casin" today

should isolate them completely from each other and expose them on all sides so that they will be clearly visible in their surroundings..."

The baluster reproduced here is of a type commonly used in palatial houses of stone and marble, for example on balconies. An old photograph shows balusters of this type on the Caillebotte property's "casin," and they can be seen there today.

"The idea of using lambrequin motifs to ornament the eaves of roofs comes from both India and Switzerland. They are commonly seen in country houses and garden pavilions today. The illustrations here show such motifs designed to be made of zinc or wood and painted in imitation of the canvas edgings of canopies, awnings, and tents." These kinds of ornament decorated the different sides of the "casin" at Yerres, as an old photograph testifies. Caillebotte's *Portraits in the Country*, painted in 1876, shows a red-and-white striped canvas awning. At Yerres the painted zinc was given the same color as the twill window shades, so that they matched.

The tradition of using striped canvas, kept up since the days of the ancien régime, was mentioned around 1779 by Carmontelle apropos of Turkish tents placed in the picturesque garden of Monceau. "These tents are striped, the first one red and white, the second blue and white. The stripes are damasked and the ornaments gilt."

Example of a baluster

Examples of lambrequin-inspired ornaments for the edges of roofs.

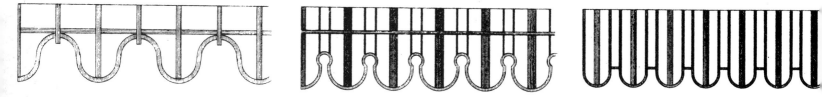

Portrait of Zoë Caillebotte, *1877*
Oil on canvas 81 × 100 cm.
Signed and dated lower left "G.
Caillebotte 77"

Edgar Degas
Billiards Room at Ménil-Hubert, *1892*
Oil on canvas, 65 × 81 cm.
Official atelier sale stamp lower right

Billiards, *c. 1875*
Oil on canvas, 60×81 cm.
When we look at this work, painted in the ground-floor
drawing room overlooking the "casin's" colonnade and
park, we are reminded of something Edgar Degas wrote
while vacationing with friends Paul Valpin and his wife
in the Orne, where Degas was inspired to paint The
Billiards Room at Ménil-Hubert. *On August 27,*
1892, Degas wrote sculptor Paul Albert Bartholomé
(Degas letter 1945 n. CLXX II pp. 193–194), "I felt
like painting and so I addressed myself to the interior of
the billiards room. I believed that I knew a little about
perspective. I knew nothing and thought I could replace
it by applying perpendicular and horizontal principles,
could measure the angles in the space by means of good
will, and I worked desperately hard."

THE LAWN

"A lawn differs from a meadow in that its grass, though equally thick, never grows high enough to be harvested and serves as grazing for domestic animals. Usually it is located in a high, dry place where a meadow would not thrive, but it serves the same purpose of pleasing the eye. A few touches such as isolated trees or thickets add to its charm. Needless to say, a lawn should be planted with the same grasses we have recommended for dry or sandy places.

"Lawns are charming visual elements widely used in modern gardens, whether irregularly landscaped or formally composed. They lighten every graceful design. As a general rule, a lawn is planted in front of the house, opening up space so that the vista is extended and the spectator can take in at a glance not only the whole composition

Yerres, on the Grass (*also known as* Woman Seated on the Grass), *before 1879* (fragment)
Oil on canvas, 42 × 31 cm.
Stamped lower right

202

Yerres, the Lawn in the Park, Seen from a Path,
before 1879
Oil on canvas, 24 × 36 cm.
Stamped lower left

but its most salient elements. Examples are given in every plan included in this book. A lawn can be ornamented with flower beds, groups of shrubs, specimen trees, even with groves and bocages, however these small scenic views must be arranged with the greatest art to fit into the overall picture and not destroy its harmony.

"Maintaining a lawn requires care. It must be mowed often, kept free of weeds and watered whenever the soil appears to be dry. Moss, if allowed to spread, can be fatal, for this cryptogamic plant destroys grass quickly. The best means of dealing with moss is to rake it several times with a fine-toothed iron rake until it is completely eradicated, then spread the ground with limestone, plaster dust, or ashes of hard coal, all very good fertilizers that will not only protect the grass but actually kill moss that has not had a chance to become too established. A lawn needs to be mowed at least four times a year, always before the plants go to seed, and bare spots must be reseeded. This last demands close attention. First, the reason for the grass's failure must be discovered. If shade from a nearby tree or other object is the offender, the remedy will be a simple matter of reseeding, preferably with wood poa, which has proved to be more resistant to shade than other grasses. Sometimes bare spots appear in a lawn because the soil is poor, and if this is the case, it should be improved with a suitable fertilizer. If the soil is sterile due to ferruginous or peat content or for other reasons, the entire surface should be dug up to a generous spade's depth and replaced.

Portrait of Jean Daurelle, *1887.*
Oil on canvas, 75 × 50 cm.
Signed and dated lower left "G. Caillebotte 1887"
Jean-Baptiste Mathieu Daurelle (June 2, 1829–April 2, 1893) was the father of Pierre Camille Daurelle (January 12, 1868–January 7, 1930)

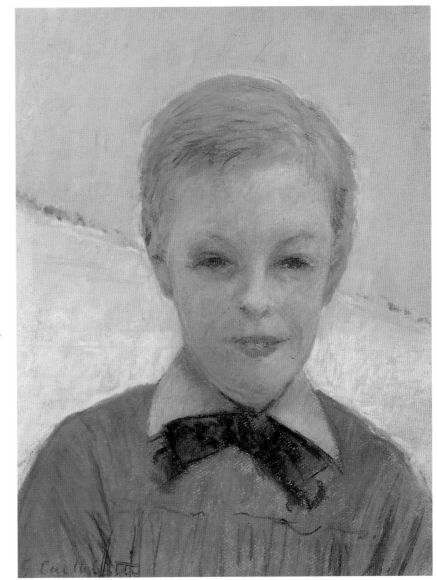

Portrait of Camille Daurelle, *1877*
Pastel, 40 × 32 cm.
Signed lower left "G. Caillebotte"
*In writing about the Salon of 1880, where this pastel
portrait of Pierre Camille Daurelle was on display,
Joris-Karl Huysmans commented ". . . and passing before
a small panel, a child in a garden, where the sin
of the terrible blue had again been committed . . ."*
Huysmans in L'Art Moderne *in 1883 said of the work
Caillebotte exhibited in 1880, "Here as in his other
works the treatment is simple and unfussy. It is the
modern formula as glimpsed by Manet and applied and
brought to fruition by a painter whose craft is more sure
and whose control is stronger. In a word, Monsieur
Caillebotte has rejected the recipe for impressionistic
daubs, which force the viewer to screw up his eyes to
make people and things fall into place and has limited
himself to the orthodox method of the Masters, altering
their execution and bending it to the demands of
modernism, in a sense rejuvenating it and making it
his own."*

"To lighten the unvarying green color of a lawn, intermingle oddly shaped or brightly colored flowers of crocus, saffron crocus, colchicum, wild orchid, and so on. For some time strawberry-leaf clover, white and crimson clover, and sweet clover have been recommended as additions.

"The best grasses for establishing a lawn are perennial rye, referred to in France as 'English meadow grass,' sheep fescue or blue fescue and, in general, all varieties of the latter species, which produces a dense, fine brilliant green turf. The main thing is to use each plant where the terrain suits it, and this is more important in lawns than in meadows because in a meadow if a plant fails another takes its place. In a lawn, which is composed of a single kind of plant and whose uniform color comprises its principal value, every individual plant must attain its best possible growth. Use rye grass in heavy dampish soil. In dry sandy places plant sheep fescue or blue fescue.

"Before seeding, the soil should be thoroughly prepared. Plough well, remove all stones, roots, and other debris, then level the surface and, if necessary, fertilize with well-rotted compost, which need not be worked in. Sowing should be done during rainy overcast weather and the seed broadcast at the rate of 50 kilos to the half hectare for rye grass or 25 kilos for fescues. The seed is raked in, harrowed and rolled with a garden roller. This last operation should be repeated as often as possible to make the plants throw out new shoots and produce a thick uniform turf. It will sometimes happen that a hill, embankment, or sloped border will need to be planted in grass. Here sodding will be useful. Squares of turf 6 centimeters thick are taken from a meadow or roadside, carried to the site and arranged paving stone fashion to fit perfectly, leaving no chinks. The sods may be anchored by wooden pegs driven in with a hammer. Level the surface with a roller or mallet and, if there is no rain, water well. If a steep slope needs grass cover and no sod is available, another procedure can be used. In a large vessel such as a barrel mix together a small amount of clay, some leaf mold and compost with enough water to give the whole the consistency of mortar. Add the correct proportion of grass seed and mix again. When the preparation is ready, the surfaces of the slope to be seeded should be pounded to make them solid but not to compact them. Water lightly, only enough to bind the surface thoroughly to the mortar and seed mixture, which is then applied with a mason's trowel or a wooden shovel to a depth of 3 to 6 centimeters. In the beginning protect all this from hard rain, which could wash it away. Soon grass will appear. When the roots have penetrated to a depth greater than the thickness of the layer the turf will be solid and require no other care than occasional watering.

"We have seen an unusual twelve-day method of producing turf in circumstances where there was no time to lose and sod was unavailable. In several centimeters of leaf mold, barley was sown and the sowing repeated six days later. Within twelve days, with careful watering, a fresh green lawn was ready for a horticultural exhibition."

OPPOSITE:
Camille Daurelle in the Park at Yerres, 1877
Pastel, 56 × 44 cm.
Signed and dated upper left "G. Caillebotte 77"
Behind the child, between him and the colonnade of the
"casin," we see an example of a sodded lawn. This
"child with flowers"—to use the title of a portrait
Edouard Manet did of Jacques Hoschedé—is Pierre
Camille Daurelle, who in 1877 was nine years old.

A "Corbeille"

"The French word *corbeille*, meaning 'basket,' usually denotes a circular flower bed, although sometimes it may take the shape of a polygon, star, and so on. A corbeille always enjoys a prominent position and contains only the most beautiful and special plants closely set in rows so that their flowers or foliage touch, giving the bed the appearance of a single bouquet. It is customary to plant a rare shrub or dazzling flowers in the center. When creating such a bed, the soil is raised 10 to 12 centimeters on the edges and as much as 30 centimeters in the center and is supported all around by an edging of box or some other bright green foliage plant amenable to clipping."

Portrait of Madame Charles
Caillebotte, *1878*
Oil on canvas, 92 × 74 cm.
Signed and dated lower right "G. Caillebotte 1878"
Outside the window near the edge of the lawn is a circular flower bed of the type known as a "corbeille."

The Park of the
Caillebotte Estate at
Yerres, *1875*
detail showing a "corbeille"

A Flower Massif

"The flower bed known [in French] as a 'massif' is also domed in the center and bordered by edging plants but does not have a well-defined central point and the form is not necessarily round; indeed it may take any imaginable shape. Such beds are found scattered here and there, taste being the chief factor in deciding on location. The plants that make them up are subject to an unvarying rule, which is that they produce handsome foliage and attractive flowers in succession throughout the season. Great care is taken to choose among continuously flowering kinds and in placing them artfully so that an individual plant going out of bloom is always next to one coming on. Space is also left for autumn flowering kinds, which are sown and cultivated in frames until needed, then brought in and set in place, sometimes sinking pot and all to its rim.

"An important point in creating these charming beds is that the lowest-growing plants are placed in the outermost rows, medium-size ones in the succeeding rows, and the tallest in the center. Then, instead of concealing and detracting from its neighbors, each variety sets off all the others."

The Exhedra before 1989.
In this wintry photograph
we see on the left the Swiss
house (the dairy), then the
entrance, decorated with
vases, of the ornamental
farm, and the Exhedra with
its statues and the site of its
former fountain. Compare
this with Frey's lithograph.
Behind the exhedra is the
aviary with its
compartments and the
buildings of the ornamental
farm.

THE EXHEDRA
"In Greek and Roman architecture an exhedra was a meeting place with benches
where people came together and conversed. The two semicircular benches at the gate
of Pompeii, which have been copied in a wooded part of the Tuileries Gardens in
Paris, are exhedras.

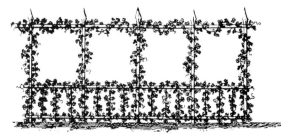

Example of ivy festoons

" We give the name exhedra to the decorative structure reproduced here. The second figure from the top shows an elevation and the next figure a plan: *a* indicates 30-to-40-centimeter-square columns made of stone or any other material, which support vases filled with flowering plants, usually geraniums and petunias. If the material of which these columns are made is of a kind to be seen, vines are used to veil them lightly. If the material is liable to deteriorate with too great exposure to weather, they are covered entirely. In the latter case, ivy is a good choice. *b* indicates vases set in front of the four columns, which form two pavilions at the exhedra's entrance (A). *c* and *d* represent other vases placed in relation to the columns, which form the outer semicircle. Row *d* of vases is higher than row *c*, and two steps *e* and *f* lead up to the terrace *g* where the benches *h* are located. In the same way, two steps also lead up to the two pavilions (A). Each column is linked to the next by festoons of vines. While waiting for ivy or other woody climbers to attain a desired size, fast-growing annual or perennial vines will give a quick effect.

"Such a plan can be modified in a number of ways. The semicircular arbor could be substituted, although the effect will not be so rich. We include it because of the sumptuous effect it would have if constructed in marble. It could have been included in the section dealing with the use of plants."

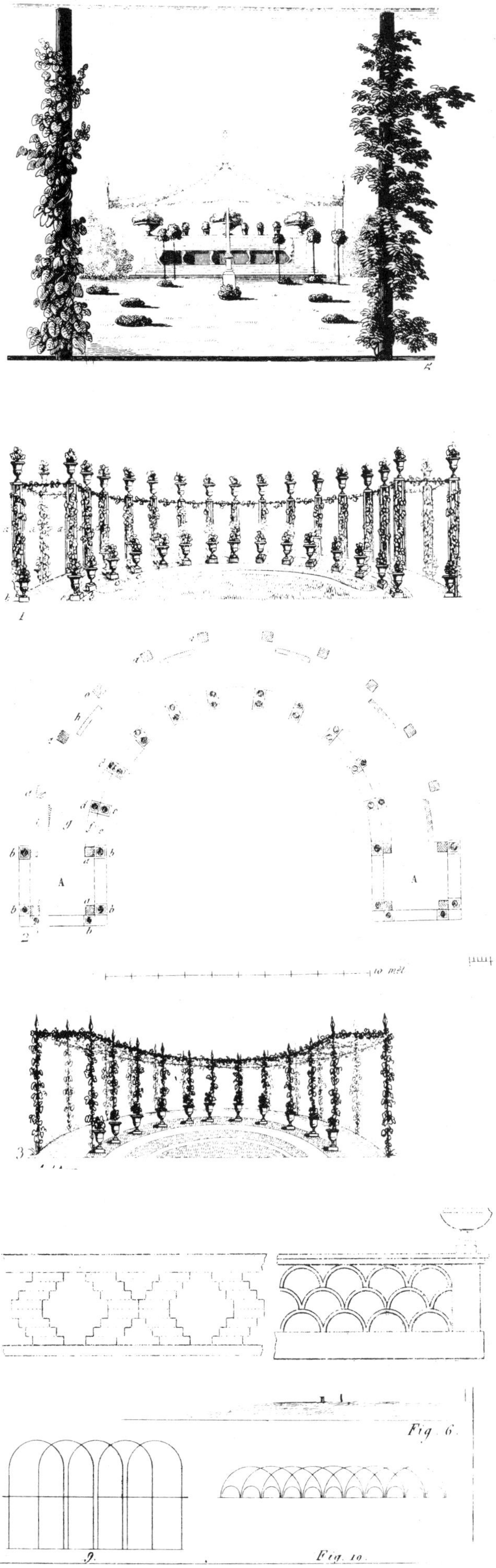

Figure at top: example of an exhedra.
Second, third, and fourth figures: plan and elevation of an exhedra; semicircular pergola.
Last two figures: details of the exhedra's balustrades.

211

Statues

"Statues are the luxuries of the rich and belong among the formal parterres of opulent palaces and châteaux. Independent of the value of the material they are made of, they are prized for the beauty of their workmanship. If it is not possible to own masterpieces, at least good copies should be found, as crude or pretentious work has no place in any garden, no matter what its style. Circumstances will arise where the use of sculpture can be justified as accessories to certain scenes..."

The statue of Aphrodite in the left-hand niche in the center of the "casin's" north side, facing the exhedra, may have played a role in young Gustave Caillebotte's unconscious when he painted his Medici Venus.

Details of statues in the exhedra. On the right is Pomona covered with ivy. These statues were stolen in 1989.

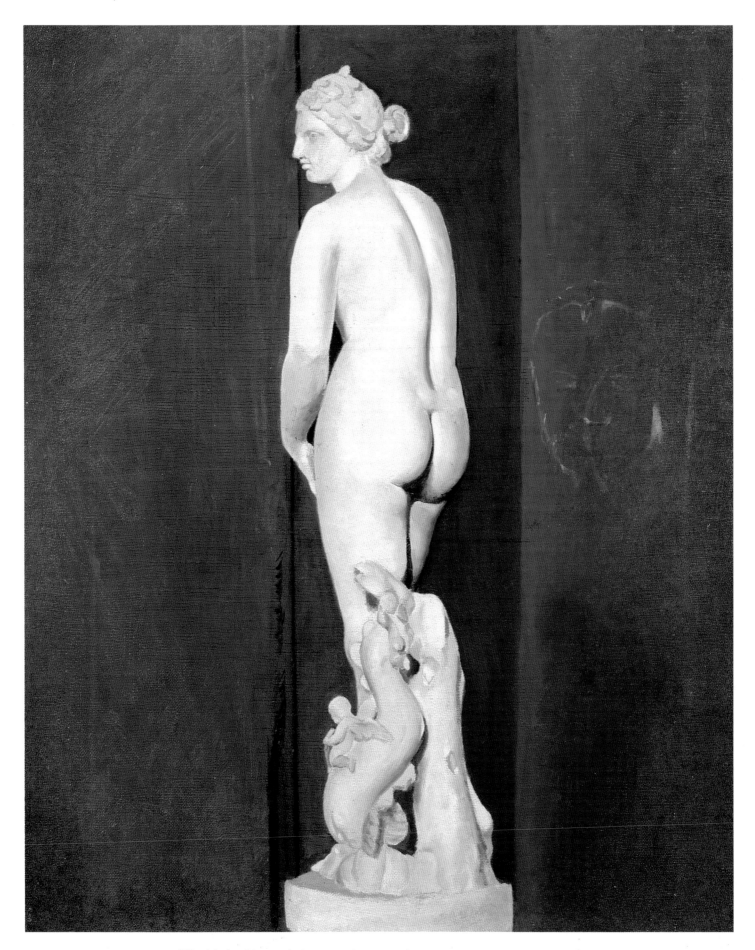

The Medici Venus, *before 1879*
Oil on canvas, 55×45 cm.
Stamped lower left

Yerres, north side of the "casin." The shutterless window on the ground floor, far right, is that of the small sitting room where Gustave Caillebotte worked. On the right of the steps is one of the Medici vases. In the foreground are paving stones.

Statues in the niches of the "casin's" north side

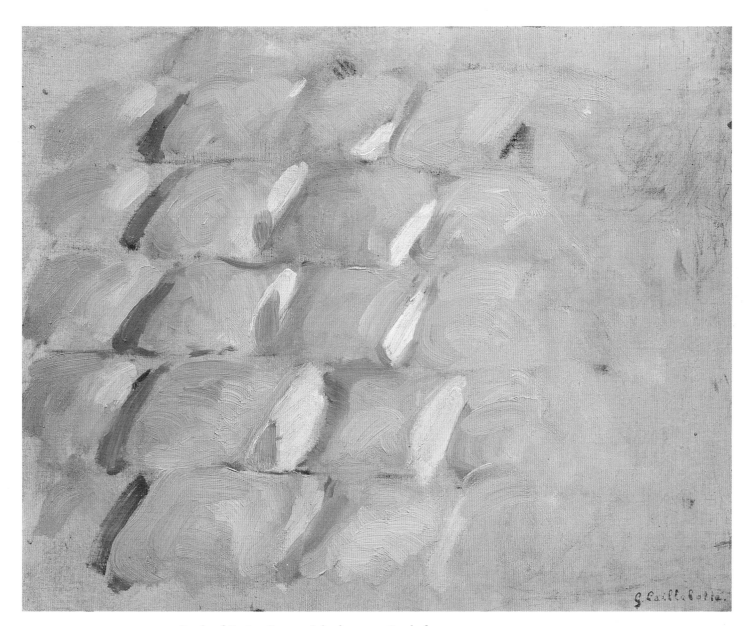

Study of Paving Stones, *(also known as* Study for
"Paris Street: Rainy Weather") *c. 1877*
Oil on canvas, 32 × 40 cm.
Stamped lower right
While making this study, Caillebotte may have been
reminded of the very handsome paving in front of the
"casin's" north entrance, opposite the exhedra and the
ornamental farm. This canvas was intended as a study
for Paris Street: Rainy Weather, *1877.*

A Fountain

"Fountains contribute to the beauty and richness of large compositions, but the accompanying house must be equally rich and beautiful. Nothing could be worse than a fountain complete with pool and sculptures next to a rustic house . . . Purely architectural forms, even if they are nothing more than simple basins, belong with formal buildings and in formal gardens . . ."

An elegant fountain like the one represented in Frey's lithograph once graced the exhedra's semicircle at Yerres, in absolute harmony with the Italianate architecture of the house; it has since disappeared. It was decorated with a copy of a third century B.C. Hellenistic sculpture, *Boy with Goose*, said to represent a son of Asclepios—Greek god of medicine, son of Apollo and the nymph Coronis—taming a goose, which symbolized malaria. The cult of Asclepios was centered at Epidaurus in the Greek region of Argolis. Under the Romans, Asclepios became Aesculapius.

This Roman copy of the Boy with Goose *from the Louvre provided the focal point of the fountain in the exhedra at Yerres.*

216

Vases

"Vases serve the same purpose as statues but are much easier to fit into a composition. As long as the style of a house is of a definite kind and the overall design is formal, they will look right. Their value depends on the beauty of their shapes and of the bas-reliefs that decorate them and the richness of their material. Vases may be placed in rows or in pairs or may stand alone on porticoes, pedestals, walls, terraces, and so on. A very elegant vase worthy of the name Medici placed next to a rustic cottage would be absurd. Some antique forms however would be in harmony with the rustic cottage . . ."

Medici vases decorated the "casin's" colonnade.

This vase, whose design shows a procession approaching an altar, is in the archaic style. Signed by Sosibios of Athens, it is in the Louvre. It is one of the sources of inspiration for the vases in the exhedra.

Horses in the Stable,
c. 1874
Oil on canvas, 33 × 46 cm.

OPPOSITE:
**Yerres, Dark Bay Horse in
the Stable,** *before 1879*
Oil on canvas, 39 × 33 cm.
Stamped lower right

THE FARM: OUTBUILDINGS[54]

"Often a country house has a farmyard as well as a place for stables and coachhouses. All the buildings adjoin each other and are arranged as if in town. They are anything but picturesque, but we propose to change all this. We shall suppose that the owner's house is in a separate place, situated as advantageously as possible, and we suggest constructing the utilitarian buildings at some distance from that. We will place the stable near the coachhouse. Farther on we will build the cowshed, the dairy, the dovecote, a small barn, the henhouse, and aviaries in which peacocks, Barbary ducks, and other exotic and ornamental birds will be housed, with their own enclosure so that they and the domestic animals cannot escape into the gardens."

François Coppée lived in this region from 1891 to 1897. His residence, La Fraizière, was situated at Mandres-les-Roses. Knowledgeable critics considered Coppée, who was influenced by Parnassian aestheticism, one of the greatest French poets. His play *Le Passant* brought him to the attention of the general public; he was Librarian for the French Senate and Archivist of the Comédie Française. Earlier he had lived at Combs-la-Ville; during the summer of 1902 he stayed at Montgeron, not far from the Great Meadow, at the watermill called Senlis after Archbishop of Paris Etienne de Senlis. Etienne de Senlis established the rule of the Benedictine Abbey of Notre Dame d'Yerres and appointed Hildegarde de Senlis, a member of his family, as its first Abbess. The Archbishops's family, and Hildegarde's, was that of Guy de Senlis, sovereign of Chantilly.

On September 19, 1897, Coppée wrote, " . . . I decided that as a reward for having worked hard I would treat myself to that small park that resembles a corner of the Trianon. In its big trees in May and June winged orchestras performed delightful concerts for me. I liked to stroll down its narrow paths at nightfall in a perfume of mignonette, in that vast garden where in a golden autumn the weight of fruit made the branches crack and the grape turned to gold on the walls, among the powdery rust-colored leaves, and where rows of long-stemmed roses reminded me of a contest among beauty queens . . . I loved all of that, all of it had entered my dreams and I gave it much of my heart. Now I must leave . . . and someone else will be its owner. I hope he will love it, I hope he will have the same illusion that I do, that the flowers that scent the poet's walk give off a more exquisite fragrance than any others and that the birds that sing for him sing more melodiously than other birds. I sincerely hope the new master of La Fraizière will be happy. I pray the shade of his trees will refresh him even more than it refreshed me, that his grass will be greener, his fruit more delicious, his flower beds sweeter smelling and more dazzling. I hope, above all, that he becomes truly attached to the old house. But I do not promise to visit him there.

Yerres, Reddish Bay Horse in the Stable, *before 1879*
Oil on canvas, 31 × 43 cm.
Stamped lower left

"I admit it. I would be angry if in my presence the new master were to enjoy my old choir of finches and thrushes. If I saw him inhale the perfume of my harem of roses, my 'Madame Bérard,' my 'Gloire de Dijon,' I would be jealous. I would suffer all over again at nature's indifference, to be made to admit that birds, like court poets, sing for everyone and that roses smell sweet to all the world.

"Still I wish my unknown successor all possible joy. I hope the merry young faun peeping out through the leaves at the top of his plaster column will welcome him with a smile, and since the rains of this miserable summer must surely have corroded the marble of the small sundial in the middle of the kitchen garden and almost entirely erased its too gloomy and philosophical inscription, *Ultima Latet* (The last hour is hidden from us), I advise the new owner to substitute the following expression of my best wishes for him: *Horas non numero nisi serenas* (I count only the finest hours). May only happiness reign at La Fraizière!

"I shall never again pass the gate over which an elderberry loses its flowers like showers of white rockets. From now on that closed gate will be for me the hostile impassive face of a woman loved not so long ago whom one meets on the arm of another. Seeing it again I would not be able to avoid muttering the oh so heartbreaking verse from *Tristesse d'Olympio*, 'My house looks at me without a sign of recognition.'

"Still, I will never become a complete stranger to the old place. Something of us, more and better than a memory, remains behind where we have made a pleasant halt and have come to love our surroundings.

"The first time I spent the month of May at La Fraizière I felt a great joy to know that my garden was full of nightingales and that they sang divinely. Some of the old people told me that before 1830, when there had been only a small cottage and a clump of trees, the place belonged to a fine violinist, the former first violinist at the Paris Opera. I don't know why I began to associate the virtuoso with the singing birds. I invented a picture of the old fellow dressed in the style of his time, trousers with flaps and shoes with buckles, choking in a triple-knotted tie and high collar à la Goethe, at a window open on all that greenery, bow in hand, Stradivarius at his shoulder, before a musical score, distracting himself from the boredom of retirement by playing his old concert successes, executing admirably, masterfully, an especially difficult bit, a tour de force, say the famous variations on a theme from 'Carnival de Venise.' An insane idea came to me that the nightingales, stung to jealousy, wishing to show the old musician they were as good as he, that their voices equalled the violin's, that they could reproduce with their throats the marvels that the illustrious Paganini accomplished on the fourth string, launched rockets of sound more and more boldly and more and more agilely, holding pauses longer, redoubling modulations, prolonging tender notes in a fury of musical competition. Of course, I knew the old master violinist was dead. I knew that generations of birds had come and gone. All the same, I wanted to believe that in my lime trees the tradition went on and that barely hatched fledglings were getting their fine musical education. And so I justified my owner's claim that in my garden nightingales sang better than anywhere else. I'm sure the old violinist is still discussed in the nests at La Fraizière.

"As for me I marked my stay there by propagating the very beautiful rose, of a velvety, dusky red, delicately perfumed, which a gardening neighbor had been kind enough to name after me. Something of me stays behind in those flowers. In those branches rustling with birds' wings something lingers, too, of the old virtuoso who spurred the birds to competition, and in the lovely spring morning the splendor of the poet's rose will continue to be celebrated in wild song by those amazing nightingales, great-grandsons of the old musician's rivals."

Landscape with Haystacks, *c. 1877*
Pastel, 44 × 61 cm.
Signed and dated lower left "G. Caillebotte 77"
At harvest time this road on the Briard plateau, perhaps near Brie-Comte-Robert, was used by hay wagons, two-wheeled carts with high-pronged racks, which allowed for maximum loads. In loading, the driver used a three-tined pitchfork to pass hay up to a helper who piled it in as orderly a way as he could so as not to "go to Versailles" (a punning idiom based on the name Versailles, then prefecture of the Seine et Oise, and the verb "verser," meaning to tip over) on the way home. A load rose as high as three or four layers of hay above the tilted prongs. Albert-André Dunoyer de Segonzac wrote, "From childhood I lived in Boussy-Saint-Antoine, a true village of the Ile de France, on the edge of the Brie plain, crossed by the winding Yerres river, near the Sénart forest . . . I have always remained faithful to this beautiful region." Around 1913 Segonzac executed a drawing with pen and India ink of "La Plaine de Brie," which is very similar to the work of Caillebotte.

Birds and Aviaries

"Birds are the natural and indispensable accessories to all kinds of settings. By their pleasant habits and lively natures, their melodious and varied songs, these agreeable guests charm our ears and sometimes, when their symphony is discordant, stir up our surroundings. The spectator admiring a vista will appreciate the distraction of a swallow's oblique swift flight and perhaps think of the story of Philomela. He will find pleasure in following until it vanishes the perpendicular path of a softly twittering lark.

"In a park every species of bird has its place. Berry-bearing shrubs will attract flocks of small birds, and we should not scorn the childish pastime of scattering hemp seeds or bread crumbs, which can convert a thicket into a natural aviary, a republic whose inhabitants will be all the more charming as they will be unconfined.

"Of course the site must be at a distance from fruit trees, which our free and easy protegés would pillage without any regard for us. To make sure that birds settle down inside our walls, we must forbid shooting. If we need to rid ourselves of a bird of prey or some other culprit, we must resort to guile and not gunpowder.

"Soon a winged population will live with us, a charming wonder of creation, which will rejoice our souls, just as a sparkling flower rejoices our eyes: a crow with its clarion call, a flock of house sparrows saluting the dawn with their odd chirping, the goldfinch, the robin, the whitethroat, the titmouse with its pleasing unbroken song, the cooing turtledove, the plaintive cuckoo announcing in the distance the return of summer and, in the evening, a pure bold song with artfully held notes in crescendoes, which produce an indescribable impression on the senses—what a powerful gift for song exists inside the nightingale's small frame! Hearing it we think of Procne!

"Not content with enjoying this seductive harmony of bird language you may wish to increase your enjoyment by locking up these little beings inside a golden prison to tame them and keep them near you.[55] Locate your aviary not too far from the house and shade it pleasantly with trees. Since the appearance of an aviary is welcome

Examples of aviaries.
The one at Yerres has seven
compartments. North of
it were rabbit hutches.

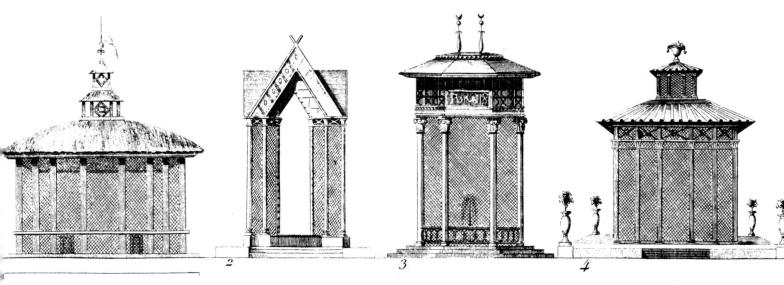

226

everywhere, it will not be necessary to disguise it. All that will be needed is to construct it in a manner that best suits the habits of the small winged chorus it is destined to confine. The form should be as elegant as possible; aviaries are in keeping with gay airy places. If you decide to conceal yours among shrubbery, the ear will be

Yerres, the Aviary in the Ornamental Farm, *before 1879*
Oil on canvas, 16 × 26 cm. Stamped lower right
On the left are the stables. Through the trees, behind the aviary, we glimpse the roof of the "casin." Zinc ornaments in the form of lambrequins or valances decorated the terrace, which faced the Rue de Conçy on the north side of the house.

struck by the pleasant song while the eye will not detect the prison and this will add a special sweetness to your woodland.

"An aviary should be divided into compartments to keep separate species of birds that cannot live together. A central access through which all the compartments can be reached will make it easy to care for the entire collection.

"The most natural kind of aviary seems to us to be one made of openwork and set among trees so that these pretty small inhabitants of the air can be seen while their jail is concealed or at least disguised among foliage. Small camouflaged sheds or similar structures can serve as shelters in bad weather."

AT THE ORNAMENTAL FARM

"We will not forget the farmer's house and even a rustic pavilion with a dining room for the owners' use when they wish to enjoy a country lunch at the farm. All the buildings will be of simple light construction, painted in different colors to make them contrast with each other attractively and naturally, and will be scattered as if haphazardly around an irregular grass plot of about half an arpent, over which trees will cast beneficial shade."

At Yerres the buildings of the ornamental farm were painted to imitate pink brick, as can still be seen on the gable of one of the buildings visible from the Rue de Concy, to the right of the ornamental farm's street entrance. The farm was situated immediately behind the Exhedra (the stables). The pink paint is also seen in

Garlic Cloves and Knife
on the Corner of a Table,
before 1879
Oil on canvas, 26 × 35 cm.
Stamped lower right

Caillebotte's *Yerres, Through the Grove, the Ornamental Farm* and in *Yerres, the Aviary in the Ornamental Farm.*

Benches

"Benches are of small importance compared to other garden structures; nevertheless the artist should give them his attention and see that they are in keeping with their settings. Form and material should be considered carefully: marble for a palace, stone

Examples of rustic furniture. The best wood for making this kind of garden seat with or without the bark left on is chestnut and the second best is maple. Knotty or twisted sections of grapevine root are good for ornaments. Oak and pine are used for pieces which will be carved. The Allée de l'Etoile at the Château de Grosbois was planted with four parallel rows of chestnuts, a tree native to Yerres.

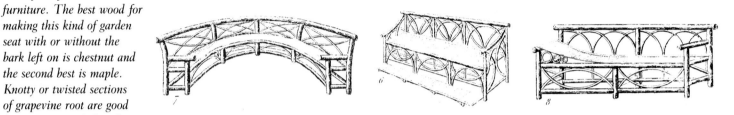

or dressed wood for the modern formal garden, rustic furniture made of unpeeled wood for a landscape garden. Location is of supreme importance; a place to sit represents a means of directing the spectator's attention and drawing it effortlessly toward detail. Wood is better than marble or stone as the latter are very cold and may be dangerous . . .

Zoë Caillebotte in the Garden, Yerres, 1877 Pastel, 47 × 59 cm. Signed and dated top right "G. Caillebotte 77" This bench stood in the path from the orangery to the "casin." In the upper left corner we see the "casin's" colonnade.

*A roofed seat
in the park today*

A Roofed Bench

"The roofed bench in the Panckoucke garden, figure 10
below, is made of undressed wood. Figure 10 above shows
a detail of the roof's underside.

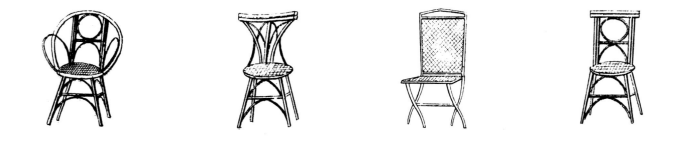

The chair on the left is the same kind Gustave Caillebotte painted in 1878 in The Painter under His Parasol. *He included one like the example on the right in* Fishing, 1878.

Chairs

"The chairs illustrated here are attractive and skillfully made. Along public walks one sees very comfortable openwork metal chairs and armchairs..."

At Yerres Gustave Caillebotte painted such openwork metal seats in his *Portraits in the Country* and *The Orange Trees*, and we see them as well in the photograph of his family property.

Fishermen on the Banks of the
Yerres, *c. 1876*
Oil on canvas, 66 × 50 cm.

A float and gazebo and the walkway along the riverbank belonging to the Caillebotte property. We are looking at the river's right side downstream of the bridge. Also in this picture are Les Charmilles, the watering place and the public washhouse with its roof of flat tiles. The roofed structure at the end of the chestnut-wood balustrade, seen here looking downstream, is the same as that in Fishing, 1878. In the latter painting the view is upstream.

Fishermen of a later day. Now as in Gustave Caillebotte's time, Guy de Maupassant's words ring true: "He stared at a motionless angler on the steep riverbank facing him. Suddenly the fellow brusquely yanked from the river a small silver fish wriggling at the end of the line."

548. Bords de l'Yerres

Fishing, 1878
Oil on canvas, 157 × 113 cm.
Signed and dated bottom right "G. Caillebotte 1878"
Zoë Caillebotte stands near the fisherman.

Nicholas de Larmessin (1684–1755), "The Isle of Cythera," published in the August, 1730, Mercure de France. After Antoine Watteau's Isle of Cythera. According to Louis Fourcauld, writing in 1904, Watteau's literary source was the 1700 three-act comedy "Les Trois Cousines" by the actor-writer Florent Carton, known as Dancourt. In the play a miller's widow living in Creteil burns with a desire to remarry but fails to provide husbands for her daughters. The complicated plot ends to everyone's satisfaction. From 1721 until his death Watteau lived at Nogent-sur-Marne.

The Reflection of a Dream

The nightingale. What swift instant of gaiety in all of nature! These new leaves, these lilacs, this rejuvenated sun! In such short moments does melancholy vanish! Let the sky cloud over; its darkness is like nothing so much as a loved one's charming pout—she will come back.

Returning home this evening, I heard the nightingale, then I heard him again, though far off. The song is truly unique, but more for the emotions it stirs up than in itself. Buffon as a naturalist is ecstatic about the flexibility of this melancholic springtime singer's throat and the varied notes it can produce. Myself, I find in its song the monotony and indefinible charm of all things that made a vivid impression. It is like watching the ocean; one always waits for the next wave, one cannot tear oneself away, one cannot leave it.

Engraving by Perelle, after Israël Silvestre, of the park of the Château de Lesigny near the Réveillon, a tributary of the Yerres. In 1616 this property belonged to Eléonora Dori, known as Léonora Galigai, wife of Concino-Concini, Marquess of Ancre, Marshal of France. Both Galigai and his wife were of Florentine origin. The historian K. Woodbridge, writing about the origins and success of the French garden and its relationship to painting, compared the work of Watteau to this local engraving.

How I despise all those rhymers with their rhymes, their glorying, their success, their nightingales, their meadows! How many of them truly convey what the nightingale makes us feel? And meanwhile their verses are only full of that. Yet when Dante speaks, he is as fresh as nature herself, and one has heard only what he describes. Everything is artificial and dressed up and intellectual. How many of them have painted love? Dante is truly the first among poets . . .

EUGÈNE DELACROIX, *Journal,* 1824

During the Renaissance the designs of parks and gardens in the Ile de France began to follow a different system of logic. The architecture of gardens does not come about by accident but is based on literary and philosophic works, one of which has had major

The third secret garden, or "garden of gold," which conveyed the idea of supreme perfection. Golden statues in niches among greenery remind the visitor of man's excellence "in God's image." The golden obelisk on the right reminds us of the Exhedra at Yerres.

Illustration from The Dream of Poliphilos *(1499 and 1546). The "Magna Porta," seen here, was inspired by the arch of Augustus (first century B.C.) at Rimini. The theory of arches, according to Léon-Baptiste Alberti, originated with Poliphilos' emergence onto the terrace of the Lower Sanctuary or Sacrarium of Aphrodite and the attack on him by the mythical dragon who guarded the "waters of life," that is, places consecrated to the arrival of life on the planet. This theory of arches was also put forward in De Re Aedificatoria.*

repercussions through the years. In this chapter we will attempt to throw light on the influence of this work as it affects the design of the park at Yerres in the first half of the nineteenth century and as it affects the oeuvre of the Impressionist painter Gustave Caillebotte.

Before entering the property, the visitor is struck by the gate. This arch, "destined to last eternally," has its origin in the *Magna Porta* in *Hypnerotomachia Poliphili*,[56] an incunabulum by an unknown author, currently attributed to Leon Baptiste Alberti.[57] We will not go into a detailed analysis of the allegorical elements of this work or their logical sequence. The book, strongly mystical, was influenced by the theological studies of the Roman Academy under Popes Nicholas V and Pius II. It describes a series of stops in an archaeological and philosophical promenade through the Roman countryside, a spiritual journey which was undertaken by Poliphilos, lover of Polia, "passionately in love with divine wisdom," which paves the way for a comparative study of non-Christian theologies and places the entire religious phenomenon within a universal perspective.

Hypnerotomachia Poliphilos inspired not only theoreticians of architecture and painters but art patrons,[58] who re-created allegories from its pages in their parks and gardens. Examples can be seen in the first garden of the Château at Fontainebleau (1528); in the garden of Isola Bella (1630); and, after 1661, at Versailles.

The landscape park at Yerres belongs within the tradition of this initiatory journey. If, as we walk through it, we keep in mind Pierre Boitard and Louis Verardi's references to antiquity, we will be aware of this. And of course in this park the twelve-year-old Gustave Caillebotte began to cultivate a taste for gardens and to grow to love them, in the footsteps of Poliphilos.

Before examining the main thrust of this "dream's reflection" and before considering a few of its allegorical elements as we find them expressed in the park at Yerres, let us look at some meanings in the place itself.

Banks of the Hière, beloved of Flora,
You entice me; I approach you.
The winds have grown still,
Buds are on the verge of bursting,
The sky smiles, the air is softer,
The tender nightingale will
Sing once more for us.

DUCIS, 1891

First, let us consider the "casin" as a symbol of the Florentine Academy. Cosimo di Medici the Elder, an admirer of Plato, founded the Academia Neo-Platonica in Florence and entrusted its control to the learned philosopher and humanist Marsillo Ficino, later closely connected with Lorenzo the Magnificent. With the death of Jean de la Mirandole on November 17, 1494, following struggles between Rome and Florence for ascendance in the control of knowledge, this Florentine academy

*Luncheon of the Boaters Beside the Yerres, c. 1872
Oil on wood, 32 × 25 cm.
Signed lower left
"G. Caillebotte"
Come with us to the isle of Cythera . . .
From which a young girl rarely comes back without a lover or a husband . . .
The village young people, dressed as pilgrims, Undertake a pilgrimage to the Temple of Love.*

DANCOURT

236

disappeared. It was within this context that in 1466 Leon Baptiste Alberti lost his post at the Vatican Chancellery and fled to the Medicis in Florence, where freedom of thought and study were encouraged and protected. A way of recounting this story about an attack on freedom of information and expression is through the legend of the nightingale, which goes as follows:

Philomela, a mythical Athenian princess, Pandion's daughter, was raped by her brother-in-law Tereus, king of Thrace, who cut out her tongue. Unable to speak, she embroidered her story and sent it to her sister Procne, who, in revenge, killed her own son and served him as a meal to her husband. Tereus pursued the two sisters, but the gods delivered them by transforming Philomela into a swallow and Procne into a nightingale.[59] The "Discourse on Poliphilos' Dream" ends with an evocation of the nightingale's song and an allusion to the fact that, beginning in 1464, humanists "had their tongues torn out" by Rome.

"While at Treviso, a grieving Poliphilos, bound by such beautiful ties of love for Polia, found himself a prisoner. May first, 1467."[60]

Components of the spiritual itinerary at Yerres

1. Relating to a search for the way:

Poliphilos, feverish after a night of grieving for the lost Polia, falls asleep.

The meadow: As dawn approaches, the unhappy man falls into a stupor and in a dream sees himself on a silent plain—a flowering meadow.

The bocage: He dreams he is in a forest, symbol of the beginning of a metaphysical quest, which will compensate him for the loss of his love. The setting of Poliphilos' dream is the Gulf of Gaeto not far from the Circeo peninsula, near the beach where Aeneas and his son Ascanius landed at the time of the founding of the city consecrated to divine love, which is Rome. In his dream Poliphilos finds his way through a labyrinth of growing trees and plants on the shores of Circeo and thence across the Pontine Marshes[61] toward a valley where he sees *Aedes Fortunae*, Palestrina's temple.

2. Relating to the initiation into truth:

Choir of shepherds and shepherdesses,
Let us leave these hamlets,
Let us go taste the sweets of love. . .
Nymph of Yerres,
With pleasure I leave my valley, my fountains
My delightful meadows:
Is there nothing in a field which one leaves without pain
To go pay homage to the nymph[s] of these places?

La Fête de Chalendre, XVIII century (extracts)[62]

Bodies of water: On the pilgrim's journey of initiation into the mysteries of life the first step was *Ninfa* in the Pontine Marshes. Travelers quenched their thirst in this garden, at springs dedicated to the nymphs *Eamus ad Nymphas*.

The pond: A lake of clear water precedes the flower garden.

The rosarium: This evokes the sacred place of Palestrina where flowers, planted long ago, have run wild but bloom again each spring among the palms, holm oaks and pines, which hide the ruins of the ancient temple of Palestrina. At the temple, the blood of victims produced the symbolic miracle of a blossoming rose, foreshadowing the sacrifice of Christ. In the month of May, which is Mary's month, the festival of roses[63] is celebrated.

The flower garden: The ancient walled enclosure contains the gush and flow of a thousand springs and small waterfalls, among tall grass, lilies, hollyhocks, eglantine, and masses of dark greenery shot through with the sun's rays.

A *gazebo*[64]: After an arduous climb, the pilgrim arrives at the gazebo, which corresponds to the belvedere on the upper part of the temple dedicated to Fortune. He seizes Fortune by the hair and by this means masters his fate. From the gazebo he sees the landscape stretching away to the horizon. All the loveliness in the world lies before his dazzled eyes, and he is in an ecstasy. His initiation continues as he descends from the belvedere and encounters, first, the Upper Sanctuary, which is the symbol of the cycle of Athena or the knowledge of destiny, then the Lower Sanctuary, where the *Magna Porta*, representing the cycle of Aphrodite or the knowledge of the origin of life, is situated.

A *grotto*: With its ornamentation, incrustations, and sea shells from different "sea caves" in the gardens of antiquity and in particular from Palestrina's Cavern of the Fates, in which the mosaic of the "sea world" must be seen under water, the grotto symbolizes the marine origin of life.

3. Relating to a knowledge of the origin of life in the physical universe:

The pilgrim, after traveling the path of "Free Choice," where his education begins, and after participating in a banquet and a ballet, and after the "Queen of Free Choice" has taught him the difference between a fate submitted to and a fate freely chosen, goes on his way. Dawn is breaking. He arrives at a festival celebrated in the gardens surrounding the palace and is led to another step in his voyage.

The landscape garden: The "Glass Garden" is consecrated to the "Richness of Nature." To the pilgrim's instruction is added human behavior, which masters the secrets.

The river: Reason shows him an aquatic labyrinth, then the "Garden of Silk," dedicated to Sweet Harmony. Beneath the arbor, poetic song awakens new harmonies in his soul and the recognition of the supreme creative activity, which is poetry.

The Exhedra: The pilgrim is then led toward the third secret garden where he gains an idea of ultimate perfection, symbolized by an obelisk.

Once the three symbolic gardens have served their purpose as vehicles of the ancient theologians' knowledge of Poliphilos, the pilgrim must choose among the three ways: the contemplative life, which is a gateway to the glory of God, the active life, which leads to the glory of the World, or the middle way, called *Mater Amoris*. He chooses the middle way and, passing through the gate, finds himself in a meadow and a bower of jasmine, which is the Persian flower of those faithful in love. At the end of the bower he finds his beloved Polia in the guise of a nymph bearing a torch, and he reaches a new degree of knowledge.

The gate to the flower garden and its lawn are the symbols of this in Yerres.

The diving board: After many adventures the pilgrim arrives in the country of shadows and, descending into hell, is initiated into the mysteries of death, after which he discovers Polia on a beach like the one onto which Aeneas disembarked.

Boats: Eros awaits the lovers, to convey them in his bark to Cythera, island devoted to the cult of the Cytheraean Venus. Nymphs singing barcaroles row the bark over a clear sea, surrounded by playful tritons. On the island, which is Ischia, Poliphilos' itinerary in the footsteps of Aeneas comes to its end and the pilgrim attains a new degree of knowledge and is initiated into the mysteries of life.

The tomb of Jean-Jacques Rousseau on L'Isle des Peupliers at Ermenonville, drawn by Hubert-Robert. The sculptor was Lesueur. According to P. Boitard, "all the resources of architecture should be deployed when erecting a monument worthy of a great man."

Alfred Roll, "Portrait of Jean-Charles Alphand." This engineer, a graduate of the Ecole Polytechique, was charged with administering the public walks of the capital and played a part in the development of, among other things, the Parc Monceau and the Bois de Boulogne.

LATER ON

The garden that I had bought along with my house was planted with common everyday bourgeois shrubbery but still possessed a certain beauty. What it basically consisted of was a superb grouping of immense trees from the old Montmorency park, clad in ivy and fanning out above a small rock formation into one of those grand sweeps of greenery with which Watteau liked to shelter the repose and siestas of his *fêtes galantes*. I wanted to keep that and rip out the rest so the bouquet of large trees would rise above a planting of smaller evergreens whose year-round foliage would give an illusion on a sunny winter day of summer. My idea was to choose shrubs from among the rarest since no matter what is said, the exceptional is almost always beautiful. Besides, given modern progress in horticulture with all its reworking and artistic recoloring of natural greenery, a possibility existed that a man of letters with the soul of a colorist could make a painter's garden and do it on a grand scale. I envisioned a palette of greens ranging from near black to the most tender wash, passing through the bluish junipers, the bronzy cryptomerias and all the varied splotchings of holly, euonymus, and aucubas, whose pale leaves in the absence of flowers give the illusion of flowers. Let it be said, in this taste for gardening, which has something about it of the knick-knack business, the elegantly branched and exquisitely shaped and daintily speckled shrub becomes a sort of objet d'art, which one dreams about behind closed eyelids and mulls over in bed at night and considers snatching from the private garden of some great horticulturist, as if it were a rare object hidden away on a shelf in a curio dealer's personal collection. The shrub, finally obtained and placed in the garden, is exactly like a fine piece of furniture installed in a room.

EDMOND DE GONCOURT, *Maison d'un artiste*, 1881

The Park at Yerres: A Garden in Town

Like the Parc Monceau in Paris.

From the French garden to the picturesque garden:

From 1773 to 1779 Louis Carrogis, a painter, architect, engraver and playwright better known as Carmontelle, redesigned the Monceau gardens for Louis-Philippe Joseph ("Philippe Egalité"), Duke of Orleans, who had acquired the "Chartres folly" in 1769. Carmontelle's remodeling in imitation of English gardens included many structures, and he intended to "unite all times and all places in one garden." The garden itself took two hours of interrupted walking to traverse. One of its features was a "Woodland of Tombs" which, according to its creator, was "... made up of Lombardy poplars, Eurasian maples, cypresses, plane trees, and Chinese thuyas. The principal pyramidal tomb is Egyptian. Inside it eight granite columns with capitals decorated with Egyptian busts are buried one-third of their length... The arch is adorned with bronze rosettes and on the right and left are two sepulchres of antique green marble. Directly in front, opposite the door, an antique marble bowl is set inside a recess. On its inner surface the figure of a woman crouches, beating her breasts... The entrance is closed by an iron grille whose jambs represent Egyptian caryatids. To the left of the tomb four steps surround a bronze urn on a marble pedestal. On its right is a crumbling fountain and, close by, a mulberry tree. The symbolism of this woodland may have to do with Pyramus and Thisbe..."[65]

From the picturesque garden to the English garden:

Later, around 1781, Thomas Blaikie set about enlarging the Monceau garden and making it even more "English" than when it had been a mere imitation.

From the English garden to the *Promenade de Paris*:

In 1861, after many changes, the Monceau was remodeled by the engineer Jean-Charles Alphand, whom Baron Georges Eugène Haussmann appointed to convert it into a public park for the city of Paris. When, on August 13, 1861, Napoleon III inaugurated the park, it covered an area of 8 hectares.

By the time Gustave Caillebotte painted the Park Monceau, all these alterations had been long completed and the place was a city garden, just as the Caillebotte park was a garden in a town—for by then the simple village of Yerres and its valley had become an agglomeration. Caillebotte's painting, *The Park Monceau*, executed around 1878, shows one of the mausoleums in the "Woodland of Tombs." Of mausoleums Audot wrote, "... cenotaphs belong in melancholic surroundings... If the designer wishes to accent such a setting with a tomb it should bear the name of one of those geniuses who now and then appear like meteors to enlighten the human race, or else of some good man relatively unknown in his lifetime but whose good works leave behind him a memento like those flowers snapped off by storms, which fade but somehow still impregnate the air with their perfume..."

White and Yellow Chrysanthemums, Garden at Petit Gennevilliers, c. 1893 Oil on canvas, 73 × 60 cm. Claude Monet owned this painting.

Edmond de Goncourt loved chrysanthemums, not because they had "the colors of God's flowers but for their fragmented tones, their fatigued, shot effect, the faded hues of artistic industry, of drapery and furniture, of the interiors of a decadent civilization." In his Journal *for Tuesday, November 12, 1878, de Goncourt wrote, "I do not know what charm winter flowers possess. They seem to me to possess something delicately sickly. Today on Nittis' table there stood an enormous bunch of chrysanthemums, supposedly yellow but so pale they seemed white, with a slight purplish tinge on the tips of their petals. I couldn't take my eyes from this bouquet. It was like the pallor of a small girl's flesh turned blue with cold."*

The architecture of funerary monuments should be more or less opulent. However, ostentation is unsuitable in a memorial erected affectionately for an ordinary man, whose tomb should be in keeping with his simpler and more modest virtues.

These gardens, companions of man,
Intermediary between the forest which precede him
And the deserts which follow.

RENÉ DE CHATEAUBRIAND

Clump of Chrysanthemums, Garden at Petit Gennevilliers, *c. 1893*
Oil on canvas, 99.3 × 61.3 cm.

Roses, Garden at Petit Gennevilliers, *c. 1886*
Oil on canvas, 89×116 cm.
Signed bottom left, by the hand of P. Renoir,
"G. Caillebotte"

Clump of Flowers, Garden at Petit
Gennevilliers, c. 1882
Oil on canvas, 54 × 65 cm.
Signed lower left "G. Caillebotte"
Photographed by Martial Caillebotte
A circular flower bed in Gustave
Caillebotte's garden. Did this "massif"
make him think of similar beds in the
lawn of the park at Yerres?

A Lost Garden at Petit Gennevilliers

To speak of the garden at Petit Gennevilliers is like conjuring up an imaginary place, since its site and surroundings have been so changed by industrialization. What gives the best idea of the house's setting is found in Claude Monet's vision of it, well before Gustave Caillebotte became its owner. Monet's painting, *Argenteuil, Boats Along the Riverbank,* shows the Argenteuil basin and the lefthand, or Petit Gennevilliers, side of the Seine, looking downstream. In this painting and in his *Boats Moored at Petit Gennevilliers,* both executed around 1872, we see the Caillebotte house. In Monet's 1873 *Hoar Frost on the Plaine de Colombes* the south side of the house as it faces the Plaine de Colombes to the east is shown on the right side of the canvas, with the garden that will also belong to Gustave Caillebotte.

Now we come to Gustave Caillebotte's works.

OPPOSITE:
Sunflowers, Garden at
Petit Gennevilliers, c.
1885
Oil on canvas, 131 ×
105 cm.
Signed lower left
"G. Caillebotte"

*Petit Gennevilliers,
Façade, Southeast of
the Artist's Studio,
Overlooking the Garden,
Spring
Oil on canvas, 80 × 65 cm.
Signed lower right
"G. Caillebotte"
Here we see a double
openwork gate similar to the
one in* The Artist's House
at Petit Gennevilliers, *executed around 1882.
In the left foreground is a
"corbeille" of garden
pansies. The mottled trunk
of the ornamental tree in the
center suggests a flowering
cherry, a small deciduous
tree that is highly decorative
in spring.*

It would appear that the Petit Gennevilliers house had been built on a rectangular parcel of land, extremely elongated and relatively narrow, judging from the proximity of the neighboring houses. One gets this feeling from the artist's 1889–90 *The Caillebotte House Seen from the Seine, Petit Gennevilliers* in which we see the length of the towpath and, in front of the house, a row of what are probably lime trees, since they remind us of the lime-bordered path along the Rue de Concy at Yerres.

In *The Artist's House at Petit Gennevilliers*, about 1882, we see how well the house and its garden were integrated into their surroundings, for example in the inclusion, in the garden behind the house, of a path designed to line up with the Argenteuil church tower so that it could be seen from the other side of the Seine. This same integration is evident in *Garden Entrance, Petit Gennevilliers* in which the spectator looks through the garden's openwork gate toward the towpath and a moored sailboat, the river and trees lining the Argenteuil path on the opposite bank. At Yerres a similar gate gave onto the Meadow Dead End.

The garden extended south into what was then countryside, the plain outside the limits of the communes of Gennevilliers and Colombes. Some of the following humid landscapes remind us, on a different scale of course, of the meadow at Yerres: *Landscape with Poplars, Petit Gennevilliers*, about 1888, and *Landscape with a Row of*

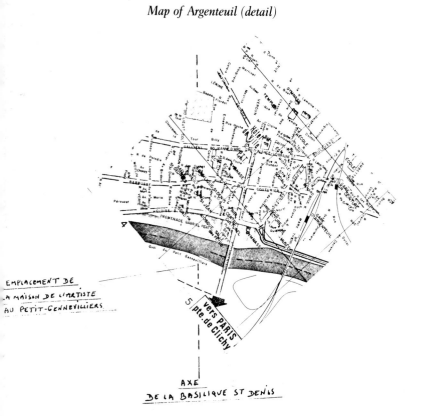

Map of Argenteuil (detail)

Site of the artist's house at Petit Gennevilliers, axis of the Argenteuil Basilica

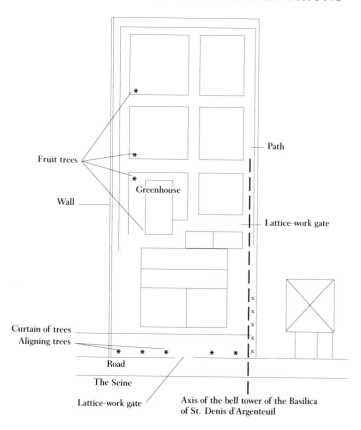

GENNEVILLIERS-COLOMBES ENVIRONS

This diagram represents an attempt to re-create the garden in accordance with clues in some of the paintings. The garden appears to have been enlarged when the house was bought and when the parcel of land on the right was acquired.

Poplars, Petit Gennevilliers, about 1893. Water is present in both these paintings or its presence is felt, for the Seine has taken the place of the Yerres; its small arm and L'Isle Marante give the large river an illusion of the dimensions of its tributary.

Other works painted over a period of ten years or so, starting in 1882, reveal the evolution and even transformation the garden went through in this time. In executing some of the alterations, Gustave Caillebotte the gardener may well have been inspired by the park at Yerres. As at Yerres, the artist's garden was a source of inspiration for his painting, as for example in *The Garden Path,* 1886.

Here is a good place to draw the reader's attention to two structures in this garden, the "sailor's house" and the studio. Other features at Petit Gennevilliers, a flower garden with trellis work and palisade fence, a greenhouse, rose garden, small woodlot and garden furniture, remind us of *The Wall of the Kitchen Garden, Yerres.* The tradition of nineteenth-century garden design and architecture has been respected and continued. In Caillebotte's painting time has stood still.

The artist's involvement in the garden at Petit Gennevilliers included not only an interest in growing flowers but in selecting their varieties; these had great importance in his life at that time. His dahlias, chrysanthemums, lilacs, peonies, daisies, pentstemons, hyacinths, poppies, and sunflowers, his blossoming fruit trees and collection of orchids inspired his painting. His flower compositions, in which we see the expression of his taste in associating and showing to advantage flowers of different species, varieties, and colors, his search for balance of form, size of the bouquet, choice of their components and the harmony of their tones, places him in the tradition of the great flower painters of nineteenth-century France.

The Artist's House at Petit Gennevilliers, *c.1882*
Oil on canvas, 65 × 54 *cm.*
Signed lower right, by the hand of Martial Caillebotte,
"G. Caillebotte"

On Observation and Color

A parallel can be established between the protected childhood of Gustave Caillebotte at Yerres and the childhoods of Marcel Proust and John Ruskin as described by André Maurois. Maurois wrote, "It is understandable that elective affinites linked Proust to Ruskin. Like Ruskin, Proust belonged to an educated upper-middle-class family. Like Ruskin he had as a child been doted on by overly solicitous parents and had spent days in a garden observing with meticulous curiosity birds, flowers and clouds."

In the last century weather observation was taken seriously in Brie. The Comte de Gasparin included in his agricultural teachings sayings on the subject by shepherds and farmers. We give a few of these below.

A pink sunset, clear or overcast, means good weather.

A red sky is a sign of wind.

A clear brilliant sky at sunset foretells wind.

A pale yellow sky is a sign of rain.

Thin ragged clouds mean good weather
    and a moderate breeze.

Small dark clouds bring rain.

A pale sun indicates rain.

As for the daily movement of the sun in a landscape garden, that has been dealt with in "A Copse."

The Briard Plain, *before 1879*,
Oil on canvas, 31 × 43 cm.
Stamped lower right

Sky Study, Clouds, Number 1,
before 1879
Oil on canvas, 24 × 37 cm.
Stamped lower left

Sky Study, Clouds, Number 2,
before 1879
Oil on canvas, 24 × 35 cm.
Stamped lower right

Sky Study, Clouds, Number 3,
before 1879
Oil on canvas, 24 × 32 cm.
Stamped lower right

Sky Study, Harmony of Violet
and Pink, *before 1879*
Oil on canvas, 18 × 25 cm.
Stamped lower right

I still have a thirty-centimeter canvas. Autumn garden, two bottle green, bottle shaped cypresses, three chestnut trees with tobacco-brown and orange leaves. A little yew with pale yellow leaves and purple trunk, two little bushes with crimson-scarlet foliage.

VINCENT VAN GOGH, Letter to his brother Theo, October, 1888

Much of Gustave Caillebotte's originality during his formative years at Yerres is seen in the diversity of his compositions, especially in their pictorial treatment. Some of these early canvases show the young painter's difficulty in breaking away from the influence of his predecessors. In others he appears to hesitate in choosing his way, especially in deciding between Naturalism and Impressionism. We have tried here to describe his strengths as they are reflected not only in the art of gardens but in that of painting.

1

During the second half of the nineteenth century a man of extremely strong personality named Eugène Chevreul left a mark on European culture and exercised a powerful influence on his contemporaries. Born at Angers on August 31, 1786, he was educated in his native city. In 1810, at the age of twenty-four, he became an assistant naturalist at the Museum of Natural History in Paris. He studied chemistry with Vauquelin. In 1829 he held the Chair of Applied Chemistry and did original research in the field, publishing an analytical work dealing with fatty animal substances, which had important industrial applications. Chevreul held his chair until his death in 1890. He was acquainted with the events of 1870–71 at the Museum; he was also a professor at Gobelins and gave highly specialized courses in the relationships of colors. Chevreul's contention was that "in the case of chemistry as it applies to painting" colors do not exist but are functions of light, and that light alone creates color and delineates form. Objects, he claimed, have no being except in relation to light, which reveals, dissolves, brings out or hides them. In 1839 Chevreul devised the first color chart, the chromatic wheel, showing the relations between the colors of the spectrum, which he divided into segments of generally equal dimensions. These ideas influenced his contemporaries, the art of garden design, and the Impressionist movement.

2

In their *Manuel de l'amateur de jardin* Decaisne and Naudin wrote as follows on "the choice of plants and their distribution in the parterre:" "As for foliage and flower color, some combinations are more likely to succeed than others. The leaves of some plants produce very strong contrasts. Villosity makes some seem almost white, the foliage of *Perilla frutescens* var. *nankinensis* is such a dark shade of purple that it appears black, and other plants may be variegated by chlorosis so that parts of the leaf look yellow, and so on. Put together, all these plants enliven the decoration of the parterre,
though they must not be used too lavishly, and it is important that they be placed symmetrically. Varieties having unusual color should be positioned near sorts whose shade of green will provide a contrast for their rare tints, for example plants with white foliage next to bright green, red or purple-black beside pale green. Avoid the too extreme contrast of white foliage with dark purple. Experience and observation will lead without much difficulty to success in producing harmonious combinations.

"The blending of flower colors is more complicated and depends on the number of species available as well as on how many individuals are to be used of each species, not to mention the different varieties' seasons of flowering and the plants' relative size . . ."

Primary colors: red, yellow, and blue
"First of all remember that the fundamental or primary colors from which all others are derived are three in number, red, yellow, and blue, and that their perfect fusion in well-defined proportions produces on the eye the sensation of white."

Intermediate colors: orange, green, and purple
"The combination of any two primary colors will result in a compound color, for example red and yellow will make orange, yellow, and blue produce green, and blue and red result in purple. The tones of these mixed colors vary depending on the proportions of the two colors entering into their composition, and since these

Yerres, the Lawn in the Park, Seen from a Path, Sunset Number 1, *before 1879*
Oil on canvas, 24 × 33 cm.
Stamped lower right

Yerres, the Lawn in the Park, Sunset Number 2, *before 1879,*
Oil on canvas, 21 × 31 cm.
Stamped lower right

Yerres, the Lawn in the Park, Sunset Number 3, *before 1879*
Oil on canvas, 21 × 30 cm.
Stamped lower right

Yerres, the Lawn in the Park, Sunset
Number 4, *before 1879*
Oil on canvas, 21 × 31 cm.
Stamped upper right

Yerres, the Lawn in the Park, Sunset
Number 5, *before 1879*
Oil on canvas, 24 × 33 cm.
Stamped lower right

Yerres, the Lawn in the Park, Seen
from a Path, Sunset Number 6, *before
1879*
Oil on canvas, 24 × 33 cm.
Stamped lower right

proportions can be altered to an infinite degree, an unlimited number of shades is possible between the two constituent colors."

Complementary colors

"A complementary color is one which, whether it is primary or not, when added to a combination of colors reconstitutes the elementary triad. Thus green (composed of blue and yellow) is the complementary of red, purple (composed of red and blue) is the complementary of yellow, orange (the result of a mixture of red and yellow) is the complementary of blue. And, reciprocally, blue, yellow, and red are complementaries of orange, purple, and green."

White

"It follows that the mixture of a color with its complementary color produces white."

Black

"Black is simply the absence or total extinction of the three primary colors."

Putting colors together

"The bringing together of colors and their various shades in twos or threes or in even greater numbers produces effects on the eye that vary according to the combinations adopted. Some colors mutually enhance each other and seem more pleasing when placed side by side. Others are diminished or become unpleasant or even shocking. Our best guide in this matter is the Museum of Natural History's distinguished Professor Chevreul who has made the most intensive study of contrasting color and who, after applying his findings to the art of dying fabrics, has not hesitated to extend them to the arrangement of flowers in a parterre. We sum up here his most essential points:

"All primary colors when pure or nearly pure contrast pleasantly with each other. When placed very close together, however, each one takes on something of the shade that would result if it were combined with the complementary color of its neighbors. For example, red next to yellow takes on a faint tinge of purple, which is the complementary of yellow, and the yellow takes on a green cast, green being a complement of red.

"In the same way complementary colors contrast with each other to great advantage. It suffices to bring together yellow and purple (composed of red and blue) or red and green (composed of yellow and blue) or blue and orange (made up of red and yellow) to see the sparkle and beauty these contrasts produce.

"The secondary combining of compound colors also yields good results, since in each of these groups the three primary colors are used and the contrasts are sufficiently pronounced. For example, purple (red and blue) goes well with orange (red and yellow) and with green (yellow and blue)...

"On the other hand disappointment or even unpleasantness will result if a primary color is combined with a compound color in whose composition it plays a part. Thus red goes badly with orange (yellow and red) or with purple (red and blue), and yellow is not successful with orange (yellow and red) or green (yellow and blue). However, if the primary color plays only a small part in the compound color it is put next to, the contrast can become pronounced enough to please the eye. Thus a bright blue will look well next to a pale or yellowish green, and bright yellow will be effective beside a deep green in which a bluish tinge predominates. As can be seen, these two cases come under the preceding rules, which establish that, in general, the more pronounced the contrast the more agreeable the result.

"All colors, whether primary or compound, are enlivened by the proximity of white and moreover contrast beautifully with it. White has the extra advantage of improving a bad combination by intervening between colors that go together poorly, as, for example, between red and orange, red and purple, purple and blue, and so on. White, which is so plentiful in nature, thus plays a large role in the decorative arts.

"With the exception of white, all colors are weakened by the proximity of black, which reduces their brilliance. Dull or very deep colors suffer from being placed next to black because of the lack of contrast. In a matter of speaking, black does not exist in the plant kingdom. Virtually the only example that comes to mind is the common broad bean with its black-spotted flower. Therefore, contrasts with it are only established between plants and the soil, and even the soil is never truly black. In the absence of black, we have replaced it, to a degree, with the deep purple foliage of plants such as *Perilla frutescens* var. *nankensis,* var. or by the very dark purple flowers of, for example, scabiosa and some varieties of dahlia, hollyhock, and so on.

"In the flower garden combinations of color may be binary, tertiary, rarely quaternary unless the green of leaves is considered to have a place in the combination. The most recommended secondary combinations are the following, listed in order of merit:

"A. All the primary or compound colors with white. The attractiveness of the contrasts will increase with the purity and brilliance of the pigments; for example, light or dark blue with white, pink or red with white, bright yellow with white, orange with white, green with white, purple with white.

"B. Primary colors together or with their complementary colors, such as red with yellow, red with blue, yellow with blue, yellow with purple, orange with blue, green with red. We have already pointed out that only ugly or mediocre effects are obtained by juxtaposing primary with compound colors which are not complementary to each other (see above).

"Tertiary combinations are much more numerous and almost always include white; often indeed the white is repeated, as can be seen in the following examples: White, red, green; or white, red, white, green. Blue, orange, blue, white; or white, orange, white, blue. White, yellow, purple, white; or white, yellow, white, purple. Yellow, red, white, yellow. White, red, blue, white; or better, white, red, white, blue. White, orange, green, white will improve if white is interposed between the orange and green. White, orange, white, purple. White, yellow, green, white. White, yellow, blue, white, or the same combination with the white inserted between the

Studio Interior with Stove
c. 1872
Oil on canvas, 80 × 65 cm.
Signed with the initials
G. C. on the left center
reverse side of the canvas;
also stamped lower right
on the face.
According to Professor
Hugo Munsterberg whom
Kirk Varnedoe consulted
about this painting, the
following Japanese objects
appear in it: two lanterns, a
plate and two porcelain
vases (Arita and/or Imari),
a print of perhaps the
Ukiyo-E type, and two
works characteristic of the
Yamato-E style of Japanese
painting. In lectures on
Japanese art in Paris and
Tokyo in 1988, the two
unframed tryptichs, which
appear to have been
mounted on paper or
cardboard and which are
seen on the wall on the left,
were said to be the work of
the Ukiyo-E painters
Yoshitora or Yoshikazu,
active in the 1860s. In the
same lecture Caillebotte's
Le Pont de l'Europe was
said to echo certain Japanese
prints that represented
foreigners being received by
geishas in a Yokohama tea
house and that had similarly
striking diagonal perspective
effects.

yellow and the blue. Such examples, of which we could cite many more, suffice to make the rule regarding such combinations clear.

"If, for lack of something better, it is necessary to use colors that are not complementary to each other, separate them by white. Finally, in mixed plantings where colors are almost always at some distance from each other, the rules we have just formulated are less rigorous than when planting a formal bed.

"In order to complete the 'gardener's palette,' the strength of the colors must be taken into consideration and special attention paid to the effects that will result from shade (tonality), brightness (value), and saturation (intensity); we must also consider the phenomenon of brilliance."

By the time Gustave Caillebotte was working at Yerres the Impressionists were aware of the physical and psychological qualities of colors and used warm tones to bring objects nearer and cold colors to make them recede. We see this in Pierre Auguste Renoir's *Banks of the Seine at Champrosay,* 1876; Claude Monet's *The Pond at Montgeron,* 1876; and Gustave Caillebotte's 1876 *Portraits in the Country.*

The studies these men made of light and color led them from that time on to fragment their brushstrokes progressively, adding to the time-honored method of mixing colors on the palette, which resulted in a gray effect, the idea of allowing them to be mixed by the eye itself, resulting in a maximum of luminous intensity. To bring out the greatest brilliance in a tone, they applied small, distinct strokes of the pure pigments of which it was comprised, without mixing beforehand on the palette. We see this in Gustave Caillebotte's *The Gardener,* painted in 1877. On this canvas Caillebotte used extremely varied brushstrokes, sometimes breaking them up, sometimes placing them as if spontaneously, in places brushing out the pigment and in others building up an impasto, which almost appears incised. *Studio Interior with Stove,* painted around 1872, is an example of this.

From this time on, ideas about representing space were altered; moreover, painters were influenced by the new way of seeing the world inspired by Japanese prints. Later on, the Pont-Aven painters and the Nabis were to continue in this vein and exaggerate its character, at a time (the beginning of the Third Republic) when the use of color was still codified according to ideas formulated during the Roman Empire.

It has been alleged that in the nineteenth century men abandoned color to women in order to emphasize the triumph of reason over intuition.

Not until the start of the twentieth century were the Fauves Maurice Vlaminck and André Derain, creators of the "Chatou School," to "throw their paint pot at the heads of the bourgeoisie," thereby breaking decisively with the traditional use of color. It would seem that in this they merely substituted a new codification for an old one; new and different colors became compulsory or were enthusiastically insisted on.

Day by Day:
A Chronology of the Life
of Gustave Caillebotte

Self-Portrait in Front of the Easel, *c. 1879*
Oil on canvas, 90 × 115 cm.
Stamped lower right
Reflected in the mirror is the reversed image of Renoir's
The Moulin de la Galette, 1876, *which hung in*
Caillebotte's sitting room. The man reading is
Caillebotte's friend Richard Gallo.

Biographical Data

PREFECTURE OF THE
DEPARTMENT OF THE SEINE
REGISTER OF BIRTHS
YEAR 1848

Twenty-one August, ten A.M.

Born, Gustave, male, the nineteenth inst. at three twenty o'clock in the afternoon at the home of his parents, Rue du Faubourg Saint Denis No. 160.

Son of Martial Caillebotte, forty-nine years old, contractor in beds to the Armed Services, and of Céleste Daufresne Caillebotte, his wife, twenty-eight years old, housewife. On inspection of the child and on representation made by the father to myself, Mayor of the Fifth Arrondissement in Paris, and in the presence of Messrs. Jean Gustave Lacoste, age forty-four, manager of the firm supplying beds to the Armed Services, living on the premises of the firm, and Pierre-Louis Ravier, age forty-nine, on duty at the company and also resident there, who have read this document and signed it in my presence,

M. Caillebotte, Lacoste, Ravier and Vée, Mayor

Certified copy from the register
Paris, 24 September, 1857
Mayor of the 5th Arrondissement

Advertisement of the Lycée Michelet at Vanves, a "recommended establishment," in L'Agenda du Voyageur—Environs de Paris, *for the 1908–9 school year. Although this advertisement was published 50 years after Gustave Caillebotte was a student there, it gives an idea of the sort of life and education the Lycée offered its pupils.*

Washhouse Interior, Laundresses at Work, *before 1879*
Pencil on paper: (paper) 31 × 21 cm., (drawing) 16 × 19 cm.
The washhouse interior by the young Gustave Caillebotte has the "form of a Roman atrium" and is of a type that can be seen today in the lower Yerres valley, on the Rue la Fontaine in Périgny (sometimes called Périgny-en-Brie and sometimes Périgny-sur-Yerres, today in the Val-de-Marne). The special interest this drawing has for us is in its original perspectives, in accord with studies the young Gustave Caillebotte was making of perspective at the time, and the attention he paid to work done by country women.

THE LIFE OF GUSTAVE CAILLEBOTTE

1848
Gustave Caillebotte is born in Paris, at 160 Rue du Faubourg Saint-Denis. His father, Martial (1799–1874), is, among other things, a judge at the Seine's Tribunal de Commerce. His mother, Céleste Daufresne (1819–1878), is the granddaughter of a notary and of a Lisieux lawyer.

1850
The Caillebotte family moves to 152 Rue du Faubourg Saint-Denis.

1851
Gustave's first brother, René, is born on January 27.

1853
Gustave's second brother, Martial, is born on April 7.

A Road near Naples, c. 1872
Oil on canvas, 40 × 60 cm.
Stamped lower right
Here the artist may have been
representing his friend Giuseppe de
Nittis who was also painting the scene.[66]
The hat seen just above the canvas
stretcher may be Nittis', as may be the
palette we see on the right, held almost
perfectly horizontal in his left hand.
Harnessed vehicles appear in a number
of Caillebotte's works having Paris
streets and squares as their settings. This
representation of Etna appears to be a
wink at Katsushika Hokusai and
Utagawa Hiroshige, who painted Mount
Fuji in Japan.

1857
On October 6 Gustave enters the Lycée Louis-le-Grand, a boarding school at Vanves.

1860
Martial Caillebotte acquires the Yerres (Seine-et-Oise) property. Gustave, at the age of twelve, begins to draw.

1868
The Caillebotte family moves into the private house that Martial has just built at 77 Rue de Miromesnil in Paris.

1869
Gustave Caillebotte passes his first law examination in April. There is reason to believe that he begins to paint at the age of 21 at the family property at Yerres.

1870

At 22 Gustave, a Bachelor of Law, joins the Seine's Garde Mobile. In a letter postdated Paris, November 14, 1870, and sent by balloon, Alexandre Perdrielle writes his brother-in-law Jean-Baptiste Mathieu Daurelle (1830–1893), an employee of the Caillebotte family, "... Poor Clarisse is still unwell, she runs on nervous energy. She doesn't dare leave the house for fear that just at any moment Monsieur Gustave will come in, though he arrives very irregularly, that is, when he can..." Clarisse is the cook for the Caillebotte family, who are away at the time, staying with Judge Daufresne on the Boulevard François I at Le Havre.

Gustave enters the atelier of the painter Léon Bonnat (1834–1922). Bonnat, who was born at Bayonne, has studied in Madrid and at the Beaux-Arts in Paris and has been a student of Léon Cogniet, who won second place in the 1858 Grand Prix de Rome and is very close to Edgar Degas (1834–1917).

Claude Monet
Interior of an Apartment, 1875
Oil on canvas, 81.5 × 60.5 cm.
Signed and dated lower center "Claude Monet 75"
This painting belonged to Gustave Caillebotte and was shown at the Third Exhibition in April 1877.

1872

Gustave travels with his father in Italy. There he paints *A Road near Naples*, which is comparable to a work of his friend Giuseppe de Nittis, shown at the first exhibition in 1874 and numbered 117, probably called *Campagne du Vésuve*.

1873

Gustave's half-brother, Alfred (1834–1896), who is referred to as the "honorary canon" of Paris, is given the task of establishing the city's Church of Saint-Georges. After the death of his father, Alfred will be called "the richest priest in Paris."

On March 18 Gustave passes a competitive examination and is accepted at the Beaux-Arts. His first known dated work, *Nude Woman on a Sofa* is done in this year.

1874

From April 15 to May, the first exhibition of the "Paris Cooperative Society of Painters, Sculptors [etc.]" takes place at 35 Boulevard des Capucines on premises previously occupied by Félix Tournachon, better known as "Nadar" (1820–1910). Giuseppe de Nittis participates. Gustave Caillebotte does not, although Edgar Degas has anticipated that he would.

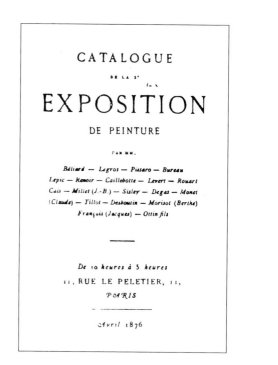

On December 25 Gustave's father dies. Gustave's mother keeps the property at Yerres.

Portrait of Jean Daurelle, c. 1885
Oil on canvas, 65 × 54 cm.
Jean-Baptiste Daurelle (1830–1893)
worked for the Caillebotte family. In
Lunch he is seen serving at the dining-
room table.

1875

Gustave Caillebotte maintains his relationships with the artists Jean Béraud (1849–1936) and Giuseppe de Nittis (1846–1884) and is a regular guest at de Nittis' Saturday "spaghetti dinners." Edgar Degas and Edouard Manet also attend these dinners. Gustave becomes the godfather of de Nittis' son Jacques.

On May 1 Gustave Caillebotte submits a painting to the Salon and is refused. At this time he is living and working at Yerres where he produces, among other works, *The Yerres, Effect of Rain*.

1876

The 28-year-old Gustave Caillebotte in a transaction made directly between himself and Claude Monet acquires Monet's 1875 Argenteuil canvas *Interior of an Apartment*.

Caillebotte paints *Le Pont de l'Europe,* in which he shows himself standing on the new 1868 bridge spanning the installations of the Gare Saint-Lazare. He becomes a member of the Sailing Club of Paris.

And then there were the rich boys like Messrs. Caillebotte and Rouart who could afford their own shows and saw no reason to tolerate the highhandedness of juries.

EMILE ZOLA, 1880

In April the second Impressionist exhibition opens at Durand-Ruel, 11 Rue Le Peletier and 16 Rue Lafitte. Eight of Gustave Caillebotte's works are shown, including three painted at Yerres: No. 22, *Garden*; No. 23, *Garden*; and No. 24, *After Lunch.* Paul Durand-Ruel's father is the great-grandson of Briard wine growers from the Yerres Valley, above Brie-Comte-Robert, at Solers.

On April 16, according to Claude Monet's ledger,

Lunch, *1876,*
Oil on canvas, 52 × 75 cm.
Signed and dated lower right
"G. Caillebotte 1876"
The man on the right is the artist's brother René.

"Man in a Top Hat"
Caillebotte with his dog at the Place du Carrousel in Paris around 1876. In the background are the Rohan and Turgot pavilions of the Palais du Louvre. Caillebotte used this snapshot to paint himself standing on the Pont de l'Europe and for his preliminary sketches for that painting.

Camille Pissarro
Red Roofs, Village Square, Winter, 1877
Oil on canvas, 54.5 × 65.6 cm. Signed and dated lower right "C. Pissarro 1877"
This painting was part of Caillebotte's collection, which also included Pissarro's signed 1876 Woods with Seated Man and Woman. The latter work, which reminds us of paths in the southern part of the landscape park at Yerres, may indeed have been painted during a visit Pissarro made to Yerres in the summer of 1876 (see "The Impressionist Movement in French Brie").

Gustave Caillebotte acquires *Argenteuil Sketch*, a work that may be the same as *Sailboat Races at Argenteuil*. In it the Petit Gennevilliers house with its familiar roof and dormer windows, which will later belong to Gustave Caillebotte, can be seen clearly.

In the summer of this year Caillebotte resides at Yerres and paints, among other works, *Portraits in the Country.* Meanwhile, Edouard Manet is at Montgeron, Claude Monet at Yerres and Montgeron, and Pierre Auguste Renoir at Draveil-Champrosay.

In the autumn Gustave's brother René dies at the age of 25.

On November 3 Gustave, who is only 28, draws up his first will, as follows, "I stipulate that the necessary monies be taken from my estate to set up in 1878 and under the best possible conditions an exhibition of the painters known as 'intransigent' or 'impressionist.' At this writing it is difficult to know what sum will be required, perhaps as much as thirty or forty thousand francs or even more. The painters to be shown in this exhibition are

Degas, Monet, Pissarro, Renoir, Cézanne, Sisley, and Mademoiselle Morisot, all names I list without excluding others. I bequeath to the State the paintings in my possession with the proviso that, since I wish this gift to be accepted and the pictures not to end up in an attic or in a provincial museum but in the Luxembourg and later in the Louvre, a certain time elapse before the implementation of this clause until the public, I do not say understands, but accepts this kind of art. This may take 20 or more years; meanwhile my brother Martial or, in his stead, another of my heirs will be responsible for the paintings. I request that Renoir be my executor and that he accept a picture of his own choosing; my heirs will see that he takes an important one. Written in duplicate in Paris, November 3, 1876. Gustave Caillebotte"

1877

On January 17 Claude Monet advises the publisher Charpentier that he has a Paris address, 17 Rue Moncey in the Saint-Lazare neighborhood. Situated on the ground floor of a five-story building, the apartment consists of a small stoveless room, bedroom, and dressing room. No mention is made of a studio. The lease is in the name of Gustave Caillebotte who pays the quarterly rent of 175 francs. This small flat allows Claude Monet to receive art collectors whom it would be difficult to persuade to come to Argenteuil, and to paint the platforms of the Saint-Lazare train station and its immediate surroundings.

In the spring Ludovic Piette de Montfoucault writes Camille Pissarro, "Do not lose courage, jettison some of the cargo and save the ship. As you value my friendship I cannot give you better advice . . . I am pleased to hear that Monsieur Caillebotte has bought some pictures from you, that will give you time to get on our feet."

Emile Zola will write in 1877, " . . . When he becomes more fluent Monsieur Caillebotte will surely be one of the strongest of the group."

In April the third exhibition of painting is organized in an apartment at 6 Rue Le Peletier near Durand-Ruel, whose help is indispensable. Gustave Caillebotte participates actively in setting up the show, which includes, among others of his works, *Portraits in the Country*. This picture was mentioned in numerous articles, extracts from some of which we reproduce here:

April 8. "Best of all is his *Portraits in the Country*, admittedly much less Impressionist but infinitely more aesthetic and infinitely more true."

Le Moniteur Universel

April 12. "[In *Portraits in the Country*] an entire family, mother, daughter, grandmother, and friend, sit decorously sewing or doing needlepoint beside a white summer house whose half-open windows emit whiffs of the bourgeois life, in a perfection that rather alarms me. Nearby, marvelously symmetrical lime trees diminish toward the distance, shading beds in which raw red geraniums edged with green make a gay, clear background for this lackluster group of bored provincial ladies."

JACQUES, in *L'Homme Libre*

April 14. "... I should like to draw attention to the charming sunlit background of *Portraits in the Country* with its true notes..."

ROGER BALLU, Inspector of the Beaux Arts Exhibition of Impressionist Painters, in "Chronicle of Arts and Curios," published in the April 23, 1877 *Les Beaux Arts Illustrés*.

"... There is, however, a very great deal to admire in Monsieur Caillebotte, who does not indulge in what critics blindly refer to as a 'debauchery of color.' Is it possible that criticism has lumped everything under one heading? Has it not wished to see, in Monsieur Caillebotte, the fine, simple, very sincere, and very realistic drawing which is his best quality? Has it not cared to recognize the search for atmosphere and light, which, I agree, may result in perhaps a certain loss of color but does not lead the less to truth... Another Caillebotte canvas... also a *Portraits in a Garden,* has extremely true tones and an unusual but valid perspective. For a man who, as one critic has said, paints in his spare time, Monsieur Caillebotte hasn't done badly. Let us hope he will spare some of his time for the next exhibition."

GEORGES RIVIÈRE (1855–1943)
L'Impressioniste, Journal d'Art No. 2

Naturalism is said to have been born during the following meal, which Edmond de Goncourt describes in his *Journal, Mémoires de la Vie Littéraire* of April 16, 1877: "This evening the young men of the naturalist, realist movement in literature, Huysmans, Céard, Hennique, Paul Alexis, Octave Mirabeau, and Guy de Maupassant, honored Flaubert, Zola, and myself, who are the three officially anointed masters of the present hour, at a most cordial and jolly dinner. The new army is in the process of forming itself." This meal took place at the Trapp restaurant on the corner of the Rue Saint-Lazare and the Tivoli arcade. On May 9, 1878, de Goncourt will inform us, "This evening Flaubert, Zola, and I paid back the young realist, naturalist writers who treated us last year. At 11 o'clock Zola left to go find out how much money his play *The Bouton d'Or* is bringing in at the Palais Royal. He is turning into a real Dennery."

Frédéric Chevallier wrote in "The Impressionists," which appeared in the May 1 *L'Artiste,* "... His *Portraits in the Country* represents a serious achievement in its tone, outlines, and total effect. Air circulates transparently in the half-tint that envelops the figures, and the geranium-splashed garden stretches away under the sun into the distance. Monsieur Caillebotte's calm and precise execution puts him in the category of realist rather than an intransigent."

On May 28 Caillebotte helps organize and contributes work to the second sale of the Impressionists at the Hôtel Drouot.

In the summer at Yerres he paints different canvases whose settings include his family's

Paris, Profile of Painter at Work,
Seated in a Voltaire Armchair,
c. 1878
Oil on wood, 32.5 × 23.5 cm.
The artist painting a still life of game
birds in his Paris apartment. The
Voltaire armchair also appears in
Portrait of Richard Gallo, *1878. The*
drawing hanging above the armchair
appears to be a reverse image of the
drawing, Portrait of a Woman. *Artists*
at work seem to have been one of
Caillebotte's preoccupations at this time.
While living in Naples he painted A
Naples Road, *c. 1872. At Yerres he*
produced The Painter under His
Parasol, *c. 1878. In Paris, around*
1874, he did The Painter Morot in His
Studio. *All these works foreshadow* Self-
Portrait in Front of the Easel, *painted*
in 1879.

drawing room, the property's park, the banks of the Yerres River, the Meadow, and the Briard plateau.

In two undated letters, one of which Caillebotte writes to Camille Pissarro and the second, which Marie Berhaut places in 1877, which he addresses to the critic Théodore Duret (1838–1927), reference is made to a trip to London. At this time the work of Caillebotte's friend Giuseppe de Nittis, a very close friend of James Tissot (1836–1902), is being shown at London's fashionable and pretigious Grosvenor Gallery. Two years before, around 1875, Tissot has painted de Nittis and German artist Ferdinand Heilbuth (1829–1889) in a drawing-room doorway in his canvas *Hush! (the Concert).* Heilbuth has belonged to the Arts Club of Hanover Square since 1870 and will be a member until 1890. Tissot
has belonged since 1873 and will continue his membership until 1884; de Nittis, who joined in 1876, will belong until 1978.

In March 1875, de Nittis has written about seeing James Tissot. De Nittis has stayed with Tissot in 1876 at 77 Boundary Road and in 1877 near Wellington Road. A secondary tendency of official

Portrait of a Woman
Pencil on paper, dimensions unknown

art in Great Britain is represented by this club, which is particularly welcoming to its London visitors. The upper floors have several rooms available for the members' use.

1878

The Paris World's Fair opens in May. Gustave Caillebotte is 30 years old. Giuseppe de Nittis becomes a friend of Edmond de Goncourt. The painter Jean Béraud (1849–1936), who frequents the studio of Bonnat, paints what many called *An Evening at the Caillebottes.*

At Yerres during the summer Caillebotte works chiefly along the riverbank on his family's property, creating the last of his "Yerres period" canvases, which will total 80 paintings. Three of these pictures, *Fishing; Bathers, Banks of the Yerres;* and *Périssoire on the Yerres,* have the river as a theme and are intended to form an ensemble.

On August 31 in Brussels the Belgian naturalist novelist and art critic Camille Lemonnier (1844–1913) publishes an article in *L'Artiste* entitled "Art at the World's Fair: Those Who Were Not Represented," in which he writes, "I regret that Messieurs Degas and Monet have not shown their work and I feel the same disappointment regarding Messieurs Caillebotte and Forain. I should like to repeat here that these men have a subtle and very modern telegraphic style, of life taken on the spot. Side-by-side with astonishing flaws, one sees in their work a gift for sensation, which at times appears to exhaust itself in its search for the extreme, sharp, almost irritating edge of feeling, of depicting such incisive moments as are caught in unretouched photographs—exaggeratedly examined intimacies, a scribbled sharp note-taking, which is extremely true to life's nervousness as we see it expressed in gestures..."

On October 20 Caillebotte's mother dies.

Study for the Portrait of Madame
Martial Caillebotte Senior, *c. 1877*
Pencil on paper, dimensions unknown

"The Property at Yerres"
The lawn in front of the "casin." Note
the state of maintenance of the house and
its grounds at the time.

Gustave Caillebotte in 1878

On December 20 Claude Monet sets up his studio at 20 Rue de Vintimille, ground floor left, in an apartment rented in the name of Gustave Caillebotte. This gives Monet the moral support and material assistance he often urgently needs. The friendship between the two artists will last until Caillebotte's death.

1879
The family property at Yerres is sold.

From April 10 to May 11 the fourth exhibition of paintings is held at 28 Avenue de l'Opéra. Fourteen of Gustave Caillebotte's Yerres-period canvases are shown.

On April 17 Louis Leroy writes in *Beaux-Arts*, "... there's a great deal of independence also in the river scene in Number 13. [Caillebotte's] grassy waves have the freshness and solidity of a green field before the harvest. Adding to its charm are the two rowers plowing effortlessly through it with their oars. Tough fellows to be able to navigate such grass..."

On April 23 J. R. Draner includes on his page of caricatures in the paper *Le Charivari* three sketches of Caillebotte's Yerres canvases.

In May Arsène Housset, who uses the pen name F. C. de Syene, writes in *L'Artiste*, "... Little by little Impressionism is imposing its character on modern art... where it feels at home, can maneuver freely, raise its voice, abandon itself to

CATALOGUE
DE LA

4ᴹᴱ EXPOSITION

DE PEINTURE

PAR

M. Bracquemond — Mᵐᵉ Bracquemond
M. Caillebotte — M. Cals — Mˡˡᵉ Cassatt
MM. Degas — Forain — Lebourg — Monet
Pissarro — Feu Piette
Rouart — H. Somm — Tillot et Zandomenighi.

Du 10 Avril au 11 Mai 1879

De 10 heures à 6 heures
28, AVENUE DE L'OPÉRA, 28
PARIS

— 2 —

6 — Une vue du Pont des Saints-Pères. (Eau forte, publiée par le journal l'*Art*.)

CAILLEBOTTE (Gustave)
31, boulevard Haussmann

7 — Canotiers.
8 — Partie de bateau.
9 — Périssoires.
10 — Périssoires.
11 — Vue de toits.
    Appartient à M. A. C...
12 — Vue de toits. (Effet de neige.)
    Appartient à M. K...
13 — Canotier ramenant sa périssoire.
14 — Rue Halévy, vue d'un sixième étage.
    Appartient à M. H...
15 — Portrait de M. F...
16 — Portrait de M. G...
17 — Portrait de M. D...
18 — Portrait de M. E. D...
19 — Portrait de M. R...
20 — Portrait de Mᵐᵉ C...

— 3 —

21 — Por... dit te b...
22 — Portrait de Mᵐᵉ H...
23 — Pêche à la ligne.
24 — Baigneurs.   Panneaux décora...
25 — Périssoires.
26 — Baigneurs. (Pastel.)
    Appartient à M. G. M...
27 — Canotiers. (Pastel.)
28 — Vallée de l'Yerres. (Pastel.)
    Appartient à M. S...
29 — Potager. (Pastel.)
30 — Rivière d'Yerres. (Pastel.)
    Appartient à M. S...
31 — Prairie. (Pastel.)

V
CALS (Adolphe-Félix)
Chez M. Martin, 52, rue Saint-Georges

32 — L'heureuse mère.
33 — Soleil couchant.
34 — Étude. Tête de femme.
35 — Bassin à Honfleur.
36 — Ferme du Butin — Honfleur — Matin de juin.

all its original verve, and take full advantage of its freedom. In the canvases of Messieurs Caillebotte, Monet, and Pissarro especially the new school shows itself at its most expressive . . . An outing of rowboats, kayaks, and canoes provides Monsieur Caillebotte with a vehicle to paint living, moving human beings, water splashing, and foliage drowning in light or bathed in transparent shadow . . ."

On May 11–13 in his correspondence with F. Bracquemond, Edgar Degas, who is involved with the launching of *Le Jour et la Nuit* (see below), a magazine devoted to the group's graphic works, writes, "I spoke to Caillebotte about the magazine; he is prepared to stand surety for us . . . Come see me so we can talk. There's no time to lose . . . Many things have to be decided and arranged about the magazine so we can present some kind of program to our backers."

May 17. Pages 6 and 7 of *Le Monde Parisien* contain a section of caricatures by Bec entitled "A Glance at the Independents." Included are the following works by Gustave Caillebotte, *Oarsmen on the Yerres,* 1877; *Périssoires on the Yerres,* 1877; and three canvases mentioned in the exhibition's catalogue and therefore undoubtedly part of the show, the 1878 *The Orange Trees, Portrait of Madame X,* and *Place Saint-Augustin, Misty Weather,* c. 1878; in Berhaut's 1978 work (see Bibliography) mention is made, on page 249 in the chapter entitled "Caillebotte's Participation in Exhibitions," of four uncatalogued and unattributed pictures, three of which would be among the Bec caricatures.

Meanwhile, in June, Charles-Albert d'Arnoux, known as Bertall, writes in *L'Artiste,* on the subject of the fourth exhibition in April, ". . . While Monsieur Manet has passed over bag and baggage into the crusaders' camp, Monsieur Caillebotte has firmly seized the helm of this ship, which would otherwise perhaps drift aimlessly . . . Among the 34 canvases of the new pundit are many amazing boatmen, prophetic boatmen, marvelous landscapes carved in vivid blue and intense green . . ."

Members of Gustave Caillebotte's family (right foreground) with friends on a path in the park, c. 1877 or earlier. This may be the same path we see in Yerres, Lawn in the Park Seen from a Path, Sunset Number 1.

In Pierre Auguste Renoir's *Boaters at Chatou*, Renoir's future wife Aline Charigot and Gustave Caillebotte serve as models.[67]

Gustave Caillebotte paints *Self-Portrait in Front of the Easel.*

Renoir's 1876 *Ball at the Moulin de la Galette*, which has been shown at the third exhibition in 1877, appears on the wall of Caillebotte's Boulevard Haussmann apartment in Paris.

1880
"Finally, Monsieur Caillebotte is a very conscientious artist who, though somewhat dry in execution, has the courage of the grand effort and pursues his goals resolutely and with the most virile determination."

EMILE ZOLA, 1880

On January 24 *Le Gaulois* announces that the first number of the magazine *Le Jour et la Nuit*, due February first, will include prints by Edgar Degas, Mary Cassatt, Gustave Caillebotte, Camille Pissarro, Jean-Louis Forain, Félix Bracquemond, Jean-Françoise Raffaelli, and Henri Rouart. *Le Jour et la Nuit* will appear at no fixed date, its price

Pierre Auguste Renoir
Boaters at Chatou, *1879*
Oil on canvas, 81 × 100 cm.

280

Pierre Auguste Renoir
Ball at the Moulin de la Galette, *1876*
Oil on canvas, 131 × 175 cm.

will vary between 5 and 20 francs depending on the number of works it contains, and the resulting profits or losses will be shared by those involved in the magazine's production. The project will remain in its planning stage.

Toward the end of January or early February Alice Hoschedé writes to Ernest Hoschedé, "Monsieur Monet asks you to let him know by wire where the *Pink Frost* is, because he has sent Monsieur Caillebotte to the Rue de Vintimille many times to take this canvas, always in vain."

Of the historian and art critic Phillippe Burty (1830–1890) Edmond de Goncourt writes in his *Journal* of April 22, "The following is typical Burty: 'Oh! do not spring Hoschedé on Edmond, spare him his visit,' he told de Nittis and the very same morning went to see Hoschedé himself to propose some articles on Japanese style."

From April 1 to April 30 the fifth exhibition of a group of independent artists takes place at 10 Rue des Pyramides in Paris. In the show are 11 pictures by Gustave Caillebotte, among them perhaps the pastel *Landscapes near Yerres*. The month before, a dispute has arisen between Edgar Degas and Gustave Caillebotte over the poster for this exhibition; Degas has not wished the names of the participants to appear. In a letter to Félix Bracquemond Degas writes, "I was forced to give in to him and allow them to be listed. When will this love of the limelight end?"

April 9. In a letter Mary Cassatt's mother Katherine Cassatt writes to Edgar Degas, she blames him for the failure of *Le Jour et la Nuit*.

"...A love of sailing was what attracted [Caillebotte] to this side of the Seine. He was Vice Commodore of the Paris-Argenteuil, a club that brought boat fanatics together. Yachtsmen as far as Rouen knew him as a trophy winner. He designed his own boats and gave them colorful names like *White Tail* and *Roastbeef*. The famous *Condor*, which he skippered with two freshwater sailors on the foredeck had a mainsail made of white silk decorated with an heraldic cat."

JEAN PRASTEAU

Caillebotte becomes Vice Commodore of the Sailing Club of Paris, founded in 1868 and given its name in 1872.

Tin tin
Is the song
Sung by all the sailors on the Seine,
Tin tin
Is the song,
Long live the Seine and good wine!

Caillebotte sails *Condor* often in 1880 and will enjoy this boat frequently in 1881 and 1882.[68]

1880–1881
Pierre Auguste Renoir appears to have used Gustave Caillebotte as a model in *Luncheon of the Boating Party* (The Phillips Collection, Washington, D.C.) at the Maison Fournaise on the island of Chatou, though this has been contested.

1881

On February 5 Caillebotte's teacher Leon Bonnat is elected to the Académie des Beaux-Arts.

In the spring the Nineteenth Infantry Regiment undergoes training.

From April 2 to May 1 the sixth exhibition of painting is held at 25 Boulevard des Capucines in Paris. For personal reasons, specifically a disagreement with Degas, Caillebotte does not participate, but he actively prepares for the show planned for 1882.

Sketches of two boats, Inès *and* Condor, *owned by Gustave Caillebotte*

On April 6 Edmond de Goncourt writes in his *Journal*, "At Nittis' I read aloud the beginning of *La Faustin* to Zola, Daudet, Herédia, Charpentier, and their families and to the young realists, and I got a surprise. The chapters most based on real life do not seem to hold up. On the other hand, the ones I think little of, the ones inspired by pure imagination, gripped my small public . . ." In this novel Goncourt examines the way in which an actress is assimilated into her surroundings.

1882

"The year 1882, which marks the end of Caillebotte's participation in Impressionist events, is also an important date in his artistic development. The works he exhibits in 1882 reveal a synthesis of the different themes that have

A Soldier, *c. 1879*
Oil on canvas, 106 × 75 cm.
Stamped lower right

inspired him so far—the Yerres river, views of Paris, interiors, and portraits. But now there also appear scenes of the countryside and the Normandy coast, which open out, in a way, to the series of landscapes and seascapes that, with still lifes, game animals, and flowers will become almost exclusively the themes of his second period."

(MARIE BERHAUT)

From May 1 to 31, probably, the seventh exhibition of the Independent Artists takes place at 251 Rue Saint-Honoré in Paris, at the Panorama de Reichshoffen, in rooms where the Messieurs Franconi's first "Olympic Circus" was constructed by Jean-Baptiste Coignet and Maximillian Heurtault. In this show Gustave Caillebotte exhibits 17 canvases including *Game of Bezique*, in which his brother Martial Caillebotte, his Yerres neighbor Maurice Brault, and other friends serve as models. Caillebotte has painted this picture in

Game of Bezique, *1881*

Oil on canvas, 121 × 161 cm.

From left to right, Edouard Dessommes, Paul Hugot, Maurice Brault, Richard Gallo, A. Cassabois, and the artist's brother Martial Caillebotte. According to Dauzat, the name "bezique" for this card game appeared around 1820. In Paul Emile Littrés Dictionary of the French Language *the game is described as similar to "brisque" or to "matrimony": "In matrimony, bezique, and quarante, brisques are tens and aces, which count as ten and take the other cards. When the hand is over, each player adds up his brisques . . ." In the August 20, 1877 review* Nineteenth Century *the term "brisque" was described as military slang for a long service stripe or badge, as in, "an old sergeant with three brisques." This composition, essentially because of its subject matter, was compared to 17th-century Flemish paintings. It might also have been compared to* The Academy, *a 116 × 145 cm. work attributed to the brothers Le Nain, which appeared in a public sale at the Hôtel des Ventes in Paris on March 1, 1875.* The Academy *represented a gathering of seven aristocrats or upper-middle-class men and clergymen gathered around a table at the home of a rich man to indulge their mutual passion. At the sale the painting was attributed to a 17th-century Flemish artist, but after the critic Champfleury wrote an enthusiastic note to the* Chronique des Arts *declaring it should be attributed to the brothers Le Nain, it was acquired by the Louvre in 1892.*

his Paris apartment on the Boulevard Haussmann. Of it Joris Karl Huysmans (1848–1907) has the following to say: "I have already expressed myself at length on the work of [Monsieur Caillebotte], in my comments on the 1880 Salon. I remarked then on the truth and exactness of his figures' attitudes and appearance and of the surroundings in which they move. This year his great qualities continue intact; he retains the same mature sense of modernism, the same calm bravura of execution, the same scrupulous study of light. Two of his canvases are extraordinary. One, *Game of Bezique* is more true to life than anything by the old Flemish painters, where almost always the players look at us out of the corners of their eyes as if posing for the public; this is especially true of the good Teniers. None of that is seen here. Imagine that a window is open in the wall of the room and that facing us and hidden from view by the casement's frame you are able to watch people smoking, absorbed, frowning, hesitating over their cards, pondering a triumphant bid of 250! . . . Since these two canvases are on a par with the ones I have already mentioned, I will not repeat myself by insisting on their originality. I shall limit myself simply, in this supplement to my comments on earlier exhibitions, to stressing the suppleness and variety of this painter who at the Panorama gave us samples of every kind, interiors, landscapes, seascapes and still lifes . . . Although literary and artistic injustices no longer have the power to upset me, I am surprised in spite of myself at the persistent silence of the press toward such a painter."

This same year Caillebotte enlarges his Petit Gennevilliers house, which is situated on the so-called "L'Isle aux Draps" between the Argenteuil bridge and Colombes. *The Seine at Argenteuil*, 1882 is painted from the Petit Gennevilliers side of the river and is the first known and dated work done near this house.

Caillebotte's name disappears from the lease of the ground-floor left apartment at 20 Rue de Vintimille and appears on a 1882–1883 lease of the ground floor right in the same building, on behalf of Claude Monet.

Caillebotte designs the sailboat *Jack*.

1883
On April 30 Edouard Manet dies.

During the summer Pierre Auguste Renoir, staying at Petit Gennevilliers, paints a portrait of Caillebotte's friend Charlotte Berthier.

On November 20 Gustave draws up a second will, which reads, "This is my testament. A previous document drawn up by me in 1876 following the death of my brother René will be found at the home of my friend Albert Courtier. I retain all that part of said will which has to do with my gift of paintings by other artists in my possession. All having to do with the exhibition of 1878 naturally becomes void. Paris, the twentieth November, eighteen hundred eighty-three. Gustave Caillebotte."

1884
On February 24 Gustave Caillebotte buys Edouard Manet's painting *The Balcony*.

Martial and Gustave Caillebotte in 1886.

The garden, greenhouse, and house at Petit Gennevilliers. The photograph was taken between 1891 and 1894 by Martial Caillebotte.

Gustave Caillebotte and his gardener at Petit Gennevilliers. The photograph was taken between 1891 and 1894 by Martial Caillebotte. Here, as in the kitchen garden at Yerres, fruit trees are espaliered in fan shapes with oblique branches. Standard roses are in the second bed.

On August 21 Giuseppe de Nittis dies at the age of 38.[69]

1885
On March 21 Gustave Caillebotte becomes the godfather of Pierre Renoir, son of Pierre Auguste Renoir and his future wife Aline Charigot. The address given on the birth certificate is 18 Rue Houdon, Paris.

1886
Gustave Caillebotte participates in Paul Durand-Ruel's New York exhibition advertised as "Works in Oil and Pastel by 'the Impressionists of Paris' at the National Academy of Design." Three of Caillebotte's Yerres-period works are included in this show.

1887
As Jean Prasteau has described it, "Across the sewage landfill a path leads toward an almost hidden, very isolated and remote spot called Petit Gennevilliers, several houses below the Argenteuil bridge on the edge of a place called L'Ile aux Draps. A boatyard there produced the vessels that appear in the Impressionist canvases. Facing Monet's view of the water, a small villa regularly caught the attention of passengers on the steamer *Le Touriste*, which on Sundays made the three-and-a-half-hour passage from Pont-Royal to Saint-Germain-en-Laye. The superb garden overflowed with roses and dahlias. The glass panes of the large greenhouse, in which the owner of this small suburban castle propagated his plants by cutting, glittered in the sunlight. A modest dock at his door permitted him to step aboard his boat. The name of this happy gardener on the banks of the Seine was Caillebotte."

In 1887 Gustave's brother Martial marries, and Gustave settles permanently into the house at Petit Gennevilliers.[70] According to Jacques Hillairet, he keeps a small pied à terre at 29 Boulevard de Rochechouart in Paris.

"From the park at Yerres to the garden at Petit Gennevilliers, Caillebotte's art evolved toward greater freedom and a spontaneity similar to that of his friend Monet... During Caillebotte's last years, this Petit Gennevilliers property situated on the banks of the Seine became an endless source of themes just as Giverny provided unending inspiration to Monet... Caillebotte shared the latter's passion for gardening... he felt the same love of the ever-present flowers that appeared in his work. Monet wrote him often from Giverny and invited him to visit his garden... Over and over Caillebotte portrays Petit Gennevilliers' paths and flower beds with their profusion of dahlias, roses, chrysanthemums and sunflowers, and borders of iris and hyacinth." (SYLVIE GACHE-PATIN)

1888
On February 6 the "Sixth Exhibition of the Twenty" opens in Brussels, with Gustave Caillebotte as a participant.

Portrait of Madame Renoir, c. 1888
Oil on canvas, 73 × 59 cm.

On May 6 and 13 he is elected Town Councillor of Gennevilliers.

By June he is a member of such municipal bodies as the Projects Bureau, Board of Education, Schools Commission, and Public Festivals Committee.

From May 25 to June 25 Caillebotte's paintings hang with the exhibition of "Impressionist and Post Impressionist Painters" at the Durand-Ruel Gallery, 11 Rue Le Peletier and 16 Rue Lafitte, which is this gallery's Paris address from 1867 to 1924.

In September Pierre Auguste Renoir and Aline Charigot are Caillebotte's guests at Petit Gennevilliers.

1890

On February 7 Caillebotte writes Armand Fallières (1841–1931), Minister of Education and Overseer of the Beaux-Arts, "In the name of a group of subscribers I have the honor of offering the State Edouard Manet's *Olympia*. In the opinion of the great majority of persons interested in French painting, the role of Edouard Manet has been useful and decisive. Not only has he played an important role as an individual but he has also been part of a great and fruitful evolution. It seems impossible to us, therefore, that such a work should not have its place in our national collection, that the master not be represented where many of his disciples are already admitted. We have also been disquieted by the ceaseless movement of the art market, by the competition from America in purchasing and carrying off to another continent so many works of art which are the joy and the glory of France . . . Our desire is to see *Olympia* hanging in the Louvre in its own time and among the works of the French school . . . We hope that in lending your support to this work to which we are devoted you will derive the satisfaction which is the reward for the simple performance of a just act." There follows the list of donors: "Bracquemond, Philippe Burty, Albert Besnard, Maurice Bouchor, Félix Bouchor-de-Bellio, Jean Béraud, Berend, Marcel Bernstein, Bing, Léon Beclard, Edmond

Launching of one of Gustave Caillebotte's boats. The photograph was taken by Martial Caillebotte between 1891 and 1894.

Bazire, Jacques Blanche, Boldini, Blot, Bourdin, Cazin, Eugène Carrière, Jules Chéret, Emmanuel Chabrier-Clapisson, Gustave Caillebotte, Carriès, Degas, Desboutin, Dalou, Carolus Duran, Duez, Durand-Ruel, Dauphin, Armand Dayot, Jean Dolent, Théodore Duret, Fantin-Latour, Auguste Flameng, (Henri) Guérard, Madame Guérard-Gonzalès, Paul Gallimard, Gervex, Guillemet, Gustave Geffroy, J. K. Huysmans, Maurice Hamel, (Alexandre) Harrison, Helleu, Jeanniot, Frantz Jourdain, Lhermitte, Lerolle, Monsieur and Madame Leclanché, Stéphane Mallarmé, Octave Mirbeau, Roger Marx, Moreau Nélaton, Alexandre Millerand, Claude Monet, Oppenheim, Puvis de Chavannes, Antonin Proust, Camille Pelletan, Camille Pissarro, Portier, Georges Petit, Rolin, T. Ribot, Renoir, J. F. Raffaelli, Ary Renan, Roll-Robin, H. Rouart, Felicien Rops, J.

Madame Renoir in the Garden at Petit Gennevilliers, *c. 1891*
Oil on canvas, 65 × 50 cm.
Signed lower left "G. Caillebotte"
Photograph by Martial Caillebotte

Sargent, Madame de Scey-Montbéliard, Thornley, De Vuillefroy, Van Cutsem, anonymous donors A. H., H. H., L. N., R. G." In the same year *Olympia* is accepted by the Musée du Luxembourg.

1891

From September 29 to October 30 Pierre Auguste Renoir stays at Petit Gennevilliers.

1892

On May 6 Gustave Caillebotte attends a dinner given by Renoir at the Café Riche[71] to celebrate his exhibition, in the tradition of Impressionist dinners. Mallarmé, Monet, Duret, and de Bellio are also present.

On February 19 Father Caillebotte, priest of the parish of Nôtre-Dame-de-Lorette in Paris, solemnizes the marriage of Pierre Camille Daurelle, son of Jean-Baptiste Daurelle, the Caillebotte family employee who has often posed as a model in Gustave's paintings.

1894

On February 21, while working on a landscape in his garden, Gustave Caillebotte is stricken by a cerebral hemorrhage and dies at the age of 46. He is buried in Section 70 of the Père Lachaise Cemetery in Paris.

AFTER THE DEATH OF THE PAINTER:
THE DISPOSITION OF
THE CAILLEBOTTE COLLECTION
AND OF HIS OWN WORKS

Ambroise Vollard in 1938:
"In your capacity as Caillebotte's executor you must have had more than one disagreement with Roujon about getting the Impressionists into the Luxembourg."

Pierre Auguste Renoir:
"To tell the truth, I have never gotten along with Roujon about anything. Not that he lacks wit nor that he is not pleasant to deal with, but to get along with him it would have been necessary for me not to pronounce the name of a single one of the painters I loved. You can imagine our discussions about the Caillebotte collection. Roujon was willing to accept the Degas and the Manets but not all of them; he rejected one or two . . . My own painting made him uneasy, and he did not try to hide this. The only canvas of mine he had confidence in was the *Ball at the Moulin de la Galette* because Gervex was in it. He considered the presence of a member of the Institute among my models a guarantee of moral probity. On the other hand, he was rather disposed to taste, not to use too farfetched a word, Monet, Sisley, and Pissarro because the art world was beginning to accept them. But when he came to the Cézannes! Those landscapes that are as balanced as Poussins, those bathers whose colors seem to have been stolen straight from ancient glazed potteries, in fact all that supremely good art . . . I can still hear Roujon: 'That one, for example, if he ever comes to understand what painting is!'"

Pierre Auguste Renoir in the garden of his house in Montmartre, winter. The photograph was taken by Martial Caillebotte, around 1891–92. The basilica was then in the process of construction.

Pierre Auguste Renoir as he appears in snapshots in Self-Portrait, *at Williamstown, Massachusetts, usually dated 1897–98.*

1894

Pierre Auguste Renoir, whom Caillebotte named as his executor and gave the opportunity to "take a painting of his choice," chooses Degas' *The Dancing Lesson*. This canvas, deposited with Paul Durand-Ruel on March 13, 1894, will be handed over to Martial Caillebotte on March 13, 1895.

March 11. In a letter to Henri Roujon, Director of the Beaux-Arts, Renoir reveals Caillebotte's bequest. Renoir has the Caillebotte collection moved from Petit Gennevilliers to his Paris studio at 11 Boulevard de Clichy.

March 19. The paintings are presented to the Director of the Beaux-Arts and to the Curator of the Musée du Luxembourg.

March 20. In an official report, the Comité Consultatif des Musées gives a favorable opinion on accepting the bequest.

March 22. The Caillebotte family donates *The Floor Scrapers* to the National Museums.

In April Martial Caillebotte prepares the necessary papers for the State's reception of his brother's gift.

April 27. The State accepts *The Floor Scrapers*.

On May 4 and 5 Renoir thanks Henri Roujon and the Minister of Trusteeships for accepting the bequest.

May 1. Henri Roujon informs Martial Caillebotte that the collection is too big and cannot be admitted in its entirety by the Musée du Luxembourg, where space is limited.

From June 4 to 16, 123 canvases by Gustave Caillebotte are exhibited in a retrospective show of his work at the Gallery Durand-Ruel, 16 Rue Lafitte and 11 Rue le Peletier. Edgar Degas buys *Yellow Roses in a Vase*, 1882.

June 22. Leonce Benedite, the Luxembourg's curator, announces that to make a selection among the works in the Caillebotte bequest would not respect the legator's wishes and that the State must accept the collection as a whole or forego all of it. A plan is put forward to divide the bequest, giving the Musée du Luxembourg twenty-five or thirty works

The Floor Scrapers, *1875,*
Oil on canvas, 102 × 146 cm.
Signed and dated lower right, "G. Caillebotte 1875"
"[Paris,] 7 September—From my window I can see a parquet layer working naked to the waist in the gallery. In comparing the color of his skin to that of the exterior wall, I notice how highly colored the flesh half-tones are compared to inert materials." Eugène Delacroix, Journal, *1856*

295

*Announcement of the Caillebotte
retrospective*

and sending the balance to the Musée de Compiègne and the Musée de Fontainebleau. This, too, does not respect the terms of the will. December 7. Leonce Benedite informs Renoir that the State has definitely accepted the bequest.

1895
Renoir paints *Portraits of Children*, a picture of Martial Caillebotte's small son Jean and little daughter Geneviève, Gustave Caillebotte's nephew and niece.

January. Rumor has it that the State is refusing the bequest.

1896
Father Alfred Caillebotte, curate of Nôtre-Dame-de-Lorette dies. Father Caillebotte has personally helped refurbish this church, which is described as follows in the catalogue of the 1900 World's Fair: "The exterior is of interest only for its portico and the tympanum representing angels adoring the infant Jesus presented to them by the Virgin. The sumptuous and smartly decorated interior makes this church one of the city's most fashionable. Most of the paintings in the nave and choir depict important events in the Virgin's life. From right to left around the nave are 'The Birth of the Virgin' by Monvoisin, 'The Consecration' by Vinchon, 'The Marriage of the Virgin' by Langlois and 'The Annunciation' by Dubois. In the choir are 'Jesus and the Doctors' by Drolling, 'The Coronation of the Virgin' by Picot and 'The Presentation' by Heim. To the left as we return toward the entrance we see 'The Visitation' by Dubois, 'The Adoration of the Shepherds' by Hesse and 'The Assumption' by Dejuinne. The chapels off the outer aisles are decorated with frescoes of the lives of the saints. On the right, starting from the entrance, are 'The Martyrdom of Saint Hippolyte' by Hesse, then 'Saint Hyacinthe' by Jeannot and 'Saint Theresa' by Decaisne. On the left, from the entrance, are 'Saint Genevieve' by Devéria, 'Saint Philibert' by Schnetz and 'Saint Stephen' by Champmartin and Couder." In the 1968 *Guide Bleu* to Paris we read, "The interior [gives] a general impression of

Pierre Auguste Renoir
Portraits of Children, *1895,*
Oil on canvas, 65 × 82 cm.
Signed and dated lower right "Renoir
94"
Jean and Geneviève , children of Martial
and Marie Caillebotte; the painter's
nephew and niece

opulence and magnificence in contrast to the austerity of the façade . . . in the nave [on the left] is an altarpiece by Etex . . ." The painter Oscar-Claude Monet, who was born on November 14, 1840, at 45 Rue Lafitte, was baptized in this church on May 20, 1841.

On February 25 it is announced that thirty-eight of the sixty-seven works in the Caillebotte collection have been accepted, along with two drawings.

On June 22 *The Floor Scrapers* is hung in the Musée du Luxembourg.

On July 15 Martial Caillebotte accompanies Pierre Auguste Renoir to Germany. Their itinerary includes a visit to Bayreuth. Fifteen years earlier, on January 14, 1882, Renoir called on Richard Wagner in Palermo, where the composer finished his opera *Parsifal*, and on the day following his call, January 15, Wagner sat for Renoir for thirty-five minutes for a portrait commissioned by the music lover Lascoux, then Judge of the Supreme Court of Appeal.

On November 23 the French Government takes possession of a portion of the works destined for the Musée du Luxembourg.

1897
In February an annex intended to house the Caillebotte collection is opened at the Musée du Luxembourg.

On March 8 eighteen members of the Académie des Beaux-Arts address an official protest to the Minister of National Education against "[this] offense to the dignity of our school."

On May 16 in an interpellation of the Government by the Senate, Senator Hervé de Saisy rails against "[this sudden] invasion of works of highly equivocal character [which sully the Musée du Luxembourg, that] sanctuary of true artists [which until now has been] pure of any compromise." Henri Roujon answers in the name of the Government: "Although many of us do not consider Impressionism to be art's last word, we do consider it an artistic expression that has the right to be uttered, and we consider the Impressionist movement, which has interested a sector of the public, to be a chapter in the history of contemporary painting which it is our duty to inscribe on the walls of our museums. It falls to visitors to the Musée du Luxembourg to judge, in the style of the day, its proper place."

1898
December 12. Following a quarrel with Edgar Degas, Renoir sells *The Dancing Lesson*, a work he has chosen in 1894 from Gustave Caillebotte's collection in accordance with instructions in the will, to Durand-Ruel for 25,000 francs. On

December 31 this picture is sent to New York and within a few weeks is acquired by Mr. and Mrs. Havemeyer.

1900

In the catalogue published by the Librairie Hachette for the World's Fair the following appears: "The Musée du Luxembourg is the Louvre's antichamber where living artists await the consecration and triumph of death. From among works on display at the Luxembourg the State chooses who shall enter gloriously and definitely into the Louvre . . . A wide eclecticism reigns at the Luxembourg. United there we find the best that each of today's schools has to offer, and the visitor is able to follow the evolution in art and especially in painting from the end of Romanticism through the Classical Revival to the present day . . . A glance at the Musée du Luxembourg's entire collection reveals the increasingly marked tendencies of painting, despite all its divergences, toward the natural and toward everything in life that is most discerning, sharp, fascinating, unexpected, and human. What dominates French art today is no longer formal composition but the often exquisite quality of intention . . . Returning to the sculpture gallery, we come to two rooms on the left reserved for the works of the Impressionist painters (the Caillebotte Gallery, named for their donor) and, in the second of these two chambers, for a number of good paintings by foreigners. In the Caillebotte Gallery, from right to left, we see *Notre-Dame de Paris*,[72] a gray almost colorless Paris scene by Raffaelli; *The Farmyard* by Sisley; *The Gare Saint-Lazare* by Claude Monet; *Olympia* by Manet, who was the father of Impressionism; and *The Church at Vetheuil* by Claude Monet. Hanging above these paintings are *The Harvest* by Pissarro, *Banks of the Seine* by Sisley, *Road Leading Upward Through Fields* by Pissarro, Manet's *The Balcony*, and Degas' *Ballet Dancers, Dancers on Stage, A Boulevard Café,* and *Woman at Her Bath*. Above the Degas pictures are *The Lunch*, a beautiful outdoor study by Claude Monet; *The Old Convalescents*[72] by

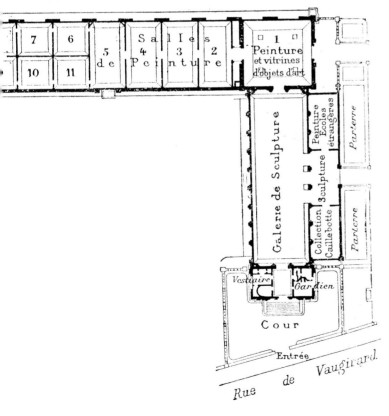

Plan of the Musée du Luxembourg in 1900 showing the room of the Caillebotte collection

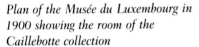

299

Raffaelli; *Frost* by Monet; *The Morning's Soup*[72] by Goeneutte; *Ball at the Moulin de la Galette* by Renoir; *Rooftops in the Snow*[73] by Caillebotte; *Young Girls at the Piano*[72] by Renoir; and Manet's *Angelina* . . ."

1902–1906

It is interesting to recall here Paul Assouline's remarks about Daniel Henri Kahnweiler in the book *Daniel Henri Kahnweiler, Man of Art*: "The first time [Kahnweiler] visits the Caillebotte Gallery he is disconcerted. He sees, of course, the difference between these pictures and others hung elsewhere in the Luxembourg, but he cannot comprehend what it is he is looking at—spots of meaningless color. He refuses to judge hastily. He resolves to come back. [Kahnweiler] has never ceased to remind himself to be modest in the presence of paintings, better still, to be humble, and a better opportunity has never presented itself to put this precept of his into practice. After several visits directly to this room, ignoring completely its 'deplorable' surroundings, he grows used to these spots of color and takes pleasure in them without trying to impute a meaning. It would not occur to him to look at a picture as an end in itself; in his view this would amount to an intellectual exercise. Little by little, under his eyes there springs from these rows of canvases 'a wonderful moving world filled with air and light,' a real painter's universe with clouds and shadows, shapes and colors in total contradiction of the academicism surrounding it. This way of painting, new and alive, comes not as a shock but as a progressive discovery, the fruit of calm reflection, of a slow maturing, of apprenticeship and getting used to."

In 1937 Ambroise Vollard writes, "I recall, after that disappointment, running into the collector's brother Martial Caillebotte and his saying, 'Vollard, you know Benedite (who was then the Luxembourg's curator), couldn't you persuade him to give asylum in the attic to the one in the lot that they refused (Renoir, Sisley, Cézanne, and Manet were the rejected paintings) so if the wind changes

Rooftops in the Snow, *c. 1878*
Oil on canvas, 64 × 82 cm.
Signed lower left "G. Caillebotte"

Edouard Manet. Compare this photograph with Gustave Caillebotte's 1878 Oarsman in a Top Hat.

he can hang them in the Museum?...' I ran to Benedite. I can still hear him: 'What, me, a civil servant the State has placed its confidence in, receive canvases the Commission has refused!'..."

1907

January 6. After Claude Monet and Gustave Geffroy intercede with Prime Minister George Clemenceau, Dujardin-Beaumetz is ordered to hang Edouard Manet's *Olympia* in the Louvre. *Olympia* is placed in the State Gallery next to *The Great Odalisque* by Jean-Auguste Ingres, and it creates an uproar, twenty-four years after the artist's death.

1910

Martial Caillebotte dies.

1921

A retrospective exhibition of Gustave Caillebotte's works is held at the Salon d'Automne in Paris.

1929

Thirty-five years after the death of their donor, paintings accepted from the Caillebotte bequest are transferred from the Musée du Luxembourg to the Louvre.

1947

The "Impressionist Museum" is founded in the ancient Jeu de Paume in the Tuileries in Paris.

1951

From May 25 to July 25 a retrospective showing of the works of Gustave Caillebotte is held at the Beaux-Arts Gallery, 140 Rue du Faubourg Saint-Honoré, Paris.

1958

After three years of work on the Impressionist Museum in the old Jeu de Paume, the Museum reopens its doors. A room on the second floor is called "The Caillebotte Gallery."

1965

From June 18 to September 5 an exhibition, "Caillebotte and His Impressionist Friends," is held at the Musée de Chartres.

1966

On February 3 Claude Monet's son Michel dies, leaving the following works by Gustave Caillebotte, which had belonged to his father, to the Académie des Beaux-Arts of the French Institute: *Paris Street: Rainy Weather* (sketch), 1877; *The Piano Lesson*, 1881; and *White and Yellow Chrysanthemums, Garden at Petit Gennevilliers*, c. 1893.

In June and July an exhibition, "Gustave Caillebotte 1848–1894," takes place at the Wildenstein Gallery, 147 New Bond Street, London.

Paris Street: Rainy Weather, *1877*
Oil on canvas, 54 × 65 cm.

Piano Lesson, 1881
Oil on canvas, 81 × 65 cm.

From September 18 to October 19 the exhibition "Gustave Caillebotte" is held at the Wildenstein Gallery, 19 East 64th Street, New York.

1976
In January the regional historian Maurice Lahaye writes as follows about Gustave Caillebotte at Yerres: "One cannot even think of writing about Yerres without speaking of this painter. As we ourselves are unqualified in the matter of art, we reproduce for our readers a short account prepared by Mademoiselle Marie Berhaut, who is at work on a book on this painter, scheduled for publication early next summer. We are deeply indebted to Mademoiselle Berhaut for her kindness on our behalf. 'Thanks to Gustave Caillebotte (Paris 1848–Gennevilliers 1894) Yerres enjoys the privilege of being among the geographical sites that illustrate the itinerary of the Impressionist painters. On the left bank of the river south of the old village the imposing Directoire-style family house where Caillebotte spent his youthful summers still exists. This painter's first period is represented by thirty-odd paintings executed between 1874 and 1881, which have as their subjects this house with its outbuildings, its green lawns and flower beds, its beautiful park planted with trees of many different species, and its kitchen garden. Often these canvases are enlivened by members of the artist's family.

"More frequently, however, Caillebotte, like his Impressionist friends, is attracted to water and paints the Yerres River above and below his property, from Brunoy to Crosne. There, among moving reflections and a changing play of light, yachts and canoes manned by colorfully dressed pleasure-boaters glide along the river's poplar-and willow-edged banks or under the shade of trees whose branches interlace to form a vault overhead. Caillebotte was a friend of the Impressionist masters; he also patronized them in their difficult early years, helping them by his many and remarkable acquistions, which formed the magnificent collection he would bequeath to the State in 1894. This body of paintings includes some of the greatest works of art that today adorn the walls of the room bearing his name at the Impressionist Museum in the Jeu de Paume. Long overshadowed by his illustrious companions, today Caillebotte is recognized as an authentic and highly individual representative of that extraordinary moment in French painting which was the Impressionist period.'"

1976–1977

A Gustave Caillebotte retrospective is held in the United States. From October 22 to January 2, 1977, the show runs at the Houston Museum of Fine Arts. From February 12 to April 24, 1977, it is at the Brooklyn Museum. Twelve of the Yerres-period canvases are included in this show.

1982

In June a Gustave Caillebotte exhibition is held at the Fondation Septentrion in Marcq-en-Baroeul. In the exhibition are three pictures painted at Yerres.

1983

March 18. At a sale in Paris *The Gardener*, which Caillebotte painted in 1877, turns up.

1984

From May 12 to October 21 the exhibition "Gustave Caillebotte 1848–1894" is held at the Musée Pissarro in Pontoise.
The previous year, in the January 12, 1983 edition of *Figaro,* Pierre Vaisse had alleged that "the Caillebotte affair is a fiction," meaning that the State never refused the Caillebotte legacy. In 1984 Martial Caillebotte's great-nephew Jacques Chardeau brings up this question again in his preface to the catalogue for the Caillebotte exhibition at the Musée Pissarro in Pontoise (May–October), pointing out that, if the State did not officially refuse the bequest, it never accepted it in its totality. Chardeau writes, "Martial

Caillebotte never ceased offering the State the rest of his brother's collection. Shortly before his death in 1910 Martial Caillebotte made his offer again. It was deemed to be of no interest, as can be seen in a 1928 letter from the Director of the National Museums, Henri Verne, who deplored his predecessors' refusal of the gift." Let us remember that among the works rejected because, according to Pierre Vaisse, they seemed to be "of insufficient merit to be shown to the public," were Manet's *The Croquet Game* (1871) and Cézanne's *Swimmers Resting*. Today, the Manet is in a Swiss collection and the Cézanne belongs to the Barnes Collection.

1985
On June 2nd Matthieu Galey writes in his *Diary 1974–1986,* "Renoir show at the Grand Palais—disappointing. When his pictures turn out well they always remind you of someone else's—Manet, Bonnard, or Caillebotte. However, a Renoir style does exist, immediately recognizable, pleasing, felicitous, but nothing beyond that, alas."

1987
May 23–June 28. The program of events at the Brunoy Museum and at Yerres includes "A Painter in His Garden, Gustave Caillebotte 1848–1894" and "The Yerres Period, 1860–1879." with visits to the Caillebotte property at Yerres on the theme of "The Traveler's Route."[74]

1989
From February 28 to March 24 an exhibition entitled "Gustave Caillebotte 1848–1894, Drawings, Studies and Paintings" is held at the Brame et Lorenceau Gallery in Paris.

THE FAMILY OF GUSTAVE CAILLEBOTTE

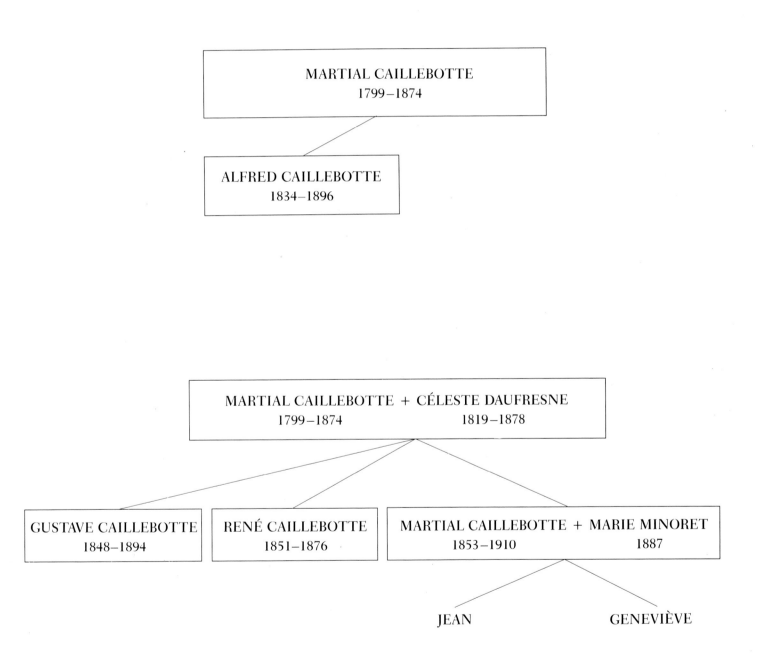

MARTIAL CAILLEBOTTE
1799–1874

ALFRED CAILLEBOTTE
1834–1896

MARTIAL CAILLEBOTTE + CÉLESTE DAUFRESNE
1799–1874   1819–1878

GUSTAVE CAILLEBOTTE
1848–1894

RENÉ CAILLEBOTTE
1851–1876

MARTIAL CAILLEBOTTE + MARIE MINORET
1853–1910   1887

JEAN   GENEVIÈVE

The Yerres River Region in Impressionist Exhibitions

Works created in the Yerres valley were shown, beginning in 1876, in various exhibitions of Impressionist painting:

1876
April. Second exhibition of Impressionist painting[75] at Durand-Ruel: 11, rue Le Peletier, Paris:

22. garden
23. garden
24. after lunch

1877
April. Third exhibition of Impressionist painting[75] in an apartment at 6, rue Le Peletier, Paris:

3. Country portraits

At this exhibition, works by Claude Monet, which were made during his stay in the Yerres valley in 1876–77, were also shown:

91. The pond at Montgeron (probably *Coin d'étang à Montgeron*)
92. Autumn landscape (probably *Sous-Bois, Automne*)
93. Dahlias (Montgeron) (probably *Les rosiers dans le jardin de Montgeron*)
101. Turkeys
108. Effect of autumn at Montgeron (probably *Sous-Bois*)

1879
April 10–May 11. Fourth exhibition of Impressionist painting[76] at 28, avenue de l'Opera, Paris:

7. Rowers
8. Boating party
9. Single-seater canoes

not in the catalogue:
10. Single-seater canoes
13. Rowing a single-seater canoe
23. Fishing
24. Swimmers
25. Single-seater canoes
26. Swimmers (pastel)
27. Canoers (pastel)
28. Yerres valley (pastel)
29. Kitchen garden (pastel)
30. Stream at Yerres (pastel)
31. Meadow (pastel)

1880
April 1–30. Fifth exhibition of Impressionist painting[76] at 10, rue des Pyramides, Paris (at the corner of the rue Saint-Honoré):

16. Landscape

Location of Caillebotte's Work from Yerres

IN FRANCE:

AGEN
(Lot-et-Garonne 47 000) at the city museum:
Bathers, Banks of the Yerres

BAYEUX
(Calvados 14 000) at the Musée Baron Gerard:
Portraits in the Country

RENNES
(Ile-et-Vilaine 35 000) at the Musée des Beaux-Arts et
d'Archéologie:
Périssoires on the Yerres

IN THE UNITED STATES:

HARTFORD
at the Wadsworth Atheneum:
The Nap

MILWAUKEE
at the Milwaukee Art Center:
Périssoires on the Yerres

Works by Caillebotte made at Yerres that have not been
located:

Washhouse on the Banks of the Yerres, c. 1875
Oil on panel, 19 × 46 cm.
Signed at lower left: "G. Caillebotte"

After Lunch, c. 1875
Oil on canvas
Georges Rivière wrote of this work in his account of the April
13, 1876 Impressionist exhibition (in "L'Esprit moderne"):
"The rower half-asleep near a table is his best picture."

Kitchen Garden, Yerres
Pastel, 41 × 54 cm.
Signed and dated at lower left: "G. Caillebotte 77"

The Garden, Flower Study, Yerres
Oil on canvas, 80 × 65 cm.
Signed (?) at lower left: "G. Caillebotte"

The Stream at Yerres
A pastel shown as No. 30 at the fourth Impressionist
exhibition in Paris, 1879

The House at Yerres, Gardener Mowing the Grass
Oil on canvas, 155 × 100 cm.

G. Caillebotte.

Notes

1. Emile Zola's dedication on Nadar's photo of him.

In his 1865 study of Hippolyte Taine, Zola wrote:

"A work is, for me, a man; I want to find in that work a temperament, a particular and unique accent . . . I completely express my thoughts when I say that a work of art is a corner of creation seen through a temperament."

This definition represents a counter-proposition to P. J. Proudhon's for whom art is "an idealistic representation of nature and of ourselves with the idea of the physical and moral perfection of our species."

2. *Sénart Cavalcade*, by Roger de Beauvoir who was really Edouard-Roger de Bully (1809–1866). He owned "La Folie Bélanger" in Santeny in the Val de Marne, which had once belonged to the architect François-Joseph Bélanger (1744–1818).

3. Earlier, in 1867, Martial Caillebotte had been nominated to the Yerres Welfare Office by the prefect of the Seine et Oise by decree dated February 3, 1867. Excerpts from the proceedings register of this office dated May 30, 1867:

"In the year 1867, Thursday, May 30, the administrative commission of the Welfare Office of the town of Yerres met in its regular meeting place on the summonings of the Mayor, under the chairmanship of his deputy M. Thomas, in accordance with the prefectorial circular of April 30 last for the regular May session.

Present: Messrs Father Beaumont, priest, Cortot, Pommier, and Chantre.

Absent: Messrs Baron Gourgaud, Mayor and Martial Caillebotte, who, by letter from Yerres today, regrets that an unexpected affair prevents him from attending this first meeting to which he is summoned.

Before opening the session, the Chairman makes public a letter from the sub-prefect dated February 16 last, in which the magistrate informs the Mayor that the Prefect has named as a member to the administrative commission of the Welfare Office of the town of Yerres by decree dated February 3, 1867: In replacement of Monsieur Louis Denis Raveneau, deceased, M. Martial Caillebotte whose mandate comes to an end December 31, 1869. Renews the mandate of Monsieur Joseph Cortot, which had expired.

The chairman declares the session open then proceeds by forming the board, which unanimously elects Father Beaumont secretary.

The Chairman invites the commission to study first the accounts of the Tax Officer and the Expenditures Officer for the Welfare Establishment for the year of 1866.

This study being carried out with the utmost attention resulted in an excess of revenue to the sum of 548 francs 35 centimes.

The sum in question will be carried over into the Heading of Additional Revenues for the fiscal year 1867 . . ."

4. At present, Place du 11 novembre.

5. See "A Walk in the Family Park: Water."

At present, Rue M. Sangnier and Rue de Concy.

6. In Brie, the wheat loft of Paris, wheat, the harvest, threshing, straw, and the wheat markets played a

determining role in regional economy. For example, in 1852 in Seine et Marne 99,178 hectares were sown with wheat with an average yield of 15.73 quintals per hectare, which had increased to 111,739 hectares with an average yield of 19.76 quintals per hectare in 1882.

The harvest with the ensuing cutting, drying, tieing up, bringing in, and warehousing began in the second half of July for central Brie. The stack was built on prepared ground and was about 4 to 5 meters in diameter. A bed of straw protected the bottommost layers of wheat. From the two-wheel sheaf wagon, the sheaves were passed to the stackers. Equipped with forks of varying lengths, depending on whether they were on the wagon or the stack under construction, the stackers in turn passed them to the rickmakers.

As the stack grew taller, its diameter widened as the sheaves slightly overhung those directly underneath, so that the base of the stack was a truncated cone with its larger base up. The broadening, which is visible in this painting, continues up to a height of 3 or 4 meters. From this height, the diameter of the successive layers narrows. Once the stack was completed, it was covered with straw by a thatcher. At the top, a rickmaker planted a cross made from two attached twigs.

In his *Journal,* Edmond de Goncourt wrote on November 27, 1876 concerning the Russian novelist and playwright Ivan Sergeevich Turgeniev (1818–1883):

"Coming up rue de Clichy, he talks to us about various projects for stories which were badgering him: among them the sensations of a being in the steppe, with grass up to mid-chest, of a being who might be an old horse. Then he stops and says, 'In southern Russia there are haystacks as tall as that house and you climb up by ladder. I have slept there several times. You can't imagine what the sky is like there, it's completely blue, a great blue with big silver stars. Around midnight a sweet, majestic warmth rises.' These are his words 'it's intoxicating'... Once I was lying on my back on top of one of the haystacks, enjoying the night, and I surprised myself—I don't know how long it lasted—I surprised myself saying out loud, 'One, two! One, two!' "

7. Meslay is, in fact, Mount Meslay in Creteil, the scene of serious combat.

8. This situation is mentioned in the correspondence, excerpts of which are reproduced below. Alexandre Perdrielle in Paris was writing to his brother-in-law Jean-Baptiste Mathieu Daurelle (1830–1893), who was working for the Caillebotte family and at that time living at M. Daufresne's house, judge and brother of Mme. Martial Caillebotte, Boulevard François I in Le Havre, in the department of the Lower Seine:

"By hot-air balloons, Tuesday morning, October 4, 1870...

As far as Yerres is concerned thanks to the good will of everyone, the Prussians must have found it sufficiently well-stocked..."

In a stamped letter dated November 21, 1870: "By hot-air balloon...

I certainly believed that Monsieur Caillebotte would have been well-advised to leave you in Paris, there would have been more advantages, first of all for Yerres where, had you been there, all would not have been lost.

In Paris things were different; your fat cook does not inspire confidence in me with all her long-winded discourses on this and that, she can't even handle the cooking. She needs a daily to help her.

And how would it be if Madame Caillebotte were in Paris and there were as many people as last year?..." (he is mentioning a cook who temporarily replaced Clarisse, the Caillebotte family cook in Paris, who was ill).

9. In *La Théorie et la pratique du jardinage* (1739) Antoine Joseph Dezallier d'Argenville wrote:

"Gates are very necessary ornaments in enfilades of walks to continue a perspective and to open a vista on the countryside.

At present, ways called ha-has are constructed, which are openings in walls without gates, and at the level of the walks. A wide, deep trench at the bottom, which is faced on both sides, retains the earth and prevents anyone from climbing up: this surprises when approached and makes one cry Ah! Ah! from whence it takes its name. These sorts of opening interrupt the view less than iron bars."

10. Alphonse Daudet (1840–1897) stays in Draveil-Champrosay:
—from 1867 at no. 2 of the present rue Alphonse Daudet in the house that belonged to Eugène Delacroix from 1852 to 1863. From 1844 on, the artist had stayed in Draveil-Champrosay near the Ris bridge on a farm. There Daudet writes *Robert Helmont—The Journal of a Solitary Man* (1873).
—from 1874 on his in-laws' estate, Monsieur et Madame Allard located within the enclosure of the present Minoret Sanatorium. There he writes *Jack* (1876), which takes place in Etiolles and the Sénart Forest.
—from 1886 until 1897 on the estate located at no. 33 on the present Rue Alphonse Daudet.

It was on this estate that Edmond de Goncourt died in 1896.

There he writes *La petite paroisse* (1894), a study of manners that also takes place in the Sénart Forest.

Edmond de Goncourt met Alphonse Daudet at Gustave Flaubert's house on March 16, 1873. The ties between them strengthened from 1874 on. During that year Edmond de Goncourt drew up his will on July 14 after having spent the day in Champrosay six days earlier. In his will he designated his friend Alphonse Daudet as his executor and instructed him to set up a perpetual literary society–the future Académie Goncourt–within the year of his death.

Edmond de Goncourt will be the godfather of Edmée Daudet, born in 1886, the daughter of Alphonse and Julia Daudet.

There would perhaps be grounds for drawing parallels between the following events in the literary world and those in the world of the plastic arts:
—1874 Edmond de Goncourt, 52, drew up his will in which he contemplated the creation of a literary society: the "young Academy whose members will be neither powerful lords nor political figures, and where election to the Académie Française will automatically bring about the resignation of that member."

—1876 Gustave Caillebotte, 28, (see "Day by Day: A Chronology of the Life of Gustave Caillebotte") drew up his will in which he contemplated his "Donation–Presentation" to the public of works by artists who have had great difficulty in being accepted, when they were, by the official Salon organized by the Beaux Arts administration.

Among the well-known writers who were to make up the Académie Goncourt:

—Emile Zola, initially, until he became a perpetual candidate for the Académie Française.

—Joris-Karl Huysmans (1848–1907), Octave Mirbeau (1848–1917), and Gustave Geffroy (1855–1926) were later added.

11. In 1884 the Belgian Félicien Rops (1837–1898) moved to Essonnes near Corbeil on an estate called La Roche Claire in Demi-Lune, where he later died. Excerpt from a letter to Armand Daudoy.

12. From the name of one of its former owners, Baron Henri de Rottembourg (Phalsbourg 1769–Montgeron 1856), an officer during the Empire.

This estate previously belonged to the family of the banker Bérard, director of the India Company and father-in-law of Charles Lebrun, consul (Saint-Sauveur-Lendelin, Manche 1739–Saint-Mesme, Seine et Oise 1824).

13. In the lower part of the park at Le Buet, a nymphaeum was built on the site of a spring. It was accessible from the main house through an archway in freestone and millstone below the main road (at present, Rue Charles de Gaulle), not far from the Isle of Virginia on which a Bald Cypress or a Louisiana Cypress (*Taxodium distichum*) was planted. The nymphaeum is still visible today.

Jean-François Boursault-Malherbe, actor, member of the Convention, speculator, and garden enthusiast was probably responsible for this construction. His family owned Le Buet between 1773 and 1807.

Within the context of the laying out of the park, designed in the English style and planted with various species of trees, there was an avenue of limes, a great iron tunnel, a labyrinth, ornamental pools, and basins with fountains, notably a Swiss cow shed. At the beginning of the century the inscription "Tripet 1780" was still visible on the balcony. J. F. Boursault had a hothouse built by the Alavoine Company, which was later known for their construction of the Colonne de Juillet, which was erected on the Place de la Bastille. The plans and perspectives of the hothouse were reproduced by Krafft in his *Plans des plus beaux jardins pittoresques de France, d'Angleterre et d'Allemagne* (1809–10).

In 1805 J. F. Boursault was designated as contractor-concessionary for the removal of sludge and sewage in Paris, a very lucrative and important position. His passion for plants being well known, he was called "Prince Merdiflore," ("Prince Dungflower"). He later was also concessionary for Parisian gaming rooms. A single flowering rose (*Rosa alpina*, Var.), the Boursault rose is named in his honor.

14. Jean Rodolphe Perronet (1708–1794) was the French engineer who directed the construction of a large number of bridges, among them, two spanning the Seine: the Neuilly Bridge (1768–72) and the Concorde Bridge in Paris (1778–91) and the Brunoy Bridge over the Yerres (1785–87). With Trudaine he founded l'Ecole des Ponts et Chaussées (National School of Civil Engineering).

15. In 1660 the fief of Narelle or Nazelle, which was in the tenure of the seigniory of Yerres, was granted to Nicolas Budé, one of the two sons of Anne Brachet and Pierre Budé, the lord of Villiers sur Marne and, in part, of Fleury-les-Meudon. In 1631 Nicolas Budé turns over his fief, which was then no more than a farm, to the Turpin family. Later the fief passed from the Turpins to the Frizons who sold it to Samuel Jacques Bernard.

16. Two commemorative plaques were placed in the St. Louis des Invalides Church. The first plaque reads:

"J. Jos de Sahuguet d'Amarzit, Baron d'Espagnac, Lieutenant General, Grand Cross of the Royal and Military Order of Saint Louis, Governor of the Invalides, born in Brives in Limousin, died February 28, 1783."

On the second was inscribed:

"Le Baron d'Espagnac de Sahuguet d'Amarzit, Lieutenant General, Grand Cross of the Order of Saint Louis, was governor of the Hôtel des Invalides from 1766 to 1783. He was the comrade-in-arms, the friend and historian of Maréchal Maurice de Saxe. Erected by his son and grandson, the Count and the Baron Charles d'Espagnac."

Maurice, comte de Saxe (1696–1750) owned the château of La Grange de Milieu in Yerres in his last years, having acquired it from Pierre Nicolas Gaudion, the Keeper of the Royal Treasury, on April 11, 1748. It was Maurice de Saxe who probably commissioned the plasterwork decoration of hunting and flag trophies in the great gallery.

Baronness d'Espagnac had the garden of her Paris mansion, located on Rue d'Anjou, designed by garden architect Gentils (according to the 1784 publication by the count of Clermont's geographer and engineer, Georges Louis Le Rouge, *Jardins anglo-chinois à la mode ou détail des nouveaux jardins à la mode*, XIth chapter).

17. Martin Guillaume Biennais was born in La Cochère, a small village in Normandy near Argentan, in 1764, and died in 1843. He was a silversmith, Rue St. Honoré at the sign of the purple monkey (at present 175 Rue St. Honoré).

18. On December 7, 1859, Edmond and Jules de Goncourt wrote in their *Journal—Mémoires de la vie littéraire*:

"Two minor historical events concerning auctions. . . . Another event. I see a sign announcing the Biennais sale at the Vignères Auction House. Bottles and stand belonging to Queen Marie-Antoinette, 23 pieces, in rock crystal. 'Oh, that must be unusual!' Vignères smiles, 'You don't know what happened? The Emperor asked to see it. It was brought to him.

He says, 'This is fine, it suits me.'

'But, Sire'

'It suits me, this is fine.'

The auctioneer is very embarrassed. 'What an imperial way of acquiring!'"

19. For an auction announced in Chartres for October 22, 1989, by J. and J. P. Lelièvre, associate auctioneers, a work which was painted of this site from the same perspective was reproduced in the trade press as well as in the sale catalogue with the following information given:

"Oil painting

48 Béraud (Jean)—(1849/1936)
The park of the château
oil on panel, signed lower left
15 cm x 22 cm"

20. A photographic reproduction (approx. 44 cm x 20.5 cm) of the plan, in very poor condition and scarcely legible, conserved at the Yerres Municipal Archives was rediscovered on April 25, 1987. It had earlier been found in the "casin" by a city employee during a cleanup, after the city's acquisition of the estate. This document was presented at Yerres during the exhibition "Gustave Caillebotte (1848–1894) au temps de Yerres" (p. 591. 13, in the exhibition catalogue).

21. On the back of the postcard, Madame Dubois wrote:
Yerres, January 11, '17
My dear little Marie,

I thank you as well as your husband wholeheartedly for your New Year's greetings. Please accept my own which are strong and affectionate. I send them with my faithful love—that all five of you are fine and that this year will bring us victory and peace and that we shall be reunited.

My affectionate best to both of you, love to the children.

B. D.
Opposite, the Hermitage at Narelle in March 1916, on a frosty day.

22. On the back of Madame Dubois' postcard:
January 11, '18
My dear Marie,

Your wishes and regards were sweet pleasure for me. I thank you wholeheartedly. Please accept my sincere wishes for good health for all. 1918, the year, let us hope, of our reunion in a victory with peace. Here we have had snow for the last four weeks. Finally it's melting. I'm leaving for Pau.

? year, for six weeks, there's no coal which is very difficult in a big house.

My best regards to all

B. Dubois
Photograph by Mulard in Yerres.

23. According to P. Boitard: "By *fabrique* we mean any construction of a picturesque style placed in the scenes of a landscape garden, such as hut, bridge, tower, pavilion, whether they be used as accommodations for man or animals, or simply for storage, or that their only purpose be to adorn the scene, to be a look-out, etc. Landscape artists also call *fabriques* the edifices that decorate their paintings."

Supplementary information concerning the use of *fabriques* in gardens in 1859 are provided during the walk in "A Utilitarian Structure: The Washhouse."

24. Garden enthusiasts can compare this park to the Garenne Lemot park, which spreads out over the towns of Clisson, Cugan, and Getigné in Loire Atlantique.

25. As for area gardeners during the Revolutionary period, the historian S. Bianchi writes concerning those in Draveil:
"The gardeners constitute a very diversified intermediate category but can be considered as of "petite aisance" (limited affluence). There are seventeen in this category who cultivate, under their own name or by lease, the gardens of important country houses of the privileged, or their hillside

orchards. Most of these are citizens who can be considered as politically active above three *livres* of direct taxes per year. Toussaint Legrand exploits one arpent 25 (½ hectare) of vineyards and one arpent 50 of orchards. He pays 604 *livres* in tallage in 1788 and has been in the past syndic of Draveil. This group, literate in general, participates fully in the deliberations of the community."

26. The high altar of the parish church in Boissy-Saint-Leger is under the invocation of Saint Leger and Saint Blaise.

The Chapel of the Saint Virgin was also under the invocation of Saint Fiacre.

27. Other villages can also be mentioned: Chaumes-en-Brie, where a banner bearing the effigy of Saint Fiacre still exists, and Gretz-Armanvilliers, where a 19th-century painting, *Saint Fiacre Preaching in Brie*, can be found in the church.

According to Messrs. J. Gautier and J. Gauchet, in Brunoy there were, in the 19th century, about one hundred gardeners and perhaps as many aids.

28. The 13th centenary of Saint Fiacre was commemorated on September 3–6, 1970 in Meaux organized by the initiative of the Saint Fiacre National Committee, 3 Rue Courteline, Meaux.

29. Concerning the park of the Château de Crosne, which then belonged to Caulet d'Hauteville, Antoine Nicolas Dezaillier d'Argenville (1741/43–1796), a Yerres resident, wrote:

"The Yerres river completely surrounds the park, making it like an island. The river was straightened out in canals on each side and two semicircles at the ends. It also fills the château moats into which it flows through two small passages. The gardens of Flora are set out in the daintiest fashion. One would say that the Goddess herself had adorned them. A prodigious variety of flowers, which change with the seasons, spread out the most lively colors and give off fragrances that perfume the air . . ."

30. At present, in part, Rue des Treillageurs.

31. Boitard notes:
"To conceal garden walls, we have seen a technique employed that is as simple as it is successful. The parts of the walls were blackened where the arbors or screens of shrubs intended to cover them have left empty spots permitting the eye to gaze through, which had destroyed all illusion and ruined the overall view. This black, broken up by branches and young plants starting off, appeared to be the shadow of a dark thicket, which did not attract the eye."

32. In 1819–20 Gabriel Thouin (1742–1824) published *Plans raisonnés de toutes les espèces de jardin* where he summarizes the trends that have governed irregular gardens in the first twenty years of the century. According to Ernest de Ganay, a second edition of this work was published in 1823, and a third in 1828 with 58 pages and 59 prints, while there were 57 pages and 57 plates in the previous editions.

33. Boitard noted:
"One day as we were visiting the park of the country cottage, accompanied by the King's architect, in a kingdom neighboring France, we showed our surprise to be following such a sinuous path. To exonerate himself from the suspicion of having laid out such a path, the artist tells us that the King himself had ordered it, by telling his gardener to take a spade

and to drag it behind him, walking around, aimlessly as his fancy dictated. This brought to mind that we had heard more than once, 'when one lays out walks in an English garden, one need only get the gardener drunk and then follow him.' One must admit that, using these expeditious means, one composes a garden worthy only of a cabaret."

34. In 1819 Monsieur de Viart published *Le Jardinier moderne, guide des propriétaires qui s'occupent de la composition de leurs jardins ou de l'embellissement de leur campagne* (*The Modern Gardener, a Guide for Owners Who Are Composing Their Gardens or Beautifying Their Countryside*).

The 184-page work included a plate on the frontispiece representing the "little valley in the park in Brunehaut." He had designed this park in Morigny-Champigny in the vicinity of the present Jeurre park near Etampes in Essonne. A 224-page second edition of this work was published in 1827. In *Monument élevé à la gloire de la langue et des lettres françaises—Dictionnaire National ou Dictionnaire Universel de la langue française* (*Monument Erected to the Glory of the French Language and Letters—National Dictionary or Universal Dictionary of the French Language*), 2nd vol., 8th edition, 1861, Monsieur Bescherelle, Sr., Librarian of the Louvre, defines "Jardiniste" (roughly, "gardenist") in the following manner: "Jardiniste, noun, masculine, root "jardin," who provides the precepts of the art of gardens or creates gardens."

"This word is new, says Monsieur Noël, but seems necessary because one must not confuse cabbage planters, and Le Nôtre and La Quintinie, and in our times, the Thouins and the Noisettes. We would willingly go along with M. Noël, although M. N. Landais considers this word to be a barbarism." *Le Jardiniste moderne*, Viart.

Louis-Claude Noisette (1772–1849), after having served in the army from 1792 to 1795, worked at Val de Grâce in Paris then founded a nursery, which acquired an excellent reputation in the Faubourg St. Jacques also in Paris. He opened a school for fruit tree husbandry in Fontenay-aux-Roses and managed a farm in Mesnil in Yonne.

Included in the 1795 real-estate auction of property belonging to Louis-Stanislas Capet, comte de Provence, *émigré*, was a "pavilion with garden called The Bakery located in Brunoy." A certain "citizen Noisette" is mentioned as cotenant of it. This person was in charge of the count's vegetable garden, and with Lambercy, who was in charge of the flower garden, were the count's head gardeners. Were these two Noisettes one and the same?

35. This is an allusion to the gardens of Academus, the mythical Greek hero from Attica where Plato (428–348 B.C.) created the school of philosophy, the Academy, in 387 B.C. It was six furlongs from Athens.

Aristotle was Plato's student there. At Plato's death, Xenocrates, Speusippus, Polemon, and Heraclitus, among others, became the directors of the Academy. This theoretical reference on the art of gardens by Boitard refers to the contents of the chapter "The Reflection of a Dream."

36. Mount Griffon to the north, which is visible from the southern section of the circuit walk. The other elements of the landscape are to the east:
—the tower of Saint Honest's, the ancient Brie church with its flat chevet from the 12th–13th centuries, which

underwent a "Byzantino-Romanesque reworking with a Constantinian pre-Romanesque side porch";
—the present A. Calmette Convalescent and Treatment Center located on an estate, which belonged to Jean Thiriot (Vignot 1590–Yerres 1647). He was master mason, contractor for Richelieu's buildings, Engineer and Architect of the King's Buildings who created the *fabrique* called Budé's Fountain near the river in his park;
—the trees on the J. P. Jazet estate, which later belonged to Jules Raingo and in the "Normandy" area, the locality where the wine growers lived.

37. Boitard noted:
"The artificial boulders of Apollo's Bath at Versailles cost during Louis XIV's reign 1.5 million francs. Those of "The Cascade" in the Bois de Boulogne were transported from Fontainbleau and must have cost a very considerable sum, which the City of Paris authorized. (A note from the 6th edition published in 1859.)

38. J. M. Morel (1728–1810) was the author of *Théorie des jardins*, published in 1776 and which underwent several revised editions, the second in 1802 and the third in 1806. Among the parks that this French architect designed, Monsieur Nicolai's in Bercy is noteworthy.

39. Boitard noted: "Its construction should take place at the same time as the garden or park is laid out; we would have preferred to describe it earlier."

40. Gustave Caillebotte was a dahlia lover during the Petit Gennevilliers period. There are about a dozen paintings that attest to it.

Claude Monet writes him and, before mentioning news concerning friends:
Giverny, by Vernon, May 12, '90

My dear friend,

I have received the dahlias. I was disturbed and therefore forgot to write you. Concerning Sisley . . . As for Renoir . . .

41. Marie François Sadi Carnot (1837–1894) became the president of the republic in 1887.

42. Boitard noted: "When there is a trellis, instead of embedding these shelters in the wall, they are stood on small wooden brackets which are stapled onto the trellis, which can be taken down when necessary."

43. Again according to J. Decaisne and M. Naudin: "Finally, the ground must furnish the necessary moisture to the seeds to bring about germination . . . in the case . . . of land plants, soil moisture must be moderate. Here, besides, there is no absolute rule to be formulated: all seeds do not adapt to the same degree of moisture. Some rot instead of germinating, whereas others develop.

"The experienced gardener must judge the amount and frequency of watering that he must do on soil that has been sown. One must observe however that direct sowing is less exposed to drying out than seeds sown in pots . . . One must be careful to keep the soil superficially moist at all times and, whenever it is necessary, to give it a light sprinkling with a watering can equipped with a wide-face spout. Whenever possible, use water that has been set out and warmed by the sun."

44. In his 1938 book *En ecoutant Cézanne, Degas, Renoir*

(*Listening to Cézanne, Degas, Renoir*) Ambroise Vollard attributes to P. A. Renoir the following: "Franc-Lamy showed me one day a letter where I wrote him, 'I am sending you a rose picked on Delacroix's grave in Champrosay.' All that seems so far away." (Eugène Delacroix was, however, buried in the Paris cemetery Père Lachaise, not far from the spot where Gustave Caillebotte would be laid to rest in 1894.)

45. Two articles in the magazine (April 1896 and April 1904) mention "Rosa Boursaultiana: Plena Multiplex, Carnea" named in memory of J. F. Boursault, a native of Yerres (see note 13).

46. Lindley, John, *Rosarium Monographia, or A Botanical History of Roses* with colored plates, London, 1820.

47. This is more than likely a reference to the *Manuel complet théorique et pratical du jardinier ou l'Art de cultiver et de composer toutes sortes de jardins* (*The Complete Theoretical and Practical Gardening Handbook or The Art of Cultivating and Arranging All Types of Gardens*) by Charles Bailly de Merlieux. This 1st edition appeared in Paris in 1829 and the 6th in 1834.

Charles Bailly de Merlieux directed the 47th installment of l'*Encyclopédie portative, ou Résumé universel des sciences, des lettres et des arts* (*The Portable Encyclopedia, or The Universal Summary of the Sciences, Letters and Arts*), a collection of separate treatises written by a learned society. It was in the offices of the l'*Encyclopédie portative* in 1830 that the Chevalier Soulage-Bodin probably revised and annotated the *Traité de la composition et de l'exécution des jardins d'ornement* (*Treatise on the Composition and Laying Out of Ornamental Gardens*) translated from English by J. M. Chopin (see above).

48. Victor Cherbuliez, writer (Geneva 1829–Combs-La-Ville, Seine et Marne 1899), successfully published a series of works in which he blended Romanesque fiction with allusions to archeology and aesthetics. He also wrote more traditional novels, which generally appeared in the *Revue des Deux Mondes*. In the August 1, 1878 issue of this magazine, he mentioned a pamphlet by the art critic Théodore Duret entitled *Les Peintres impressionnistes Claude Monet, Sisley, C. Pissarro, Renoir, Berthe Morisot*. In a letter dated September 9, 1878 from Cognac, Duret confided to Camille Pissarro, "Since my departure, I have no news from the art world, but I suppose that times are still hard for Impressionism. I was pleasantly surprised when I saw that the August 1 *Revue des Deux Mondes* brought my pamphlet to the attention of their readers under the pen of Victor Cherbulliez and moreover, to criticize it."

49. In 1777 the gondola used by the comte de Provence when he stayed at his Folly in Brunoy was being repaired.

50. By 1859 Boitard had already published a four-volume work entitled *Amusements de la Campagne* (Country Pastimes), which, he added, was "in hands of all the lovers of country pleasures."

"Swings, ring games, seesaws, archery, pistol and rifle shooting, jump rope, the bladder game, and giant's step or vindas are in fashion. They are at once games and for some, the most salutary of exercises at a period when sport had started a rapid development thirty years earlier."

In the *Grand Dictionnaire Universel du 19ième siècle* by Pierre Larousse (1817–1875), which he undertook at Concy near Yerres and where he lived from 1863 to 1869, Eugène Chapus, the founder of the newspaper *Le Sport* in 1853 wrote: "Sport implies three things simultaneously or separately: the outdoors, wagers and the use of one or more physical aptitudes."

Authors also echo these activities. Edmond de Goncourt wrote in his journal on Thursday, June 21, 1883:

"Afternoon spent at Zola's in Médan with the Daudets and the Jourdains. Went canoeing where Daudet gallantly bent over his oars and directing sailors' songs to the banks in a loud voice, is a pleasure to see in the midst of this gay intoxication that nature showers on him. As for Zola, with his boat *Nana*, accompanied by Alexis, swims arounds heavily, moving like a fat roach, a tubby awkwardness in his physical exertions. His great pleasure is, from time to time, to cry with a laugh that rolls off the corner of his mouth, 'Who has read Noris? Oh! Noris! Noris!' *Noris* is the novel that Claretie published in *Figaro*."

51. The action of Alphonse Daudet's *Robert Helmont—Journal d'un solitaire* takes place principally in the Draveil-Champrosay Hermitage in the Sénart Forest between September 3, 1870 and January 30, 1871.

52. Boitard then furnishes various elements concerning the Swiss house which Jules Janin (1804–1874) had constructed. He was a literary critic, author, and journalist who gravitated around the Realist movement. Jules and Edmond de Goncourt wrote about him in their journal (April 21, 1857):

"Saw Janin . . . Spoke to us about his move from his 60,000-franc chalet in Passy. Decorative paintings on the wooden ceilings; a magnificent chimney given him by Prince Demidoff into which he embedded mosaics from Rome and other things of a like taste. Tells us that everything is for sale in his house. We propose to buy his Louis XV dining room chairs. He prices them at 6 francs. It's a deal, then he goes back on his word."

Jules Janin had acquired the Silvestre mansion, Rue de Passy, in Paris from Nicolas Deyeux's son, whose father had been the pharmacist to the Emperor Napoleon and a member of the Academy of Sciences. The latter had enlarged the park by buying former quarries that he laid out as a miniature valley by adding landfill. This mountain chalet was shown in the frontispiece illustration by E. Lebel entitled "Maison Suisse dite : le chalet J. Janin" ("Swiss house called J. Janin's chalet"), of which Boitard also gives "the plan of the charming little garden . . . designed by the owner himself" while mentioning that Mr. Jules Janin could only praise himself for the temperature in his Swiss house all year round.

"In scrupulously employing the shape and the materials from the Oberland valleys, the architect, who was born in the region, knew how to a give a more animated appearance to the dwelling of the man of letters for whom he worked and to enhance inside with all that is attractive in interior ornamentation and objets d'art, those which brighten an abode and speak to the mind and the heart. In the drawing room–library the most beautiful books are gathered together in great number and in their most brilliant finery that a bibliophile, perfect connoisseur, has been able to acquire by dint of investigation and expense for his use or recreation. It is the most beautiful ornament of what he calls his "cabin," however what wouldn't we say about his statuettes, bronzes, paintings, drawings, decorations from the masters' brushes, mosaics, parquet floors, cabinetwork, and furniture, all which are so well chosen! There is nothing more charming than a Carrara marble chimney, richly adorned in gilt bronze and on top of which this beautiful face is smiling, one worthy of the pastels of the famous Quentin de La Tour!

"It is clear that the most brilliant, the most precious, the most cheerful objects can be assembled in a cabin. However, since a Bernese house must present on its principal façades one or two inscriptions that reveal the master and occupant, Mr. Jules Janin has written the following inscriptions:

—on the pediments of his dwelling: to the north two lines from Clément Marot, his favorite poet:
'May heaven preserve us, here in this base world,
From hunger and the importunate, from worries, from cold.'
—to the south, these lines from Horace were marked:
Sumite materiam . . .
'Writers, before taking on a subject, consult your forces and wit.'
(By a rather subtle play on words this line also means:
Writers, if you build, choose materials commensurate with your fortune.)
—under the two lines form Horace's *Ars poetica*, could be read this charming line (and very suitable here) from *Art poétique* by Despréaux:
'He who limits himself not, knows not how to write.'

"And it is left to each person to smile at this gentle philosophy, the kind feelings, the limited ambition, human fortune, at work past and present, at the happy and comfortable life of this worthy writer, who has been a part of us for such a long time already. His lively ways and appeal have always led him and brought him back to us.

"Two architects presided over the erection of this wooden palace: Monsieur Seiler, a Swiss builder, a promoter of houses in this material, and Monsieur Godde, a young French artist very accomplished in the art of giving space, appearance and well-being to the joists and planks raised on a small brick wall. . . [This building includes: on the ground floor, a kitchen, a model of comfort, a stove which is capable of heating the entire space and a bath room. There is also an indoor staircase, besides the one which leads to the outside porch. On the second floor, there is the drawing room-library, which is 7 meters long, a dining room and a boudoir. On the third and even the fourth, bedrooms and private studies.]

"The above-mentioned Monsieur Seiler has founded in Paris a gigantic enterprise for the construction of chalets and Swiss houses. In La Villette at number 40 rue de Flandre, prodigious piles of wood can be seen that are constantly being shaped, cut and implemented by a steam-powered machine with the force of forty horsepower. An architect from Bern draws up the plans and directs the construction in such a way that one can very rapidly enjoy a perfectly dry residence without having to wait two or three years for the plaster to be aired. But Monsieur Seiler's immense factory is not limited to the production of wooden walls for houses. Its powerful steam-powered machine cuts parquet floors with incredible speed, from the most simple to the most rich and graceful. A comparable mechanical sawmill is necessary to execute at a reasonable price work, which, in the past, would have been impossible . . ."

Benjamin Delessert, French industrialist, financier, and philanthropist (1773–1847), owned Lauzun's former estate on Rue Basse in Passy (at present, Rue Raynouard, Paris 16th) where he had the main house built by Leroy in a neo-Louis XVI style (colonnade and balusters) with some Italian influences brought about by the steep slopes of the hills of Passy, which encouraged the use of stairs and terraces. This was the inspiration for the "Italian casin" to use the expression from the architect Marie Joseph Peyre, Sr. (1730–1785) in his 1765 publication *Oeuvres d'Architectures*. Delessert had a "Swiss House" constructed in his park. On the façade he had painted the coat of arms of the twenty-two Swiss cantons, after the addition of the cantons of Valais and Neufchâtel in 1815. A 1829 print by Villeneuve entitled "View of Monsieur Delessert's chalet in Passy" is preserved at the Carnavalet Museum in Paris.

Other mountain houses were constructed in the "Hameau Boileau à Auteuil." This hamlet was built at the initiative of the printer Lemercier around 1839.

53. Antoine Joseph Dezallier d'Argenville (1680–1765) illustrates his work *La Théorie et la pratique du jardinage,* (the third edition was published in The Hague in 1739) by a plate which reproduces "la veduta del casino nel giardino in Castelazzo" ("a view of a 'casin' in a garden in Castelazzo)." His son Antoine Nicolas had acquired the fief of Dannemois and its dependencies on June 6, 1761. On his return from Rome the painter, architect, and garden designer Hubert Robert presents paintings and drawings at the *Salon*, notably:

—in 1773 *View of the Casin Mattei near Rome
A Staircase of the Casin Albani*
—in 1779 *An Italian Casin*

Alexandre-Théodore Brongniart (1739–1813), an architect, as well as a garden and interior designer, who worked in Montgeron (Essonne), executed a project for a "casin" in the Italian style: two elevations in ink and pencil (INV B 780).

There is also good reason to mention the house built for Caron de Beaumarchais in Paris by Paul Guillaume Lemoine le Romain (1755–after 1808), which was inspired by this type of architecture. Although the style underwent a revival at the end of the 18th century and the first half of the 19th century, its roots are decidedly much older. The château de Monsieur de Léry, the king's butler, built in Auvers in 1635 by Zanoby Liony, who arrived in France in the entourage of Marie de Médicis, is a "casin."

Overlooking the Oise, the "casin" was inspired by the Villa d'Este in Tivoli. Part of the gardens are laid out on hillsides, in a series of terraces with an axial perspective from top to bottom, following the arrangement that was common to Italianate Mannerist gardens of the times.

54. Concerning the "Rustic and the Vernacular" in Alexandre-Théodore Brongniart's work, Monique Mosser writes in 1986: "One of the most remarkable of Brongniart's

drawings depicts an elevation of a *fabrique* or country house, which was probably part of an ornamental farm. It can almost be considered as a manifesto of the irregular style. From the choice of materials, the brick that appears under the crackled outer coating to the climbing vines wrapping around a high balcony; from the bays, each one different from the other, to the chimney stacks; without forgetting the two poplars that enter into the composition, this architecture condenses all the ingredients of the Vernacular into one example... It was particularly during the Empire that this type of architecture became more generalized. There are, however, earlier examples, which seem to be the case for Brongniart. Moreover, while some projects attest to direct Italian influence, others draw on the local repertoire (wood panels, play of stone against brick)." The example given is the ornamental farm at Yerres.

55. Boitard is the co-author with Corbié of *Les Pigeons de Volière et de Colombier* (*Pigeons for Aviaries and Dovecotes*) published in 1824 by Audot and Corbié in Paris.

56. Elaborated before 1467, this work was published in Venice in 1499 and in Paris in 1546 under the name of *Discours du Songe du Poliphile* (*The Discourse of the Dream of Poliphilos*).

57. Italian humanist and architect (Genoa 1404–Rome 1472). From an important Florentine family, he studied humanities in Venice and Padua and law in Bologna, and received an office in the papal chancellary in 1431. In his dialogues, *Theogonius* and especially in his treatise *On the Family* (1437–41), Alberti proposed the ideal of harmony and moderation, which he himself tried to reach, confident in human virtue to attain it. He was one of the first to defend the common language and compiled the first Italian grammar.

The physical sciences and mathematics interested him as much as ethics and literature. Architecture was the converging point of his various interests. He composed *Della Pittura*, which he dedicated to Brunelleschi (1436), and *De Statua*. His interest in Vitruvious led to *De Re Aedificatoria*, dedicated to Laurent de Medicis (1485), in which he presented architecture as the art of the city par excellence. The monument itself is an organic entity whose elements must be in harmony with the whole and in respect to one another with a musical rigor. As an archeologist, Alberti was well versed in antiquity, especially in the Latium, Palestrina, and the Campania. As a philosopher, he was in keeping with the neo-Platonists, and he commented on and annotated Virgil's *Aeneid* at the Camadoli Congress in 1468. The purpose of this congress was to define the research to be carried out within the Platonist Academy. It took place in the Tuscan Valley, where Saint Romuald had founded a religious order in 1010. Monks of this order settled in the Boiron Woods in Yerres in the 17th century.

58. "The Chapel," while not being a part of the "The Dream's Reflection," is an occasion to evoke allusions to *The Discourse of the Dream of Poliphilos* in William Shakespeare's work. Poliphilos is the brother of the "Passionate Pilgrim" erring since his exile from the Garden of Eden.

Wander, a Word for shadows like myself,
Philomela sits and sings...

The vision comes to an end on the nightingale song (see following note).

59. Please refer to "Birds and Aviaries" as well as "Water." A walk through the forest on the domaine of the Château de Grosbois, which is not far from the former convent of the Camaldules, was called "Nightingale walk."

60. "Tarvissii, Cum Decorissimis Poliac Amore Lorulis distincretur Misellus Poliphilus... M.CCCC.LXVII Kalendis Maii."

Pyramus arrives and, thinking that his beloved has been devoured, stabs himself in despair. On her return Thisbe discovers Pyramus dead and in turn stabs herself. According to the legend, this would explain why the fruit from the mulberry tree, which had been initially white, became dark red at the sight of so much spilled blood.

This was, during the Renaissance, a very popular myth as can be judged by the play-within-the-play put on by the craftsmen in celebration of Prince Theseus's marriage in Shakespeare's *Mid-Summer's Night Dream* (1595).

66. On Wednesday February 25, 1880, Edmond de Goncourt writes in his journal, *Memoirs of a Literary Life*, concerning Giuseppe de Nittis:

"De Nittis had lunch at my house and, as he ate, recounted the story of his life—one of those stories that one recounts only once in certain conditions of happiness, pleasure, and effusiveness.

"He began drawing at the School of Fine Arts in Naples but refused to study in museums. He found old paintings all black, and outdoors the atmosphere was gay, light, and fair. He then left for his family's estate in the country. He left with seven bladders filled with paints, taking with him, as his brother would say, all the colors of the rainbow. Then without master, guide, or counsel, he started painting with joy and fury.

"After a year's time he returned to Naples to show his work with success. But the problems that he had with his brothers, who were hostile to his vocation and completely disdainful of his occupation, made him decide to leave Naples with the idea of going to Paris. He went to Rome where he sold a painting for 25 francs, then reached Florence, where he was sensitive only to the Primitives. He then got to Milan, where, at an inn, he was robbed by thieves, whom he considered true artists, of 500 francs of the 650 he had left. Therefore 150 francs was his entire fortune and the trip to Paris in third class cost him around a hundred francs. He did not hesitate, and here he was in France of which he knew nothing and where he knew no one.

"He heard of a Neopolitan sculptor who lived in Place Montparnasse. He has himself driven there directly by omnibus from his train. From above his small truck and big paint box are thrown down to him; the latter opens as it falls and the brushes and paints are scattered about in the gutter. He gathers them up as best he can, goes into a small hotel, which was indicated to him, takes a 2-franc garret room and throws himself on the bed. It is one of those sunless summer days and, through a skylight, a sad, back-courtyard light falls on his face, a light he sees on himself like on a cadaver. In this great unknown city, without any relations, not a single letter of introduction, with not even knowledge of the native language, he is suddenly overcome by an immense sense of discouragement in the midst of which he falls asleep.

"Night had fallen when he awakens. He starts to look for a place to eat and enters into a cheap eating-house where he pays 7 francs for his dinner. He returns to the street, directing himself at random, and after two hours, ends up on the Boulevard des Italiens. There, in the comings and goings of the men and women, in this movement, in the life of the Parisian crowds, the gaslights, suddenly the blackness the young man feels in himself disappears. He is transported, enthused by the modernity of the spectacle. And after severals instants in a café on the corner of rue Richelieu, several 'Oh! What? You, here?' from compatriots remove all anxiety, all worry and preoccupation about the future..."

Giuseppe de Nittis enters into Léon Gérome's studio (1824–1904), receives counsel from Meisonnier (1811–1891), and is introduced to Adolphe Goupil (1806–1893) by Emile Edouard Brandon (1831–1897). He first shows at the Salon of 1869 and rapidly obtains success in France and England. G. Caillebotte will represent Aimé Nicolas Morot (1850–1913) in *The Painter Morot in His Studio* and will add a personal dedication on the back. Morot was L. Gérome's son-in-law who was married to one of Goupil's daughters.

67. If the figure sitting in the boat, painted in 1879, is compared to *Self-Portrait in the Park at Yerres* executed earlier, it seems hardly plausible that Caillebotte was Renoir's model.

68. Considering the following:

On the one hand, in Marie Berhaut's 1978 monograph (p. 15): Gustave Caillebotte regularly took part in regattas and won numerous prizes. His sailboats "Condor," "Inès," and "Cul Blanc" for which he had drawn up the plans himself are often mentioned by columnists. One of them studying the necessary qualities of boats used for river navigation cites the example of the "Condor" belonging to M. Caillebotte, the leader and the most likeable of the independent painters from rue des Pyramides." ("La Vie Moderne," May 8, 1880). And on the other hand, excerpts from the magazine *Le chasse-Marée* (nos. 5–6) in answer to Mme. Gilles Outin from Chatou that the "Condor" was the model for the "Monotype de Chatou."

I was lead to write about the artist's role in the evolution of naval architecture in the preface of the exhibition catalogue (Feb. 28–March 24, 1989, see Bibliography) in the following terms: "As a navigator and naval architect, his research led to the 'Monotype de Chatou.'"

Daniel Charles has done important research in the field and has established a "Catalogue of sailboats conceived by Gustave Caillebotte and sailboats which he owned." He has pointed out that in his opinion:

1) Texier, Jr., was the architect of the "Condor."

2) The directory of the Paris Sail Club lists Martial, Gustave's brother, as owner. But the brothers may have co-owned the boat, and in any case Gustave often sailed the boat and the maquette conserved by the Yacht Club of France lists Gustave Caillebotte as the owner. It seems that Gustave Caillebotte owned a sailboat as early as 1876. I would like to thank Daniel Charles for these clarifications and details.

69. Edmond de Goncourt mentions Giuseppe de Nittis' death in his journal on the following dates: August 19, 21–25, 29, 30–31, and September 1, and the role he played for Madame de Nittis during this period.

According to the art historian Christopher Lloyd, Gustave Caillebotte probably executed and dated drawings during the summer and fall of 1884:
—in Vetheuil on June 13, July 11, 17, 28;
—in Chaudry not far from Vetheil on August 18;
—near to Chérence, not far from La Roche Guyon, on August 25;
—in Paris at the Louvre on October 9;
—in Chérence once again on October 25;
—in Chaudry on October 29;
—in Vetheil on November 4;
—in La Désirée on November 16.
The same drawing book was later used:

in 1885	on May 12 in La Désirée;
	on September 28 in Vetheuil;
	on September 30 in Millonets near Vetheuil;
	on October 5 in Paris.
in 1886	on June 18 at M. Coutois' residence;
	on August 12 in Vetheuil;
	on August 19 in Blois in the Loire et Cher;
	in September in Chaumont-sur-Loire in the Cher.

70. It is worth noting that a steamboat line operated on the Seine. "Le Touriste" linked Pont Royal in Paris and Saint-Germain in 3½ hours. There was a café-restaurant aboard. It stopped at Ile de la Grande Jatte, Asnières, Bousquin Baths, Restaurant Fournaise in Chatou, and Bougival Grenouillère among other places. Argenteuil was then 45 minutes from Chatou and 50 from the Grenouillère.

71. At the corner of Le Peletier and the Boulevard, this establishment, which opened in 1785 and closed in 1916, was the mecca of Paris gourmet cooking. The kitchens were modernized in 1865, and Zola was an habitué. A scene in *La Curée* takes place there. On a visit in 1880 Madame de Nittis eats crayfish à la bordelaise "with all sorts of childish coyness." On June 8, 1894 Edmond de Goncourt wrote indignantly: "Oh! the Café Riche's new decor, I have never seen anything so coarsely ugly as Forain's macabre frescos and Raffaelli's colored caryatids..."

72. Works that were not part of the bequest. Concerning *Olympia* see "The Life of Gustave Caillebotte" 1890.

73. Works that were donated by the artist's family.

74. A photographic exhibition, "A Walk in the Painter Gustave Caillebotte's Landscape Garden 1848–1894" took place at the Brunoy museum during July and August 1987, which was a continuation of the May 23–June 28 Caillebotte exhibition. Its purpose was to draw attention to the historical importance of the garden.

75. Gustave Caillebotte's address was then at his parents' house, 77 rue de Miromesnil in Paris.

76. Gustave Caillebotte's address was then 31 boulevard Haussmann in Paris.

List of Illustrations

*Unless otherwise noted, works of art
are by Gustave Caillebotte.*

PAGE 158
Riverbank, before 1879
Oil on canvas, 28 × 41 cm.
Signed lower right "Gustave Caillebotte"
Private collection
Photo: Laurin-Grilloux-Buffetaud

PAGE 158
Brunoy, the Soulins Bridge, before 1879
Oil on canvas, 30 × 22 cm.
Stamped lower right
Private collection
Archives Galerie Brame et Lorenceau

PAGE 160 (above)
Banks of the Yerres, c. 1878
Oil on wood, 15 × 22 cm.
Photo Earl Ripling (Collection John C.
    Whitehead Photograph Archives;
    Achim Moeller Fine Arts, New York)

PAGE 160 (below)
(left) Banks of the Yerres in the Meadow
(right) Yerres—the Meadow and the
    banks of the Yerres
Photographs
Collection Tailleur-Renous, Paris

PAGE 161
Périssoires on the Yerres, 1877
Oil on canvas, 103 × 156 cm.
Signed and dated lower left "G.
    Caillebotte 1877"
Collection Milwaukee Art Center, Gift
    of the Milwaukee Journal Company in
    honor of Miss Faye McBeath

PAGE 162
Sailing Dinghy on the Yerres, 1878
Oil on canvas, dimensions unknown
Signed and dated lower right "G.
    Caillebotte 1878"
Photo: Archives Durand-Ruel, Paris

PAGE 163
Boaters on the Yerres, 1877
Pastel, 52 × 86 cm.
Signed and dated lower right "G.
    Caillebotte 1877"
Private collection, Paris
Archives Galerie Brame et Lorenceau

PAGE 164 (above)
Périssoire on the Yerres, c. 1878
Oil on canvas, 65 × 82 cm.
Signed lower left (by P. A. Renoir) "G.
    Caillebotte"
Private collection, United States
Photo: Martial Caillebotte, c. 1894
    (Private collection, Paris)

PAGE 164 (below)
"Yerres—Banks of the Stream, the
    Meadow"
Postcard
Collection Tailleur-Renous, Paris

PAGE 165
Périssoires on the Yerres, 1878
Oil on canvas, 157 × 113 cm.
Signed and dated on the right "Gustave
    Caillebotte 78"
Collection Musée des Beaux-Arts de
    Rennes

PAGE 166
*Boater Pulling in His Périssoire, Banks of
    the Yerres*, 1878
Oil on canvas, 73 × 91 cm.
Signed and dated lower right "G.
    Caillebotte 1878"
Virginia Museum of Fine Arts,
    Richmond, Gift of Mr. and Mrs. Paul
    Mellon

PAGE 167
Oarsmen on the Yerres, 1877
Oil on canvas, 81 × 116 cm.
Signed and dated on the right "Gustave
    Caillebotte 1877"
Private collection, Paris
Photo: B. L. Giraudon

PAGE 169
Yves Jannès
The Yerres river today
Photograph

PAGE 170
Models of boats
from L. E. Audot, *Traité de la
    composition et de l'ornement des jardins*

PAGE 171
Oarsmen in a Top Hat, c. 1878
Oil on canvas, 90 × 117 cm.
Signed lower left "G. Caillebotte"
Private collection, Paris
Archives Galerie Brame et Lorenceau

PAGE 172
Cautin et Berger, Paris
The Yerres river seen from the park,
    looking upstream, after 1879
Photograph
Private collection, Paris

PAGE 173 (above)
*Bather Preparing to Dive, Banks of the
    Yerres*, c. 1878
Oil on canvas, 117 × 89 cm.
Signed lower right
Private collection, United States
Photo: Christie's

PAGE 173 (below)
Bathers, Banks of the Yerres, 1877
Pastel, 75 × 95 cm.
Signed and dated lower left "G.
    Caillebotte 77"
Collection Musée d'Agen, France
Photo: B. L. Giraudon

PAGE 174
Sketch for *Bathers, Banks of the Yerres*,
    1878
Pencil, (paper) 40 × 26 cm. (drawing)
    28 × 21 cm.
Private collection, Paris
Archives Galerie Brame et Lorenceau

PAGE 175
Bathers, Banks of the Yerres, 1878
Oil on canvas, 157 × 117 cm.
Signed and dated lower right "G.
    Caillebotte 78"
Private collection, Paris
Archives Galerie Brame et Lorenceau

PAGE 176
Yves Jannès
The washhouse of the property today
Photograph

PAGE 177
Laundry Drying, Petit Gennevilliers,
    c. 1888
Oil on canvas, 54 × 65 cm.
Photo: Martial Caillebotte, c. 1894
    (Private collection, Paris)

PAGE 178
Diagram of the pond from a 20th-century
    map
Private collection, Yerres

PAGE 179
Landscape, Banks of the Yerres, c. 1875
Oil on wood, 40 × 49 cm.
Collection Etienne Dulière, Brussels
    (*formerly* Collection Gaston)

PAGE 180
A. Riocreux
(left) "Yellow pond lily," c. 1862–71
(right) "Common water lily," c. 1862–71
from J. Decaisne and Ch. Naudin,
    *Manuel de l'amateur des jardins—Traité
    générale d'horticulture*, vol. 1

PAGE 181
Yerres, on the Pond, Water Lilies, before
    1879
Oil on cardboard, 19 × 28 cm.
Private collection, Paris
Archives Galerie Brame et Lorenceau

Bibliography

Adams, W. H., *Les jardins en France 1500–1800: Le rêve et le pouvoir*. L'Equerre, Paris, 1980.

Alexandre-Théodore Brongnart, 1739–1813: Architecture et décor. Exhibition catalogue, Musée Carnavalet. Imprimerie Alençonnaise, Alençon, 1986.

Aries, M., *Faïences Creil-Choisy Montereau*. ABC Collection, June 1980.

Arneville, M. B. d', *Parcs et jardins sous le Premier Empire— Reflets d'une société*. Tallandier, Paris, 1981.

Assouline P., *L'Homme de l'Art D. H. Kahnweiler: 1884– 1979*. Balland, 1988.

Audot, L. E., see Boitard

Autour du pont de Maincy de Cézanne: le pont dans la peinture. Exhibition catalogue, Musée de Melun, 1983.

Balanda, M. J. de, *Gustave Caillebotte: La vie, la technique, l'œuvre peint*. Edita, Lausanne, 1988.

Bannour, Wanja, *Edmond et Jules de Goncourt, ou le génie androgyne*. Persona, 1985.

Barron, L., *Les environs de Paris—Ouvrage illustré de cinq cents dessins d'après nature par G. Fraipont et accompagné d'une carte en couleur*.

Barthélémy, G., *Les jardins du Roy*. Short history of Paris gardens. Le Pélican, Librairie du Muséum, Paris, 1979.

Batho, C., *Giverny: La mémoire d'un jardin*. A.D.A.C. Aurillac, 1986.

Belugou, P., *Monotypes et voiliers de course*. Librairie nautique du Yacht, Paris, ca. 1948.

Berhaut, M., *Caillebotte l'Impressionniste*. Lausanne, 1968.

Berhaut, M., *Caillebotte sa vie et son œuvre: Catalogue raisonné des peintures et pastels*. Fondation Wildenstein, La Bibliothèque des Arts, Paris, 1978.

Berhaut, M., "Gustave Caillebotte et le réalisme impressionniste." In *l'Œil*, N° 268, November 1977.

Berhaut, M., "Gustave Caillebotte." In *Le Monmartel*, N° 7, June 1980.

Berhaut, M., *Le legs Caillebotte: Vérités et Contre Vérités*. Etude Bulletin de la Société de l'Histoire de l'Art Français, Paris, 1985.

Berrail, J. S., *Histoire illustrée des jardins*. Del Duca, Paris, 1968.

Berthier, François, *Le jardin du Ryoanji—lire le zen dans les pierres*. Adam Biro, Paris, 1989.

Besson, Georges, "Gustave Caillebotte et ses amis" (originally preface to exhibition catalogue, Musée de Chartres, 1965). In *Galerie des Arts*, N° 140, September–October 1974.

Boccara, Jacqueline, *Ames de laine et de soie*. Editions d'Art Monelle Hayot, St-Just-en-Chaussée (Oise), 1988.

Boitard, Pierre (pseud. Louis Verardi). *Traité de la composition et de l'ornement des jardins*. With 168 plates, representing garden plans, structures appropriate to their decoration, and devices for irrigation. The sixth edition was augmented with a great number of new drawings by L.

E. Audot, Ex-Secretary of the "Comité de la Composition des jardins à la Société Centrale d'Horticulture de Paris." Published by L. E. Audot, Publisher, in 1859 (sixth edition). (Reprint of the 1859 Paris edition by L.V.D.V. Inter-livres, 55, passage Jouffroy, 75009 Paris.)
This work, sometimes better known under the name of Audot, was edited for the first time in 1818 during the reign (1814–24) of King Louis XVIII (1758–1824); a second edition was published in 1823; the third edition was published in 1825 during the reign (1821–30) of King Charles X (1757–1836); the fourth edition was published in 1834 during the reign (1830–48) of King Louis-Philippe (1773–1850); 3,000 copies were printed of the fifth edition, published in 1838.

Bordeaux, P., *Recherches historiques sur le couvent des Camaldules de Grosbois.*

Bosch, R., *Couleur: la palette des sens.* In *Le Point*, August 26, 1985.

Bourges, R. M., *Le jardin de Cézanne—L'époque des Lauves.* Aix-en-Provence, 1984.

Brosse, J., *Les arbres en France. Histoire et légendes.* Plon, Paris, 1987.

Camille Pissarro 1830–1903. Exhibition catalogue, Arts Council of Great Britain; Museum of Fine Arts, Boston; Galeries Nationales du Grand Palais. Editions de la Réunion des Musées Nationaux, Paris, 1981.

Cartes des environs de Paris, 1/20.000 No 29: Boissy-Saint-Léger. Drawn and engraved by the Service Géographique de l'armée, revised in 1887. Plon, Paris.

Cartes des environs de Paris, 1/20.000 No 35: Brunoy. Drawn and engraved by the Service Géographique de l'armée, revised in 1887. Plon, Paris.

Catalogue de l'Exposition Universelle de 1900. Librairie Hachette, Paris, for the Salle Caillebotte at the Musée du Luxembourg.

Centenaire de l'Impressionnisme. Exhibition catalogue, Grand Palais. Editions de la Réunion des Musées Nationaux, Paris, 1974.

Chantilly—Historique des jardins. Illustré par des gravures du XVIIe au XIXe siècle. Association pour l'Animation Culturelle du Domaine de Chantilly, Chantilly, 1987.

Chardeau, Jean, *Les dessins de Caillebotte.* Editions Hermé, Paris, 1989.

Charles, Daniel, *Catalogue des voiliers conçus par Gustave Caillebotte et des voiliers lui ayant appartenu.* April 20, 1989. With Corinne Renié.

Cherbuliez, V., *La ferme du Choquard (1882).* Presses du Village, Etrepilly.

Chimay, J. de, *Les jardins à travers le monde.* Hachette, Paris, 1962.

Côté jardin—L'art des jardins dans les collections de la Bibliothèque Forney. Exhibition catalogue, Hôtel de Sens, 1984.

Cochet-Cochet, *Notes historiques sur la Brie Ancienne.* Les Editions du Bastion, 1929, 1982.

Corpechot, L., *Parcs et jardins de France. Les jardins de l'intelligence.* Plon, Paris, 1937.

Courcel, R. de, *La forêt de Sénart: étude historique—Mémoires de la Société de l'Histoire de Paris et de l'Ile-de-France.*

Volume I. H. Champion, Paris, 1930.

Courtine, R., *Le ventre de Paris—de la Bastille à l'Etoile, des siècles d'appétit.* Librairie Académique Perrin, Paris, 1985.

Courtine, R., *La Vie Parisienne: cafés et restaurants des Boulevards 1814–1914.* Librairie Académique Perrin, Paris, 1984.

Crespelle, J. P., *Les Maîtres de la belle époque.* Hachette, Paris, 1966.

Curtat, P., "Bernard Niewvenhuyssen (fils) Maître jardinier du Comte de Provence à Brunoy—Premier Maire d'Epinay-sous-Senart." In *Le Monmartel*, No 11, December 1984.

Curtat, P., *Brunoy côté jardin 1722–1795: Les grandes eaux.* Les lettres libres, Paris, 1984.

Daix, Pierre, *L'ordre et l'aventure.* Painting, modernism, and totalitarian oppression. Arthaud, Paris, 1984.

Daudet, A., *Robert Helmont, Journal d'un solitaire, 1873.* Drawings and watercolors of Picard and Montégut. E. Dentu Edit., Paris, 1888.

Daulte et Richebe, C., *Monet et ses amis—Le legs Michel Monet, la donation Donop de Monchy.* Exhibition catalogue, Musée Marmottan, 1971.

Daulte, F., *Auguste Renoir.* Diffusion Princesse Fratelli, 1974.

A Day in the Country: Impressionism and the French Landscape. Exhibition catalogue, Los Angeles County Museum of Art, Art Institute of Chicago. Richard R. Brettell, et al. Abrams, New York, 1984.

De Bagatelle à Montceau 1778–1978: Les folies du XVIIIe Siècle à Paris. Exhibition catalogue, Domaine de Bagatelle; Musée Carnavalet. Edition Imprimerie Alençonnaise, 1978.

De Cayeux, J., *Hubert Robert et les jardins.* Herscher, Paris, 1987.

Decaisne, J., *Manuel de l'amateur des jardins—Traité général d'horticulture.* Firmin Didot, Paris, after 1863. Published in four volumes, 1862–1891. Illustrations by A. Riocreux.

De Ganay, Ernest, *Bibliographie de l'Art des jardins.* Introduction: Geneviève Bonté. Preface: Monique Moser. Bibliothèque des Arts Décoratifs, September 1989.

De Goncourt, Edmond et Jules, *Journal-Mémoires de la vie littéraire.* Robert Laffont S.A., Paris, 1989.

Delacroix, E. *Journal 1822–1863.* Plon, Paris, 1931, 1932, 1981

De Renoir à Matisse. 22 masterpieces from Soviet and French museums. Exhibition catalogue, Grand Palais. Editions de la Réunion des Musées Nationaux, Paris, 1978.

Dezallier d'Argenville, A. J., *La théorie et la pratique du jardinage.* Third edition, The Hague, 1739. L. J. Toth Milano reprint.

Dumesnil, R., *Le réalisme et le naturalisme.* Del Duca, Paris, 1968.

Duthuit, C., *Renoir.* Stock, Paris, 1923.

1874 Hommage à Paul Durand-Ruel 1974—Cent ans d'Impressionnisme. Exhibition catalogue. Imprimerie Steff, Paris, 1973.

Endrès, A., *Tourisme Nord de Seine-et-Marne.* Volume I : *Meaux et environs.* Editions Amatteis, Le Mée-sur-Seine, 1987.

Ernouf, Baron A. A., *Traité pratique et didactique: l'art des jardins*. Paris, J. Rothschild, after 1868.

Etienne Carjat 1828–1906—Photographe. Exhibition catalogue, Musée Carnavalet. Imprimerie Alençonnaise, 1982.

Et les jardins en France? Exhibition catalogue, l'Institut Français d'Architecture, Paris, 1988.

Eve A., *Les rosiers anciens, arbustifs, botaniques*. Pithiviers. Sale catalogue, Fall 1986–Spring 1987.

Exposition rétrospective d'œuvres de G. Caillebotte. Catalogue. Galerie Durand-Ruel, June 1894, Paris.

Extraits intéressants Yerres. Document from the Municipal Archives of Yerres.

Fatoux, H., *Histoire d'eau en Seine-et-Marne*. Volumes I and II, 1986–1988. Editions Amatteis, Le Mée-sur-Seine.

Félicien Rops, 1833–1898. Exhibition catalogue, Musée des Arts Décoratifs, Paris. Edition Flammarion, Paris, 1985.

Ferre, J., "Gustave Caillebotte, prophète et grand bourgeois." In *Le Figaro Magazine*, January 24, 1981.

Fillacier, J., *La pratique de la couleur*. Dunod–Bordas, 1986.

Fleurent, M., *Le Monde secret des jardins*. Flammarion, Paris, 1987.

Foerster, K., *Stauden Katalog Zugleich ein Wegweiser Durch das Staudenreich*. Bornim bei Potsdam, Sanssouci, 1930.

Fosca, F., *Renoir*. F. Rieder et Cie, Ed., Paris, 1923.

Fontaine, R., *Draveil et son histoire (dont Champ Rosay)*. Imprimerie de Milly-la-Forêt, Essonne, 1981.

Foucart, B., "Caillebotte, le militant de l'impressionnisme." In *Beaux Arts*, N° 31, January 1986.

Fournier, A., *Les dictons de Seine-et-Marne, 1873*. Editions Amatteis, Le Mée-sur-Seine, 1984.

Galey, Matthieu, *Journal 1974–1986*. Grasset, Paris, 1989.

Ganay, E. de, *André le Nostre 1613–1700*. Edition Vincent Fréal et Cie., Paris, 1962.

Ganay, E. de, *Châteaux et Manoirs de France XI—Ile-de-France*. Vincent Fréal et Cie, Paris, 1938.

Gauchet, J., "Us et coutumes à Brunoy . . . La confrérie de Saint Fiacre." In *Le Montmartel*, N° 7, June 1980.

Gatinot, J. C., *Histoire de Montgeron*. Imprimerie Laubin, Paris, 1986.

Gautier, Jean, et Gauchet, J., *Histoire de Brunoy*. Editions J. Laffitte, Marseille, 1980.

Gérard, Robert, "Le flageolet ou l'histoire du haricot de M. Chevrier" In *Jardins de France*, April 1988.

Grandes et petites heures du Parc Monceau—Hommage à Thomas Blaikie (1750–1838); Jardinier écossais du Duc d'Orléans. Exhibition catalogue, Musée Cernuschi. Firmin Didot, Paris, 1981.

Greaves, R., *Nadar ou le paradoxe vital*. Flammarion, Paris, 1980.

Grenier, J., *La Brie d'autrefois, 1883*. Editions Amatteis, Le Mée-sur-Seine, 1986.

Grimal, P., *Les jardins Romains*. Fayard, Paris, 1984.

Gromort, G., *L'art des jardins*. Ch. Massin, Paris, 1983.

Guide Clause 23e édition—Traité pratique du jardinage. Brétigny-sur-Orge.

Guide Vilmorin du jardin—9e édition Vilmorin-Andrieux. La Menitre, Beaufort-en-Vallée.

Guillaud, J. et M., *Degas le modelé et l'espace*.

Guillaud, M. et J., *Claude Monet au temps de Giverny*. Exhibition catalogue, Centre Culturel du Marais à Paris, 1983.

Guillaud, M., *Pissarro: Monde rural, art, politique*. Centre culturel du Marais, Centre de recherches pour les expositions et le spectacle, Paris, 1981.

Guillemard, Roger, *Grosbois. Une demeure tranquille en Ile-de-France*. Boissy-Saint-Léger, Val-de-Marne, 1977.

Gustave Caillebotte 1848–1894. Exhibition catalogue, Fondation Anne et Albert Prouvost, 1982. Marcq-en-Barœul.

Gustave Caillebotte 1848–1894. Exhibition catalogue, Musée Pissarro, 1984. With contributions by J. P. Lachenaud, E. Maillet, Jacques Chardeau, Marie Berhaut.

Gustave Caillebotte 1848–1894: Dessins, Etudes, Portraits. Exhibition catalogue, Galerie Brame et Lorenceau, Paris, 1989.

Gustave Caillebotte: A Retrospective Exhibition. With contributions by Kirk Varnedoe, Marie Berhaut, Peter Galassi, and Hilari Faberman. Catalogue by Kirk Varnedoe and P. Lee Thomas. Preface by William C. Agle. The Museum of Fine Arts, Houston, The Brooklyn Museum, New York, 1976–1977.

Hobhouse, P., *Les couleurs de votre jardin*. Nathan, Paris, 1985.

Hommage à Claude Monet 1840–1926. Exhibition catalogue, Grand Palais. Editions de la Réunion des Musées Nationaux, Paris, 1980.

Hoog, M., Distel, A., Gache, S., *L'impressionnisme*. F. Hazan, Paris, 1977.

Hoog, S., *Louis XIV. Manière de montrer les jardins de Versailles*. Editions de la Réunion des Musées Nationaux, Paris, 1982.

Hudelot, M., *Brunoy en cartes postales anciennes*, Bibliothèque européenne, S.F.L. Paris, 1979.

Hure, G., *Notice historique de Yerres en Brie*. 1943, unpublished.

Jardins en France 1760–1820. Exhibition catalogue, Caisse Nationale des Monuments Historiques et des Sites, Paris.

Jardins en France 1760–1820 Pays d'illusion, Terre d'expérience. Exhibition catalogue, Caisse Nationale des Monuments Historiques et des Sites, Paris, 1977.

Jardins de Paris. Exhibition catalogue, Bagatelle, 1984.

Joanne, P., *Environs de Paris*. Hachette, Paris, 1889.

Johnson, H., *L'art des jardins*. Nathan, Paris, 1980.

Joyes, C. et Toulgouat, J. M., *Claude Monet et Giverny*. Chêne, Paris, 1985.

Kayser, B. et R., *L'amour des jardins célébré par les écrivains*. Arlea, 1986.

Kretzulesco-Quaranta, *Les jardins du songe—Poliphile et la Mystique de la Renaissance*. Les Belles Lettres, Paris, 1986.

Lahaye, M., and Berhaut, M., *Gustave Caillebotte dans "Promenade entre l'Yerres et la forêt."* Quincy-sous-Sénart, 1976.

Lalos, J., *De la composition des parcs et jardins pittoresques*. A useful and instructive work for property owners and amateurs. Paris, 1824.

Lanoux, A., *Maupassant le bel ami, 1967*. Grasset, Paris, 1979.

Laroque, A., *Yerres (Seine-et-Oise): Ses origines et curiosités historiques avec vues illustrées, indicateur des rues et plan.* A. Desbouis, Villeneuve-Saint-Georges, 1931.

L'Art en France sous le Second Empire. Exhibition catalogue, Grand Palais, Paris. Editions de la Réunion des Musées Nationaux, Paris, 1979.

Lebègue, E., *Boursault-Malherbe—Comédien, conventionnel, spéculateur 1752–1842.* Félix Alcan, Paris, 1935.

Le Buet Yerres: d'après les titres de propriété; historique; principaux propriétaires 1773–1925. 2 typewritten pages, ca. 1981. Courtesy Mme de Pallières, 1985.

Lecoufle, M., Bert, G., *Orchidée.* Catalogue 1985. Boissy-Saint-Léger.

Legarrec, B., *Photographies: Parc et Château de Rottembourg à Montgeron: Sur les "traces" de Claude Monet à Montgeron.* October 25, 1986, Musée de Brunoy.

Le "gothique" retrouvé. Exhibition catalogue, Caisse Nationale des Monuments Historiques et des Sites. Paris, 1979.

Le Japonisme. Exhibition catalogue, Galeries Nationales du Grand Palais. Editions de la Réunion des Musées Nationaux, Paris, 1988.

Le potager du Roy et le Parc Balbi. Ecole Nationale Supérieure d'horticulture, Versailles.

Lequenne, F., *Olivier de Serres, agronome et soldat de Dieu.* Berger-Levrault, Paris, 1983.

Les peintres entre Seine et Loing. Exhibition catalogue, Musée de Melun, 1986.

Lévêque, J. J., *Guide des parcs et jardins de Paris et de la région parisienne.* P. Horay, Paris, 1980.

Leymarie, J. *Renoir.* F. Hazan, Paris, 1978.

Lloyd, Christopher, "An Unknown Sketchbook by Gustave Caillebotte." In *Master Drawings*, Volume XXVI/Number 2, Summer 1988. Published April 1989. Meriden-Stinehour Press, Lunenburg, Vermont.

Maupassant, G., *Œuvres complètes.* 15 volumes. Librairie de France, Paris, 1934.

Magnol-Malhache, V. et Weill, G., *Jardins et paysages des Hauts-de-Seine—de la Renaissance à l'art Moderne.* Exhibition catalogue, Archives Départementales des Haut-de-Seine, Nanterre, 1982.

Manet: 1832–1883. Exhibition catalogue, Metropolitan Museum of Art, New York; Grand Palais, Paris. François Cachin et al. New York, The Metropolitan Museum of Art, 1983.

Martin, F., *Notice sur l'église d'Yerres—Canton de Boissy-Saint-Léger.* C.A. Arts 3. Commission de l'inventaire des richesses d'Art, arrondissement de Corbeil. Notices et inventaires. Archives de Seine-et-Oise, Versailles.

Moissinac, C., et Romera, A. M. "Le château et le parc de Lery à Auvers-sur-Oise." In *Panorama du val d'Oise—Le Val d'Oise, pays de l'Impressionnisme.* Revue trimestrielle du Conseil Général, Septembre 1988.

Monnier, C., *Pastels du XIXᵉ siècle.* Inventory of French public collections. Musée du Louvre, Cabinet des dessins, Musée d'Orsay. Editions de la Réunion des Musées Nationaux, Paris, 1985.

Monuments historiques—Jardins des provinces, Nᵒ 143. (Inventory, department of Essonne) February–March, 1986. Editions de la Caisse Nationale des Monuments Historiques et des Sites, Paris.

Moreau, J., *L'Eglise Saint-Honest d'Yerres.* April 1982.

Note concernant le Château de la Grange. 3 handwritten pages. Château de La Grange du Milieu, Yerres.

Peintres de fleurs en France du XVIIᵉ au XIXᵉ siècles. Exhibition catalogue, Petit Palais, Palais des Beaux Arts de la Ville de Paris, 1979.

Perruchot, H., "L'affaire Caillebotte." In *Jardin des Arts,* Nᵒ 140–141 July–August 1966.

Pierre Joseph Redoute, Le Raphaël des Fleurs: 1759–1840. Catalogue produced by the Centre d'Action Culturelles de la Communauté d'Expression Française (CACEF) and the Centre Culturel de la Communauté Française de Belgique à Paris.

Plan général commune d'Yerres. By A. Ferret. A. Desbouis, Villeneuve-Saint-Georges, 1931.

Plancke, R. C., *Histoire de Seine-et-Marne—Vie paysanne.* Editions Amatteis, Le Mée-sur-Seine, 1987.

Plancke, R. C., *La Vie rurale en Seine-et-Marne—1853–1953.* Editions Amatteis, Dammarie-les-Lys, 1982.

Poisson, G., *Charenton-le-Pont, cinq mille ans d'histoire.* Albatros, Paris, 1982.

Prasteau, J., *Voyage insolite dans la banlieue de Paris.* Librairie Académique Perrin, 1985.

Promenade dans l'histoire des jardins Français; Images de jardins; Gardens Image. Sang de la Terre, Paris, 1987.

Queffurus, G., *Notice concernant Louis Victor Maurice Mulard—Photographe éditeur à Yerres, 1875–1925.*

"Rapport soumis par Prudent Gaudefroy aux membres du Conseil Municipal d'Yerres sur sa gestion depuis le 8 septembre 1870, époque à laquelle il a commencé l'exercice des fonctions de Maire, en l'absence de celui-ci et de son adjoint." In *Le Monmartel,* Nᵒ 11.

Renoir. Exhibition catalogue, Arts Council of Great Britain; Museum of Fine Arts, Boston; Réunion des Musées Nationaux, Paris, 1985.

Revue de la Société Nationale d'Horticulture de France (S.N.H.F.), Paris.

Rewald, John. *History of Impressionism.* The Museum of Modern Art, New York, 1973.

Riousset, M., *De Lagny à Charenton: Les bords de Marne du Second Empire à nos jours.* Editions Amateis, Dammarie-les-Lys, Seine-et-Marne, 1984.

Roure, J. *Alphonse Daudet.* Julliard, Paris, 1982.

Roux, E. de, "Les bâtisseurs de ruines." In *l'Express,* Paris, May 10–16, 1985.

Ryout, Denys, *Les écrivains devant l'impressionnisme.* Editions Macula, Paris, 1989.

Serullaz, Maurice, *Delacroix.* Fayard, 1989.

Staes, G. et Cavailler, P., *Les seigneurs d'Yerres.* Bulletin de la Société Historique et Archéologique de Corbeil, d'Etampes et du Hurepoix, 1978, Nᵒ 48. Corbeil-Essonnes, 1979.

Shikes, R., Harper, P., *Pissarro.* Flammarion, Paris, 1981.

Signac, P., *D'Eugène Delacroix au Néo-impressionnisme.* Introduction and notes by F. Cachin. Savoir—Hermann, 1987.

"Talma et les roses." In *Le Monmartel,* Nᵒ 5, May 1977.

The New Painting: Impressionism 1874–1886. Exhibition catalogue, The Fine Arts Museums of San Francisco;

National Gallery of Art, Washington, 1986.

Toussaint, Hélène, *La liberté guidant le peuple de Delacroix.* Catalogue of the files of the Paintings Department. Editions de la Réunion des Musées Nationaux, Paris, 1982.

Troquet, C., *La banlieue Est pendant le siège de Paris, La Vie militaire quotidienne de Septembre 1870 à Janvier 1871.* C. Troquet, Vincennes, 1981.

Une promenade dans le parc. Brochure by Madame Bergery and Madame Payen, preface by Francis Salet, curator at the Domaine de Chantilly.

Un peintre dans son jardin: G. Caillebotte 1848–1894, Au temps de l'Yerres 1860–1879. Exhibition catalogue, Musée de Brunoy, 1987.

Un sentier pour découvrir Yerres. Guide by fifth-level students of the Collège Budé, Yerres. Imp. Yerres Impression, 1980–1981.

Vacquier, J., Soulange Bodin, H., Jarry, P., *Les anciens châteaux de France,* series no. 8, Contet, Paris, 1925.

Vaisse, P., *Le legs Caillebotte d'après les documents.* Communication Soc. Hist. Art français, séance du 3 décembre 1983.

Van der Kemp, *Une visite à Giverny.* Edition d'Art Lys, Versailles, 1980.

Varnedoe, Kirk, "Caillebotte's Pont de l'Europe: A New Slant." In *Art International,* April 20, 1974.

Varnedoe, Kirk, *Gustave Caillebotte.* Editions Adam Biro, Paris, 1988.

Varnedoe, Kirk, *Gustave Caillebotte.* Yale University Press, New Haven and London, 1987.

Verardi, L.: see Boitard

Vincent, M., *Maisons de Brie et d'Ile-de-France.* Les Presses du Village, Etrepilly, 1981, 1988.

Vollard, A., *En écoutant Cézanne, Degas, Renoir, 1938.* Grasset, Paris, 1985.

Vollard, A., *Souvenirs d'un marchand de tableaux, 1937.* Albin Michel, 1984

Wengel, T., *L'art des jardins au fil des âges.* Editions Leipzig—R.D.A., 1987.

Wildenstein, D., *Claude Monet: Biographie et catalogue raisonné.* Volume I, 1840–1881, Paintings. Bibliothèque des Arts, Lausanne and Paris, 1974.

Winninger, C., *Le jardin. Ministère de l'Education Nationale.* Direction des bibliothèques et de lecture publique, Bibliothèque centrale de prêt de Seine-et-Marne. Melun, 1970.

Wittmer, P., *Les origines des jardins du Comte de Provence à Brunoy vers 1479–1491–1774.* Proposal for an exhibition at the Musée de Brunoy, February 1989. (unpublished).

Woodbridge, K., *Princely Gardens—The Origins and Development of the French Formal Style.* Thames and Hudson, London, 1986.

Works in Oil and Pastel by the Impressionists of Paris. National Academy of Design; Special Exhibition, 1886, under the management of The American Art Association (Archives Durand-Ruel) Paris.

Yerres. H. Lussaud, Imp. Ed. Fontenay-le-Comte, 1923.

Zola, E., *Le bon combat, de Courbet aux impressionnistes.* Anthology of his writings on art. Hermann, Paris, 1974.

Index

Page numbers in italic refer to illustrations.

H

I

J

K